THE LEGENDS OF
BURNLEY

THE LEGENDS OF
BURNLEY

by Mike Jackman

breedon **books**
PUBLISHING

First published in Great Britain in 2006 by
The Breedon Books Publishing Company Limited
Breedon House, 3 The Parker Centre,
Derby, DE21 4SZ.

ISBN 1 85983 538 4

Printed and bound by BIDDLES LTD,
King's Lynn, Norfolk.

Contents

Dedication

This book is dedicated to
Steve Lord and Daniel Lord,
two generations of Burnley supporters who have remained faithful
to the Claret and Blue through good times and bad.

Introduction

The difficulties in a book of this type are obvious. Firstly, what are the requirements needed to achieve legendary status? What criteria can be used to qualify a player, manager or, indeed, chairman for inclusion within the pages of this book? Of course, for many of the people included in this book, a combination of length of service and achievement would guarantee their inclusion in most supporters' selection of 100 legends. However, some of the selections have been rather more personal in nature. I've looked at players who began their careers at Burnley but enjoyed their greatest success away from Turf Moor – players like Tommy Lawton and Trevor Steven. On the other hand, I have also incorporated some players who came to Burnley at the end of their careers but enjoyed a glorious 'Indian Summer' in the Claret and Blue – Ian Wright being an obvious candidate for this group.

The one thing that all 100 entries have in common is that they have all made a contribution to this wonderful club. That alone should merit them legendary status, and yet, as I have said before, so many others could easily have been included. I hope you can agree with some of my selections, and hopefully you will enjoy the discussions that are bound to follow with regard to the various merits of those that I have not included.

Notes on the text

In the statistical section for each player the following should be noted:
European – includes appearances and goals in the European Cup and the Inter-Cites Fairs Cup.
Other – includes appearances and goals in the FA Charity Shield, the Associate Members' Cup, including its many and varied names after sponsorship, the Anglo-Scottish Cup, the Watney Cup and the Texaco Cup.

Acknowledgements

I am grateful to Steve Caron for his continuing support throughout this project. Thanks too go to Michelle Grainger and Sarah Allard for their editorial work on this book. I am grateful for the input of Steve and Daniel Lord with regard to the selection of subjects for inclusion in this book, and Mike Davage for help with births, deaths and career records. Once again, I am indebted to Howard Talbot for his excellent photographic work and grateful thanks also go to Edward Lee of the *Burnley Express* and Ray Simpson for providing many of the photographs used in this book.

Jimmy Adamson

Date of birth: 4 July 1929, Ashington

Burnley record:
Appearances: League 426, FA Cup 52, League Cup 3, Europe 4, others 1
Goals: League 17, FA Cup 1
Debut: League, 10 February 1951 v Bolton Wanderers (a) drew 1–1
Manager: February 1970–January 1976

Also played for: Ashington YMCA, East Chevington Juniors, England B (1 cap),
    Football League (1 appearance)
Also managed: Sunderland, Leeds United

During a career with Burnley that spanned some four decades as a player, coach and manager, Jimmy Adamson, to this day, continues to be held in the highest esteem by the Turf Moor faithful.

Plucked from a north-east mining community, Adamson almost ended his career at Turf Moor before it had really begun. Within a fortnight of joining the groundstaff he had returned home, suffering from homesickness. Fortunately, he returned and then signed professional forms in January 1947. During the early stages of his career at the club, he came under the watchful eyes of coaches Ray Bennion and Billy Dougal. Indeed, it was Dougal who suggested he switch from a forward position to the half-back line.

National Service interrupted Adamson's career, but once he had made his debut, replacing Reg Attwell for the trip to Burnden Park in February 1951, he was in the first team to stay. He made the right-half spot his own, and, although not the quickest of players, his masterful reading of the game enabled him to always be in the right place at the right time. His control of the ball was almost artistic, and when having won possession he rarely wasted a pass. Always calm and collected under pressure, he developed into a player of exceptional quality, a fact recognised by the international selectors in March 1953, when he was chosen to represent England B against Scotland B at Easter Road, Edinburgh.

With the emergence of Bobby Seith, Adamson happily switched to centre-half to cover for the injured Tommy Cummings during the latter stages of 1956–57. The long-term injury to Cummings meant Adamson continued in that position for the whole of the next campaign before switching to left-half when Cummings regained full fitness. His ability to play anywhere along the half-back line with equal aplomb merely underlined his ability. Not just an outstanding individual footballer, he was also an inspirational captain.

It was during the late 1950s and early 1960s that he was at the zenith of his game. Adamson led the club to the Championship in 1959–60, and in 1961–62 he almost led the team to a League and FA Cup double, finishing runners-up in both competitions. His individual efforts were recognised when he was named the Footballer of the Year for 1961–62, the only Burnley player to be afforded that honour.

The honour was testimony to a classy, skilful and intelligent footballer who was a keen student of the game. He gained his full FA Coaching Badge at 28 and was then taken on as a staff coach at the newly-developed Lilleshall Complex. It was here that he formed a strong bond with Walter Winterbottom, the England manager.

'I met Walter during those sessions at Lilleshall. We got on well, and he invited me to go to the World Cup Finals in Chile in 1962 as his assistant,' Adamson recalled in a later interview. The hierarchy at the Football Association were sufficiently impressed to offer him the England manager's job when Winterbottom resigned. However, not wanting to uproot his family from their Burnley home and feeling that he perhaps lacked a little in experience, he turned down the opportunity. Alf Ramsey took the job, and the face of English football was changed forever.

In September 1964 Adamson was appointed the chief coach at Burnley in a move that was to prove beneficial to both club and player. He had been troubled with knee problems for some time and so a move into coaching on a full-time basis proved ideal. For several years he worked under manager Harry Potts and seemed the natural heir apparent. In February 1970 he stepped up to take charge of the team, while Potts moved upstairs to become General Manager.

Adamson suffered an early blow in his managerial career when what he described as the 'team of the 70s' slipped into the Second Division. Unperturbed, he continued to tinker with his youthful squad and guided them to the Second Division Championship in 1972–73. The next two seasons found the Clarets in highly-respectable sixth and 10th positions in the First Division. These were commendable positions for a small-town club, particularly at a time when finance was becoming a dominant factor in the game.

Unfortunately, the 1975–76 campaign proved disastrous, and after a defeat at Blackpool in the third round of the FA Cup Adamson left Turf Moor. He coached for a short time in Holland before serving both Sunderland and Leeds United as manager.

Adamson left the game for good in 1980. Since then he has continued to live quietly in Burnley, and although in recent years he has not enjoyed the best of health he remains one of the town's favourite adopted sons.

Joe Anderson

Date of birth: 1895, Thornliebank

Burnley record:
Appearances: League 121, FA Cup 4, others 1
Goals: League 64, FA Cup 8
Debut: League, 20 March 1920 v Sunderland (h) won 2–1

Also played for: Thornliebank, Vale of Leven, Airdreionians, Dumbarton Harp,
Royal Scots Fusiliers, Clydebank, Vale of Leven, Glasgow Pollack

Every successful team needs a goalscorer: a player who will prowl around the penalty area like a hungry predator awaiting its prey. In the 1920–21 Championship-winning side, that man was Joe Anderson.

'Joe Andy', as he became known to the Turf Moor faithful, only enjoyed the briefest period at the cutting edge of the Burnley attack. Indeed, he was only at his peak as a goalscorer at Turf Moor for two seasons, but the first of those campaigns delivered the League title for the first time in the club's history. Little wonder then that, as the leading goalscorer, he etched his name forever in the history of Burnley Football Club.

Anderson was born in Scotland and, apart from his brief flirtation with the Clarets, spent the whole of his football career in his native land. He scored goals on a regular basis with a string of Scottish clubs without ever really breaking into the 'big time'. He then joined Clydebank in August 1919 and enjoyed a fairly successful campaign with his new club, as they ended the season in fifth position in Division One in Scotland. However, before the season reached its conclusion, he had been poached by John Haworth for Burnley in March 1920. At the time of his signing, the *Burnley Express* reported that Anderson '...is a player of a dashing type and knows where the goal is, as will be evidenced from his being the chief goalscorer in the Scottish League.' When he left Clydebank he had scored 30 goals from his 32 appearances that season.

Anderson made his debut at Turf Moor against Sunderland in front of 27,590 supporters. The correspondent of the *Burnley Times* commented that 'Most interest centred on Anderson, who, without making a sensational debut, pleased the crowd, and the outstanding feature of his work was his fast first-time shots, while on occasions he distributed the ball in excellent style.' He went on to complete the final eight League games of 1919–20 and netted six goals, including a hat-trick in the 5–0 win over Everton.

The Burnley public immediately took to Anderson, a robust and hard-working forward who was particularly fond of the shoulder charge. In the days when goalkeepers were not a protected species, this was an important weapon in the armoury of top-class forwards, and Anderson was a master exponent of this particular art. Although not the biggest of men, he would dip his shoulder and head towards many a

startled goalkeeper, who found himself and the ball in the back of the net before he could take evasive action – another victim of the famous 'Anderson charge'.

The 1920–21 campaign didn't open particularly well for the Clarets with three straight defeats and just one goal, naturally coming from Anderson, to show for their efforts. It was at this point that the ageing legs of Bert Freeman were withdrawn from the action, and Benny Cross was introduced into the team. Anderson and Cross quickly became an instant success as an attacking partnership. The shrewd probing and passing from Cross was created chances galore for Anderson and Bob Kelly, as the Clarets embarked upon a 30-match unbeaten run that took them to the Championship.

Anderson scored 25 League goals that season, 13 of which came in just three matches. He hit four goals in the 7–1 win over Oldham Athletic and then bagged another four in the 6–0 demolition of Sheffield United. On 5 February 1920 he went one better and scored five goals in the 7–1 thrashing of Aston Villa. All three of these victories came in front of an adoring public at Turf Moor, but he could also be just as lethal away from home. In the first round of the FA Cup that season he hit four goals in the 7–3 win over Leicester City at Filbert Street. It was, perhaps, no coincidence that Anderson was out of action on the day that the Clarets were beaten by Hull City in the third round of the Cup competition.

Anderson was again top scorer in 1921–22 when the Clarets finished in third place in the First Division. However, the following campaign revealed that his goalscoring powers were on the wane as he approached his 30s. Unfortunately, he had shown flaws in his game that were covered up by his goalscoring ability, and when the goals dried up his wayward distribution and erratic ball control became more noticeable.

At the start of the 1923–24 campaign there were rumours circulating the town that Anderson was destined for a move to Chelsea. However, nothing developed, and he continued to lead the Burnley attack. When the Clarets travelled to Bramall Lane to face Sheffield United on 20 October 1923, a contingent of officials from his former club were more than interested spectators. After some protracted negotiations, he returned to Clydebank before ending his career with short spells at Vale of Leven and Glasgow Pollock.

John Angus

Date of birth: 2 September 1938, Amble

Burnley record:
Appearances: League 438+1, FA Cup 45, League Cup 25, Europe 10, others 2
Goals: League 4
Debut: League, 3 September 1956 v Everton (h) won 2–1

Also played for: Amble Boys' Club, England (1 cap), England Under-23 (7 caps),
Football League (1 appearance)

Homesickness almost cost the Clarets the services of John Angus before his career at Turf Moor had even begun. Fortunately, he was persuaded to give the club another chance after manager Alan Brown travelled to Amble and refused to give up on this talented full-back. Brown's persistence meant that Burnley were able to utilise Angus's unique talents in over 500 League and Cup games. Angus collected a League Championship medal and a full England cap as well as seven Under-23 caps and an FA Cup Finalists' medal.

Having arrived at Turf Moor on the recommendation of Charlie Ferguson, Clarets' shrewd north-east scout, Angus had to bide his time in the junior teams. However, when promotion came it came rapidly. He made the breakthrough in the early stages of the 1956–57 season when he was drafted into the first team just a week after his Central League debut. For the next few seasons he vied with David Smith for the right to inherit the mantle of Harold Rudman at right-back. Ultimately, it was Angus who prevailed, and the latter stages of the 1958–59 season found him firmly ensconced in the number-two shirt.

Angus's game was multifaceted. Not only was he an excellent defender, but he was also able to use his immaculate right foot to initiate many attacking moves. Jimmy McIlroy described him as one of the best full-backs he had either played with or against, and few would argue with such a revered figure. Above all, Angus, who was regarded as the quiet man of the Championship team, had the perfect temperament for a defender. Never rash in the tackle or in judgement, he held his nerve no matter how great the pressure. This steely resolve was accompanied by excellent ball control and perfect balance.

Such qualities ought to have been recognised more at international level than they were. Angus collected seven England Under-23 caps between 1959 and 1962, and in May 1961 he made his full international debut against Austria in Vienna. Brian Miller also made his England debut that day, but, inexplicably, neither man was to appear for their country again. Angus, who played at left-back against an Austrian side that inflicted a 3–1 defeat on England, enjoyed a fine debut for this country, which made it even more difficult to understand his lack of further opportunities. However, with Jimmy Armfield the automatic choice at right-back and Ray Wilson about to oust Mick McNeil at left-back, he found himself out in the cold when it came to international football.

During the Championship-winning season of 1959–60, he missed just one game and only five during the 1960–61 campaign, when Burnley finished fourth in the League and reached the semi-finals of both the FA Cup and the fledgling Football League Cup. In 1961–62, when the Clarets almost achieved a League and Cup double, he was again a model of consistency at right-back. Indeed, throughout the 60s, as many of the big names departed from Turf Moor, he continued to give distinguished service. In a sea of change, he remained a constant and a rock at the heart of the club.

As the 60s drew to a close, Angus found himself under pressure to retain the right-back spot, primarily from the challenge of Fred Smith. Nonetheless, as the club battled unsuccessfully against relegation in 1970–71, it was Angus who continued to fill the position. Sadly, injuries and an Achilles tendon operation brought his career to an end after 18 years at Turf Moor.

On leaving Burnley, Angus chose to make a complete break from the game, and he and his wife returned to Amble where they bought a small business. Twelve months later he returned to Turf Moor for a well-deserved testimonial, which attracted a crowd of over 15,000. Today he is happily retired and enjoys fishing, playing golf and walking around the beautiful Northumberland countryside.

Reg Attwell

Date of birth: 23 March 1920, Oakengates, Shropshire
Died: 2 December 1986, Burnley

Burnley record:
Appearances: League 244, FA Cup 25, Wartime 15
Goals: League 9, FA Cup 2, Wartime 1
Debut: League, 9 November 1946 v Luton Town (h) drew 1–1

Also played for: Morley Place FC, Conaby St Andrews, Conisbrough Welfare, Denaby United, West Ham United, (wartime guest for Leeds United, Chelsea, Doncaster Rovers, Preston North End, Queen's Park Rangers, Blackburn Rovers), Bradford City, Darwen, Football League (1 cap)

The son of a former Shrewsbury Town goalkeeper, Reg Attwell first strode onto the scene at Turf Moor during the final season of wartime football. He made his first appearance for the club on 10 November 1945 against Leeds United at Turf Moor. At that time he was still a registered player with West Ham United, but, despite a 3-2 defeat on his debut, he went on to make 15 guest appearances for the Clarets before returning to the London club for the 1946-47 season. Nonetheless, manager Cliff Britton had seen enough of him during those games to recognise the potential of the 26-year-old player. During his own playing career, Britton had been a cultured international half-back and therefore was well qualified to spot the qualities required for the position. Attwell, who had made his debut for the Hammers at Sheffield United in April 1938, appeared in four of the opening five games of 1946-47 for West Ham United. As a result, it took Britton several attempts to persuade West Ham to part with him, but, eventually, the Burnley manager succeeded in signing his man.

Attwell made his senior debut on 9 November 1946, when Luton Town visited Turf Moor and held the Clarets to a 1-1 draw. It was the first time that he teamed up with Alan Brown and George Bray, and this formidable half-back trio, together with Arthur Woodruff and Harold Mather at full-back and Jimmy Strong in goal, formed what became known as Britton's 'Iron Curtain' defence. By the end of his first season at Turf Moor, the club had not only won promotion to Division One but had also won through to an FA Cup Final meeting with Charlton Athletic. Sadly, the Final ended in defeat, but Attwell had done enough to fully justify the confidence that Britton had placed in him.

Colleague Jimmy McIlroy summed up Attwell's attributes as a player: 'Blessed with magnificent ball control, a beautiful passer, and one of that rare breed of player who always appear to have so much time to do things. No matter how tight the situation, Reg just seemed to extricate himself with ease. He made it look so simple that I'm convinced a lot of people failed to recognise the man's genius.'

Attwell appeared for the Football League against the Scottish League at Ibrox Park in March 1949. Yet, inexplicably, this was the only representative honour that he gained, despite unquestionably being one of the finest half-backs of his generation. Undoubtedly, if he had played with one of the fashionable London clubs he would have won England caps.

Attwell continued to display the same high levels of consistency until the early 1950s when, having passed the age of 30, he found himself under pressure from the youthful Jimmy Adamson. Unable to oust Adamson from the right-half spot, he languished in the reserves for a time until Bray's switch to the coaching staff enabled him to return to left-half. He proved just as successful on the opposite flank, but sadly, just as he had re-established himself, he was struck by a personal tragedy when his father died. He returned to Denaby to attend the funeral in December 1952 but then stayed to look after his mother who had been taken ill. Unfortunately, he failed to contact the club and, as a result, missed a game against Arsenal at Turf Moor.

Although Attwell returned, the event proved something of a watershed in his Turf Moor career. He was now no longer regarded as an automatic choice and his ageing legs found the challenge of Adamson and Seith difficult to resist. Restricted to 20 League appearances in 1953-54, he made his final appearance for the club on 4 September 1954 when Everton, under the management of Britton, visited Turf Moor and enjoyed a 2-0 victory. The following month he accepted the chance to move to Bradford City.

Attwell stayed just one season at Valley Parade before ending his playing career with Darwen in the Lancashire Combination. After the curtain came down on his playing career, he continued to make Burnley his adopted home.

Attwell, away from football, liked a drink and a bet. He was the most mild mannered of men. His easy going attitude was reflected by the fact that he never complained, despite suffering rather poor health in his final years, but always accepted his fate without a grumble. He was also said to have a keen sense of humour, and McIlroy, at the time of Attwell's death, told the story of how he played with him in one particular game. Burnley won a corner, and in his broad Northern Ireland accent McIlroy asked Attwell 'Shall I take the corner?' Attwell looked somewhat nonplussed, replying 'What?' McIlroy then repeated the question twice more. 'I haven't a clue what you're talking about Jim, but take the bloody corner.'

Attwell was truly one of the unsung and most underrated of all of Burnley's legends.

Alf Bassnett

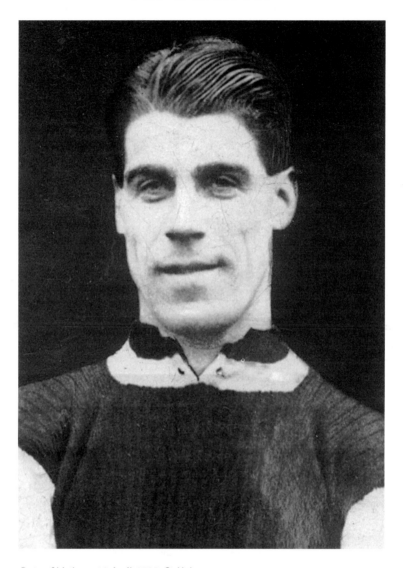

Date of birth: 10 April 1893, St Helens
Died: 24 June 1966, Burnley

Burnley record:
Appearances: League 147, FA Cup 9, others 1
Goals: League 5
Debut: League, 28 February 1920 v Derby County (h) won 2–0

Also played for: Star Rovers FC, Skelmersdale United, St Helens Town, Eccles
Borough, Lincoln City, Nelson
Managed: Ballymena, Hereford United

'From first to last a sticker, Alfred Bassnett had rendered the Burnley club much valuable service as a half-back, and, though he has not reached the heights of his immediate predecessors as a player, his wholeheartedness has carried him through.' That was the verdict of one scribe of the *Burnley Express* with regard to the contribution that Bassnett made to Burnley Football Club. Considering that he had to follow the trio of Halley, Boyle and Watson, it is no mean epithet and certainly one that was fully justified. He took the rough with the smooth and always came up smiling. He was the perfect professional and a loyal servant to Burnley Football Club.

When Bassnett joined the Clarets in June 1919, he had already turned 26 and had yet to appear in the Football League. Prior to World War One, he had gained a wealth of experience in the Lancashire Combination with the likes of Skelmersdale United, St Helen's Town and Eccles Borough as a workmanlike half-back. During the war he had served with the Royal Engineers in France. Gassed at Ypres and sent home invalided, he made a full recovery, played football for the military and won an Army Championship before he returned to Ypres.

In the summer of 1919 Burnley snapped up Bassnett to strengthen their options at half-back. Of course, prior to the war, the half-back line at Turf Moor had largely picked itself, with George Halley, Tommy Boyle and Billy Watson being the undisputed first-choice trio. Only in the final season of peacetime football had there been a threat to this settled line up, with Thorpe challenging Halley at right-half. With all four of these players still on the books at Turf Moor in 1919, Bassnett had to bide his time in the reserves. He was restricted to half a dozen senior games during his first season with the Clarets, filling in for Thorpe at right-half after the latter had been sold to Blackburn Rovers.

During the Championship-winning season of 1920–21, Halley was at his imperious best at right-half, and so Bassnett spent a large part of the season playing Central League football. However, when Halley went down with a bout of pneumonia, Bassnett stepped up to play in the final 15 matches of the season and so gained a Championship medal. At that point he would have walked into any side, but at Burnley he was again faced with the prospect of the role of understudy when the 1921–22 campaign began.

However, when Tommy Boyle slipped out of the Burnley team in February 1922, Bassnett stepped up to fill the centre-half berth. It spoke volumes for his professionalism and ability that he wasn't overawed by being faced with the task of replacing one of the club's all-time greats. He did sufficiently well to retain his place for virtually the whole of 1922–23 and impressed everyone with his consistency in defence. The following season he reverted to his right-half position following the arrival of Jack Hill at Turf Moor.

In November 1926, at the age of 33, and after appearing in 147 League games for the Clarets, Bassnett left Turf Moor to join Lincoln City. At the time of his departure he had lost his place in the team to John Steel, who had been signed from Hamilton Academical in November 1925. Although the quality of those around him limited his appearances at Turf Moor, he was fondly remembered as a tough competitor who was particularly good at breaking up opposing attacking moves. Perhaps his fondness for the physically competitive side of the game came from his Rugby background because as a youth, coming from the Rugby League stronghold of St Helens, he had been extremely talented with the oval ball. Nonetheless, his ability to fill any of the half-back positions made him a useful asset at Turf Moor.

Bassnett joined Lincoln at a time when the Sincil Bank club's fortunes were on the up. The club had invested heavily in the likes of Albert Iremonger, the famous goalkeeping veteran, and wingers Charlie Bosbury from Preston and Frank Pegg from Sunderland. However, when Bassnett arrived in November 1926, results had not reflected this investment, and Lincoln finished the campaign in a disappointing 11th position in the Third Division North.

The following season, Bassnett missed only one League game as the Imps narrowly missed out on promotion by finishing runners-up to Bradford Park Avenue. At that time, only one club was promoted to the Second Division from each of the two regional third tiers. He made his final appearances for Lincoln in 1928–29, and the following summer he joined Ballymena in Northern Ireland as player-manager. He led them to the Irish Cup Final in 1930 before taking the player-manager's role with Hereford United. He returned to East Lancashire in August 1931 to join Nelson.

In later life Bassnett became a licensee in Burnley, being mine host at the Bridge Inn and later the White Bull. After his retirement, he continued to live in the town until his death in 1966, following a prolonged illness.

George Beel

Date of birth:	26 February 1900, Bracebridge Heath, near Lincoln
Died:	30 December 1980, Maidstone

Burnley record:

Appearances:	League 316, FA Cup 21
Goals:	League 178, FA Cup 9
Debut:	League, 5 May 1923 v Birmingham (h) lost 0–2
Also played for:	Lincoln Schools, RAMC (Blackpool), Lincoln City, Merthyr Town, Chesterfield, Lincoln City, Rochdale
Managed:	Tunbridge Wells Rangers, Maidstone

Beel had the misfortune to arrive at Turf Moor just as John Haworth's Championship-winning side was breaking up. The club's fortunes were on the wane, and although he made some 337 senior appearances, in which he scored 187 goals, medals and trophies eluded him during his stay at Burnley. Nonetheless, during his time at the club he was able to rewrite the goalscoring records and thus earn his own place in the history of Burnley Football Club. A seasonal record of 35 League goals in 1927–28, 11 hat-tricks, and top scorer in six of his nine seasons as a first team player all reflected the fact that he was simply a goalscoring phenomenon.

'One of the most hard-working players they have ever had, Beel could always be relied upon to put heart and soul into a game, and many a time he had been the rallying force for a dispirited side. Many spectators will remember his prodigious energy and 'do or die' tactics on grounds inches deep in mud. At his best he was a clever schemer and a prolific goal-getter.' These were the thoughts of one local journalist with regard to the contribution that Beel made during his time at the club.

Beel was signed by John Haworth as the long-term replacement for the fading Joe Anderson. He arrived from Chesterfield in April 1923 in part-exchange for John Fisher. Beel had gained previous League experience with Lincoln City and Merthyr Town, but it was at Saltergate, with 26 goals in 39 appearances for Chesterfield, that he really made his mark.

A record of 19 goals from 34 League games in 1923–24 easily made him the leading goalscorer. Bob Kelly and Benny Cross, who played at inside-forward, scored eight and five goals respectively as the Clarets suffered a stuttering season, which brought an appearance in the semi-final of the FA Cup but a lowly 17th position in the First Division.

The following season Tom Roberts took the centre-forward position in October, and Beel was successfully switched to inside-forward. Restored to centre-forward, he passed the 20 goals in a season mark for the first time during his stay at Turf Moor in 1926–27. The 24 goals that he netted helped the Clarets to finish in fifth place in the First Division.

In 1927–28 Beel was on fire and notched an impressive 35 goals in 39 League appearances. Unbelievably, the Clarets finished in 19th place, just one point above the relegation places. It was all the more remarkable as Louis Page had chipped in with 22 League goals. Fortunately, in what was the tightest ever First Division – only five points separated fourth-placed Derby County from Portsmouth who finished in 20th position – the goals that he and Page scored ultimately saved the club from relegation. Indeed, as the Clarets finished the season with the worst defensive record in the top flight with 98 goals conceded, it merely underlined the importance of Beel's contribution to the club.

The 1928–29 season brought another relegation struggle as the Clarets again finished with the worst defensive record of all top-flight clubs, 103 goals conceded. Once again the club relied heavily on his goalscoring exploits and his 30 League goals ensured survival with another 19th-place finish.

Sadly, there was to be no escape from relegation during the following campaign. Beel moved to inside-right for a spell but the goals didn't flow quite so freely. A relatively meagre haul of 10 goals, as the Clarets slipped into the Second Division, merely emphasised how important his goals had been in previous seasons.

Beel found his scoring touch again the following season and finished top scorer with 25 League goals, as the Clarets finished in eighth place in the Second Division. During the latter part of his career he lost much of his speed, but that didn't prevent him from scoring goals. '...even on days when he has touched very low form he has scored,' commented one local scribe during Beel's final days at Turf Moor.

Beel was offered the opportunity to enter management at the end of 1930–31 but chose instead to remain at Turf Moor. He was still scoring freely in 1931–32 when he was surprisingly sold to Lincoln City in February 1932. The club, like so many others at that time, was suffering financially as a result of the trade depression that had affected the Lancashire cotton towns. Nonetheless, it still came as something of a shock when it was revealed that he had been allowed to leave.

Arthur Bellamy

Date of birth: 5 April 1942, Blackhill

Burnley record:
Appearances: League 204+13, FA Cup 9, League Cup 16, Europe 6, others 1+1
Goals: League 29
Debut: League, 26 March 1963 v Manchester City (a) won 5–2

Also played for: Consett Iron Company, Chesterfield

Bellamy is typical of that band of footballers who give long and loyal service to a club without ever winning honours or achieving national recognition. While he might be somewhat anonymous outside of Burnley and its surrounds, to the Claret and Blue faithful he remains the archetypal one-club man who gave a lifetime of service to a club and, as a result, wins the hearts of the followers of that club. In Bellamy's case, his contribution to Burnley Football Club means that he is held in the highest esteem by those who support the club.

Like so many of the club's most faithful servants, he was spotted while playing junior football in his native North East. An apprentice welder at an iron works, he caught the eye of Jack Hixon, the Clarets' north-east scout. He was invited to Turf Moor for a trial and joined the club as a junior in February 1958, in the same week that Harry Potts took the helm at the club. He arrived at a time when Burnley were on the brink of greatness thanks to a squad of hugely-talented players. As a result, Bellamy had to ply his trade in the youth and reserve teams for some time. In 1961–62 he helped the A team win the Lancashire League title and also appeared for the reserve team that lifted the Central League Championship. However, with Jimmy McIlroy and Jimmy Robson still at their peak in the inside-forward positions, breaking into the first team was no easy task for young Bellamy.

His chance came in March 1963, following the controversial departure of McIlroy to Stoke City. He made his debut in the 5–2 victory over Manchester City at Maine Road and celebrated his first-team call up with a goal. He went on to appear in 13 League games that season, and the following campaign, although in and out of the team, he managed to score eight goals in 17 League matches. Indeed, on his first appearance in 1963–64 he bagged a hat-trick in a 4–3 win over Everton at Goodison Park.

Throughout his 10 seasons as a first-team player at Turf Moor, he proved a valuable member of the Burnley squad without ever really establishing himself as an automatic choice in one particular position. Although he amassed some 250 senior appearances for the club, it was his final year with them that brought his highest seasonal total with 27 starts in the League and a further four substitute appearances. His lack of opportunities was due to the excellence of those ahead of him at Turf Moor, with Gordon Harris and Brian

O'Neil holding down the midfield places for most of the 60s. However, Bellamy was sufficiently versatile to adapt to the changing nature of the English game, and for a time he proved a very successful sweeper behind the Burnley defence.

Bellamy suffered the agony of scoring an extra-time own-goal against Swindon Town in a semi-final replay of the Football League Cup in December 1968. He also had to suffer relegation to the Second Division in 1970–71. His final game for the Clarets came against Sunderland, ironically the club he had supported as a boy, in April 1972. The following July, aged 30, he was sold to Third Division Chesterfield for £10,000. He made 133 League appearances for the Saltergate club, all in the third tier of English football.

When Bellamy was released by Chesterfield in April 1976, he returned to Burnley, bought a milk round and then tried his hand at running a chip shop. He then received the call to rejoin the Burnley backroom staff in 1979 as coach to the B team. In 1986 Brian Miller returned to the club as manager and invited Bellamy, a former playing colleague, to step up to the position of assistant manager. It was while he held this post that the Clarets reached Wembley in the Sherpa Van Trophy in May 1988. When Frank Casper took over the manager's job, he stepped down from his role and took over as the club's head groundsman, a position that he holds today.

Marlon Beresford

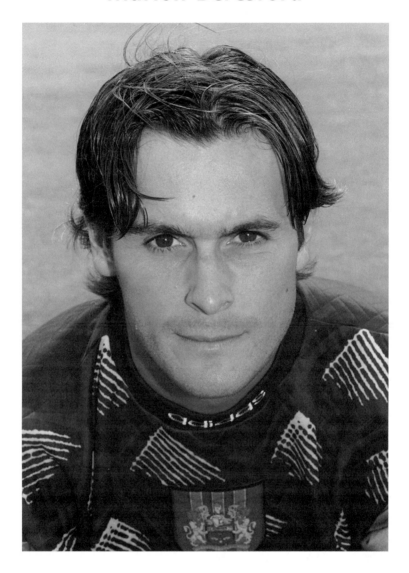

Date of birth: 2 September 1969, Lincoln

Burnley record:
Appearances: League 286+1, FA Cup 25, League Cup 22, others 16
Debut: League, 29 August 1992 v Rotherham United (h) drew 1–1

Also played for: Sheffield Wednesday, Bury, Ipswich Town, Northampton Town, Crewe Alexandra, Northampton Town, Middlesbrough, Sheffield Wednesday, Wolverhampton Wanderers, York City, Bradford City, Luton Town, Barnsley, Luton Town

Burnley Football Club and Marlon Beresford shared a special relationship for over a decade. Although he travelled far and wide during his career, he continually returned to the familiar surroundings of Turf Moor. The club and its supporters always welcomed him back with open arms.

It was Jimmy Mullen who first signed him in August 1992 for a fee of £95,000. The Sheffield Wednesday custodian, yet to make a senior appearance for the Hillsborough club, had made 34 League appearances while on loan to the likes of Bury, Northampton Town and Crewe Alexandra.

After witnessing five 'keepers try to make the position their own during 1991–92, it was perhaps unsurprising that the sure handling of Beresford should find favour with the supporters. Throughout his first season at the club, he produced a string of breathtaking saves that demonstrated his agility to the full. A good shot stopper, with a particularly good record of saving penalties, he was voted Player of the Year by readers of the *Burnley Express* at the end of his first season at the club. His fellow professionals also recognised his qualities when they voted him as the best 'keeper in the Second Division.

The following season Beresford helped the Clarets to promotion via a wonderful victory over Stockport County, at Wembley in the Play-off Final. He was an ever present that campaign and was again rewarded with the accolade of the Division's best 'keeper by his fellow professionals.

Dismissed twice for professional fouls during 1994–95, he was unable to prevent the Clarets from suffering relegation after just one season at a higher level. Suddenly, inconsistency began to creep into his performances. Brilliance could often be followed by unexpected and elementary errors. The struggle to find his best form in 1995–96 was not helped by continued hernia and back problems.

The following season found Beresford in more commanding form as his contract neared its end. He expressed the desire to play at a higher standard of football, and, as a result, the club allowed him to move to Middlesbrough in March 1998. The return of £400,000 was excellent for a player whose contract was about to expire.

During the remainder of the 1997–98 campaign, Beresford made three appearances for Middlesbrough. Although they won promotion to the Premiership, he found himself as understudy to Mark Schwarzer.

Beresford made 10 appearances for Middlesbrough in the League – two of which were as a substitute – and was also loaned out to Sheffield Wednesday and Wolves before rejoining the Clarets in January 2002, initially on a month's loan. Ironically, he found himself in a similar situation to the one which had caused his departure from Turf Moor. 'I am out of contract at Middlesbrough in the summer, and I'm looking to get away and play some football, so I can hopefully make an impression here and put myself in the shop window,' he explained.

Beresford spent a couple of months on loan at Turf Moor as cover for regular 'keeper Nik Michopoulos. During that time he hardly put a foot wrong with his safe handling and spectacular shot stopping. It was hoped in the summer that he would return to Turf Moor on a permanent basis.

During pre-season Beresford remained with the club, but the financial situation meant that Stan Ternent couldn't offer him a contract. As a result he moved to York City on a short-term contract in the hope that the finances would improve at Turf Moor.

A disastrous start to the 2002–03 campaign, coupled with the fact that the Clarets only had one other senior 'keeper, enabled Ternent to persuade the directors to sign Beresford on a one-month contract. 'I just can't keep away,' was his reaction on returning to training at Gawthorpe. He continued to renew his short-term contracts with the club and featured in 34 League games that season. Unfortunately, he didn't enjoy the best form during his final spell with the Clarets. The team suffered some unexpectedly heavy defeats, and at the end of the campaign both he and Michopoulos were released.

Beresford continued to ply his trade in the Football League and was never short of employers. He played briefly with Bradford City before joining Luton Town and then Barnsley. In July 2005 he rejoined Luton and made 38 appearances for the Hatters in the Championship. At the start of the 2006–07 campaign he remained the first-choice custodian at the club.

Adam Blacklaw

Date of birth: 2 September 1937, Aberdeen

Burnley record:
Appearances: League 318, FA Cup 44, League Cup 12, Europe 8, others 1
Debut: League, 22 December 1956 v Cardiff City (h) won 6–2

Also played for: Blackburn Rovers, Blackpool, Great Harwood, Scotland (3 caps),
                   Scotland Under-23 (2 caps)
Managed: Clitheroe

When Colin McDonald broke his leg playing for the Football League in March 1959, it fell to Adam Blacklaw to pick up the mantle of Burnley's England 'keeper. For many it would have been an unenviable task, as McDonald was one of the outstanding goalkeepers of his generation. Fortunately, he was up for the task, and as McDonald's career came to a tragic end Blacklaw's began to blossom.

The son of a ship's carpenter at Hall and Company in his native Aberdeen, Blacklaw hoped to follow in his father's footsteps. He described him as 'a really good footballer, an old-fashioned centre-forward,' who played for his work's football team. Blacklaw, however, soon forsook his dreams of being a goalscorer when he was persuaded to become a goalkeeper when at school. His natural ability for the position brought him Scottish international selection at Schoolboy level and the offer of an apprenticeship with Burnley. While learning his trade as a 'keeper, he also served his apprenticeship as a bricklayer.

In October 1954 Blacklaw turned professional and was promoted to the Central League team at Burnley at the age of 16. He made his senior debut when McDonald was ruled out by injury in December 1956. He spent the next two seasons as understudy to McDonald until fate intervened and ended the England 'keepers career.

Blacklaw proved remarkably consistent, and during his first six seasons as the senior custodian he only missed two matches. On one occasion international duty kept him out of action for Burnley, while the second occasion occurred when Harry Potts rested the whole team before a European Cup clash with SV Hamburg.

Blacklaw was also a key member of the Championship-winning team of 1959–60. 'We had no real stars, but we worked hard for each other. If any of us was having an off day, everyone else would dig in even deeper to help them through it. We played for each other – that was the secret of our success,' he explained. He was also in goal when the Clarets were beaten by Tottenham Hotspur in the 1962 FA Cup Final and was an ever present as the men from Turf Moor finished second in the First Division that same season.

Having already won a couple of Under-23 caps for Scotland, Blacklaw gained the first of his three full caps in June 1963 against Norway in Bergen.

Consistency and bravery were the hallmarks of Blacklaw's his game. He was never overawed no matter how intense the atmosphere and simply took everything in his stride. When the Clarets visited Naples for a Fairs Cup clash in February 1967, he was no longer first-choice custodian at Turf Moor. In the game that became known as the 'Battle of Naples', the Clarets held out for a valiant 0–0 draw, thus winning the tie 3–0, thanks to the brilliance of Harry Thomson in the Burnley goal. When Thomson was attacked after leaving the pitch, it was Blacklaw who waded in to rescue his colleague before the Burnley players were whisked away by military escort to the airport. The previous season he had been involved in a skirmish at Ewood Park when a Blackburn fan ran onto the pitch to confront him during a local derby. The fan soon realised the folly of his actions and left the pitch in rather worse shape than when he entered.

Undoubtedly, one of Blacklaw's happiest memories of European football had occurred during the European Cup campaign of 1960–61. He made a miraculous save from a goal-bound header from the legendary West German star Uwe Seeler. Such was the quality of the save that Seeler simply stood in shock for a moment before he joined in the applause for Blacklaw.

In the summer of 1967 he left Turf Moor to make the short journey to Ewood Park. He gave three years' excellent service to Blackburn Rovers before ending his career with a season at Blackpool as backup to Harry Thomson, the man who inherited his number-one spot at Turf Moor. Ironically, both men were released by the Seasiders at the end of the season. He was involved locally in the non-League games for a while, with both Great Harwood and Clitheroe.

When Blacklaw retired from the game he ran a Burnley newsagent's for seven years before he became the steward at Burnley Cricket Club. He then ran a pub for several years and in more recent times has worked as a caretaker-handyman at Nelson and Colne College.

Robbie Blake

Date of birth: 4 March 1976, Middlesbrough

Burnley record:
Appearances: League 103+17, FA Cup 6+1, League Cup 11
Goals: League 42, FA Cup 4, League Cup 5
Debut: League, 3 February 2002 v West Bromwich Albion (h) lost 2–0

Also played for: Darlington, Bradford City, Nottingham Forest, Birmingham City,
Leeds United

Stan Ternent had been a long-time admirer of Robbie Blake, Bradford City's goalscoring forward who had suddenly found himself out of favour at Valley Parade after a change of management. Blake, who had begun his career at Darlington, where he scored 21 goals in 68 League appearances, had scored 40 goals in 153 League outings with the Bantams. He had been loaned out to Nottingham Forest and was the target of other clubs before Ternent made his move to bring him to Turf Moor.

The Burnley manager had expressed an interest in signing him in December 2001 but felt he was overpriced. However, the following month Barry Kilby, the Burnley chairman, backed his manager to the hilt when he paid £1,000,000 for him, with the promise of another £250,000 going to Bradford if the Clarets won promotion during his time at Turf Moor.

Unfortunately, a series of niggling injuries limited Blake's involvement during his first few months at Turf Moor. Stomach strains, a hernia problem and perhaps being a little overweight, he certainly didn't enjoy the best of starts to his Burnley career.

However, in 2002–03 Blake demonstrated to the Burnley faithful exactly why their manager had rated him so highly. Sometimes employed up front and sometimes behind the strikers, he displayed his full range of trickery as he struck up an excellent understanding with Glen Little. He was an immensely skilful player in possession and had the ability to take the ball to an opponent, almost invite him to rob him and then, sleight of foot, he would spirit the ball away and leave the defender floundering. Although he hit 13

goals in 41 League appearances that season, it was somewhat of a disappointing tally for a player who could strike the ball with venom using either foot. Nonetheless, he created numerous goalscoring opportunities for his colleagues. He was at his best with the ball at his feet and the play developing around him. He quickly became the focal point of all the best attacking moves that the team put together.

In 2003–04 the club's survival in the First Division owed as much to the efforts of Blake as anything else. He bagged 19 goals in his 45 League appearances but proved, once again, that there was more to his game than just scoring goals. He was not a goal poacher in the classic sense of the term. He wasn't one to loiter around the penalty area to snap up half chances. He did, however, possess the ability to mesmerise opponents and continually drag defenders out of position. He liked to run at the opposition and unleash his shots from all ranges and angles. Although not the tallest of men, he was immensely strong and was difficult to shake off the ball once in possession.

Steve Cotterill appointed him as captain in 2004–05, and Blake responded with some excellent performances, particularly when asked to plough a lonely furrow up front on his own. During the first half of that season, the Clarets relied heavily on his goals and his creative ability. He celebrated his 100th League appearance for Burnley with a magnificent solo effort against Wolves early in the season. Cotterill waxed lyrical about his star forward, 'He is a wonderful player who expects high standards from himself...'

With Blake in such electrifying form, it was little wonder that other clubs began to show an interest in the Burnley captain. In December 2005 Wigan Athletic made several unsuccessful attempts to prise him away from Turf Moor. However, the bids unsettled him, and in January 2005 he left Turf Moor to join Birmingham City for an initial £1,250,000, plus various add-ons.

Surprisingly, the move to St Andrews didn't work out quite as expected, and in July 2005 Blake was sold to Leeds United for £800,000. He started just two Premiership games for Birmingham while making another nine appearances as a substitute. During his first season at Elland Road he helped Leeds to reach the Play-off Final but found himself on the losing side at the Millennium Stadium when Watford romped to a 3–0 win.

Tommy Boyle

Date of birth:	29 January 1888, Hoyland near Barnsley
Died:	5 January 1940, Whittingham

Burnley record:

Appearances:	League 210, FA Cup 25, Wartime 63, others 1
Goals:	League 36, FA Cup 7, Wartime 13
Debut:	League, 30 September 1911 v Barnsley (a) drew 1–1

Also played for: Hoyland Star, Elescar Athletic, Barnsley, Wrexham, England (1 cap), Football League (4 appearances)

Tommy Boyle was the first Burnley captain to lead his side to League Championship success and remains the only Burnley skipper to lift the FA Cup. Not only was he a great footballer, but he was also a captain in every sense of the word. His attributes as a player are well documented: 'He was magnificent in judging a ball, untiring, a great intervener, deadly with his head, unsurpassed in sweeping passes to the wings,' wrote one local scribe. Little wonder that Boyle is still held in such high esteem by the followers of Burnley Football Club.

A Yorkshireman by birth, Boyle had enjoyed a highly successful career with Barnsley prior to joining Burnley in September 1911. In 1909–10 he had led the Tykes to an FA Cup Final against Newcastle United, which, despite defeat in the replay, ensured his own niche in the history of the Yorkshire club. Indeed he was so highly thought of in Barnsley, having played 178 League and Cup games for them, that the Clarets had to pay a club-record fee of £1,150 to persuade the Yorkshire club to allow him to come to Burnley.

Boyle was the player around whom John Haworth built one of the all time great Burnley teams. Promotion to Division One in 1912–13, FA Cup success the following season and a League Championship in 1920–21 all meant that he more than repaid the huge investment that the club had made in him.

Boyle was part of the famous half-back line of himself, George Halley and Willie Watson that wrote its name in the annals of the club. Future generations of Burnley supporters were weaned on stories of this famous trio that had become synonymous with the glory days of Burnley Football Club. Although not the tallest of men at 5ft 7in, Boyle was a powerful header of the ball and scored many vital goals this way. Perhaps his most celebrated headed goal was the one that he scored in March 1913 in a fourth-round FA Cup tie, against neighbours Blackburn Rovers. His aerial power was matched by his ability on the ground. He was a strong tackler and once the ball was won his distribution was immaculate.

Despite his success in domestic football, Boyle was only selected for England on one occasion. He played at centre-half in Belfast in February 1913, when Ireland beat England 2–1. He did appear in a military international at Goodison Park in May 1915 when he played for an England team that beat a Scottish team 4–3. One of the scorers for England that day was Eddie Mosscrop, Boyle's colleague at Turf Moor. He was also selected to represent the Football League on four occasions between 1912 and 1919.

Boyle might well have achieved even greater success at the club but for the outbreak of World War One. Like all players of his generation, his career was severely affected. Although he made appearances for the club during the somewhat meaningless wartime competitions, he also served his country with distinction. As a Bombardier, he fought in France and suffered serious injuries in 1917. Many men might well have called it a day at that point in terms of football, but Boyle was made of sterner stuff. He returned to action at Turf Moor in March 1919 and appeared in the final nine games of wartime football.

In 1919–20 Boyle led the Clarets to second place in the First Division, and the following season he helped Burnley lift the Championship for the first time in the club's history. However, at the age of 33 he was starting to slow down a little, and the 1921–22 campaign proved to be his last as injuries began to take their toll. Fittingly, he made his final League appearance for the club at Turf Moor in the 1–0 win over Arsenal on 20 February 1922. After that, his centre-half berth went to Alf Bassnett, and Boyle became player-coach at the end of the season. Restored to fitness, he played in the reserves for a spell before joining Wrexham in June 1923 as player-coach.

Boyle spent a season in Wales before working for a time in Germany as a coach. However, he returned to England, settled in Blackpool and prepared for a life outside of football. At one time, Boyle, whose favourite pastime was bowling, was a licensee. Sadly, financial difficulties blighted his life, and led to a nervous breakdown. He was under medical treatment for practically the rest of his life, and his health remained fragile until his tragically early death at Whittingham Hospital in January 1940.

George Bray

Date of birth: 11 November 1918, Oswaldtwistle, Lancashire
Died: 13 February 2002, Hapton, Lancashire

Burnley record:
Appearances: League 241, FA Cup 18, Wartime 59
Goals: League 8, FA Cup 1
Debut: League, 1 October 1938 v Luton Town (h) won 3–2

Also played for: Great Harwood, (wartime guest for Charlton Athletic, Crystal Palace, Royal Artillery, Glentoran)

When George Bray arrived at Turf Moor as a promising young 18-year-old, few could have predicted the colossal contribution he would make to the club over the next seven decades. As a player, his career stretched over both sides of World War Two, while his coaching roles ranged from the youth team to the senior squad. In short, he was the very epitome of the loyal one-club man.

Bray arrived at Turf Moor in October 1937 and quickly made an impression with his lively displays in Central League football. After a year in the second team, he made his senior debut in the home clash with Luton Town in October 1938. From that day until his retirement in 1952, he became the automatic choice for the left-half position.

Like so many players of his generation, the outbreak of war robbed Bray of what should have been the most profitable years of his career. He appeared in 59 wartime matches for the Clarets, including the two opening League games of the 1939–40 season, which were declared void when the Football League was suspended for the duration of the war. He played as a guest for Charlton Athletic and Crystal Palace, and, while serving in Northern Ireland, he also represented Glentoran. Indeed, he played in the 1942 Irish Cup Final when one of his teammates was Reg Kirkham, who later joined him at Turf Moor.

When the Football League began operations again in 1946–47, Burnley were under new management. Cliff Britton constructed a new half-back line that consisted of Reg Attwell, Alan Brown and, of course, Bray at left-half. The trio became the cornerstone of Britton's 'Iron Curtain' defence.

Bray missed only one League game as promotion was won during that first memorable season of peacetime football. He also played in every match of the FA Cup run and appeared at Wembley when Charlton Athletic inflicted a 1–0 defeat on the Clarets in the FA Cup Final. As Burnley established themselves in the top flight, he proved himself to be a tough-tackling half-back who never shirked a challenge or gave less than 100 percent. Curiously, his brother Jack was also a wing-half, who enjoyed a successful career with Manchester City and won half-a-dozen caps for England.

Bray played his final game for the Clarets at the Victoria Ground, Stoke, on 29 September 1951. The emergence of Jimmy Adamson challenged the ageing legs of Bray and Reg Attwell for one of the half-back positions, and, ultimately, it was Bray who lost out.

After a season of Central League football, Bray called time on his playing career and joined the backroom staff at Turf Moor. Initially, he was asked to look after the youngsters in the A team and was then promoted to perform the same task with the Central League side. In the 1960s he succeeded Ray Bennion as first-team trainer and worked alongside both Harry Potts and Jimmy Adamson in that role. In 1974, when Adamson rearranged his backroom team, Bray left Turf Moor to work in a local hospital. However, he wasn't away from the club for long and returned to become the kit manager. Sadly, while in this new role, he witnessed the club's fall to the Fourth Division. He finally retired at the age of 73, but he remained a fierce champion of the Burnley cause and was a keen supporter of the club until his death in February 2002.

Cliff Britton

Date of birth:	29 August 1909, Bristol
Died:	1 December 1975, Hull

Burnley record:

Manager:	May 1945–September 1948
Played for:	Hanham Athletic, Hanham United Methodists, Bristol St George, Bristol Rovers, Everton, England (9 caps+12 wartime caps)
Also managed:	Everton, Preston North End, Hull City

When, in May 1945, the Burnley directors appointed Cliff Britton as manager, it was something of a leap into the unknown. Alf Boland, who had been in control prior to the outbreak of World War Two, had left the club in 1940. The years before the war had been disappointing ones for the Clarets, and it was in a bid to move the club forward that the directors turned to the former England international.

As a player, Britton had been a cultured half-back who, after turning professional with Bristol Rovers, made almost 250 appearances for Everton. He won 21 caps for England, nine at full international level and 12 during wartime football. Burnley was his first managerial appointment, and it gave Britton the opportunity to try out his progressive ideas with regard to tactics and training.

Military service (Britton was a sergeant-major instructor in the Physical Training Corps) meant that he didn't take over at Turf Moor until October 1945. He used the final season of wartime football to study his players and assess their potential. At the club's annual meeting in February 1946, he announced an ambitious three-year plan to take the Clarets back into the First Division, not that he thought it would be an easy task. 'Things were not too good. Burnley had been in the doldrums for a long while,' he later reflected when explaining the job he faced.

The restoration of the Football League in 1946–47 ended with the Clarets winning promotion from the Second Division and reaching the FA Cup Final. While defeat at Wembley at the hands of Charlton Athletic, was disappointing, it couldn't overshadow the tremendous progress that the club had made under Britton's management. He had welded his players into a unit and empowered them with a team spirit that was to become a vital factor in their success. This success at Burnley was built on what popularly became known as his 'Iron Curtain' defence. It consisted of Jimmy Strong in goal, Arthur Woodruff and Harold Mather at full-back and a half-back line of Reg Attwell, Alan Brown and George Bray. Together this defensive barrier kept 20 clean sheets, including a run of six games in November and December 1946, and conceded just 29 League goals.

Britton followed the exploits of 1946–47 with a hugely respectable third-place finish in the First Division the following season. Despite heavy away defeats at Manchester United (0–5) and Manchester City (1–4), the 'Iron Curtain' looked just as impenetrable in higher company.

In the wake of his success, it was a major blow to the Clarets when Britton was lured back to his beloved Goodison Park in September 1948. Long-serving Bob Johnson, the captain of the Central League team at Turf Moor, described him as '...a great football tactician.' Mr E.D. Kay, the Burnley chairman, while disappointed at losing his manager, spoke highly of him when he said 'In Mr Britton we are losing a man who had given outstanding service, and he takes with us our best wishes for his future success. He will leave Burnley with the respect of a host of friends.'

After his success at Turf Moor, Britton endured difficult times at Everton. In 1949–50 he took them to an FA Cup semi-final but lost out to neighbours Liverpool in the quest for a place at Wembley. The following season also proved disastrous, with the club dropping into the Second Division. He had returned to Turf Moor in October 1950 to sign Harry Potts, but his former Burnley player couldn't help Everton retain their First Division status. However, he managed to guide Everton to promotion in 1953–54.

In 1956 Britton parted company with Everton over an internal dispute with the directors at Goodison Park. However, he wasn't out of work for long as Preston North End appointed him manager in the summer of that year. Having finished the previous season just one point above the relegation zone, Britton had an immediate galvanising effect at Deepdale, and his first season in charge ended with Preston in third place on the same points as second-placed Tottenham Hotspur. In 1957–58 he led Preston to the runners'-up spot in the First Division. Sadly, things then began to slide, and in 1960–61 Preston were relegated, and Britton parted company with the club.

Once again Britton was not out of work for long, and in July 1961 he accepted the managerial position at Hull City. It was to prove a profitable move for both him and the club. In 1965–66 he guided Hull to the Third Division Championship and turned them into a strong outfit in the second tier of English football.

However, no matter what Britton achieved elsewhere in his managerial career, his period in charge of Burnley was one of success for both club and manager. His legendary status at Turf Moor is well deserved.

Ian Britton

Date of birth: 19 May 1954, Dundee

Burnley record:
Appearances: League 102+6, FA Cup 1+2, League Cup 7, others 11+1
Goals: League 10
Debut: League, 23 August 1986 v Torquay United (a) drew 1–1

Also played for: Hillside Rangers, Chelsea, Dundee United, Arbroath, Blackpool,
Burnley Bank Hall, Nelson

To the neutral observer there is nothing in Ian Britton's record, in terms of goals and appearances at Turf Moor, to suggest the need for his inclusion in a book such as this. However, to the Claret and Blue faithful the events of 9 May 1987 and Britton's role in them will ensure his name remains at for the forefront of Burnley folklore for generations to come. Quite simply, it was the diminutive Scot who scored the goal that saved the club from the unthinkable – relegation from the Football League.

Britton, aged 32, had a wealth of experience behind him when he joined the Clarets, initially on loan, in August 1986. At Stamford Bridge he had made 289 League and Cup appearances for Chelsea in the top two Divisions of English football. After a very brief flirtation with Scottish football, during which he won a Scottish League Championship medal with Dundee United, he had returned south of the border to appear in 106 League games for Blackpool. Although approaching the final stages of his career, Brian Miller, the Burnley manager, believed that Britton could provide that extra spark and touch of class in football's basement.

Britton arrived at the club as Burnley were about to embark upon their second season of Fourth Division football. He made his debut on the opening day of the campaign, having appeared in the pre-season Lancashire Manx Cup competition. The Clarets had not fared too well in that annual tournament, and it proved a foretaste of things to come. A promising start, which brought just one defeat from the opening seven games, quickly evaporated, and the Clarets became involved in a desperate battle against relegation. Britton, who made 37 starts and two substitute appearances in the League that season, was one of the few bright spots in an otherwise disastrous campaign. Even so, if it hadn't been for his heroics on the last day of the season he might well have disappeared into the mists of time without registering a footnote in the annals of Burnley Football Club.

Fate, however, decreed that Britton would be viewed as a saviour of this famous old club. The position on the last day of the season was quite simple. Burnley had to win their final match at home to Orient and then hope that results elsewhere went in their favour. Ultimately, relegation was between Burnley, Lincoln City and Torquay United. The visitors, on the other hand, needed the three points if they were to stand any chance of winning a place in the Play-offs. The match caught the imagination of a wider audience, as the prospect of a founder member of the Football League losing its status captured the headlines.

As the first half moved into injury time, and with the game goalless, Britton broke down the right wing and found Neil Grewcock with a perfect pass. Grewcock cut inside and from 20 yards sent a left-foot drive into the net to give the Clarets a 1–0 lead. As the game had started 15 minutes late due to crowd congestion, the men from Turf Moor also had the advantage of knowing how other results were going. The key moment came three minutes into the second half when Grewcock floated in a free-kick that Britton, the smallest man on the field, headed home with great aplomb. The visitors pulled a goal back after 56 minutes, but the Clarets held on and survived, while Lincoln City took the drop after losing their last-day battle. 'It's a day I'll remember for the rest of my life' he recalled. 'People have called me their hero and thanked me for keeping Burnley in the Football League. That's very special. I always get a nice feeling that the fans are so grateful and that they still remember.'

Britton remained at the club for a further two seasons before bowing out of League football as he approached his 35th birthday. Like so many former Clarets, he has continued to live in the area and has been active on the non-League scene, working with clubs like Burnley Bank Hall, Nelson and Accrington Stanley.

Alan Brown

Date of birth:	26 August 1914, Consett
Died:	9 March 1996, Barnstable

Burnley record:

Appearances:	League 88, FA Cup 10
Debut:	League, 31 August 1946 v Coventry City (h) drew 1–1
Manager:	August 1954–July 1957

Also played for:	Corbridge United, Spen Black & White, Huddersfield Town, Huddersfield Police Force, (wartime guest for Blackburn Rovers, Halifax Town, Liverpool, Manchester United, Nottingham Forest, Barnsley, Fulham, Notts County), Notts County, Football League (1 appearance)
Managed:	Sunderland, Sheffield Wednesday, Sunderland, Ham-Kam Hamar

Even if he hadn't returned to Turf Moor in August 1954 as the manager, Alan Brown would still have ranked as one of the greatest captains and centre-halves to have represented the club. However, when his contribution as manager is added to his achievements as a player, it is easy to see why he ranks among the legends of Burnley Football Club.

The son of a painter and decorator, Brown came from footballing stock as his cousin was Aussie Campbell, the former Blackburn Rovers, Huddersfield Town and England international half-back. Indeed, Campbell was still at Huddersfield when Brown joined the Leeds Road club in March 1933. He became understudy to Alf Young, Huddersfield's England international centre-half, and Brown, a keen student of the game, learnt at first hand the finer arts of defending from Young. However, the consistency of England's man limited his exposure to League football. Furthermore, the hopes he had harboured of furthering his education while at Huddersfield came to nothing, and, as a result, he left to join the local police force. He spent two and a half years with the Huddersfield Constabulary, but the lure of football proved too great and he returned to Leeds Road as he was obliged to do so under the regulations of the time.

The war years brought a round of guest appearances for various clubs, and Brown also played for the RAF in inter-service matches. He was signed by Cliff Britton for Burnley in February 1946 for a fee of £25,000 and made his first appearance for the club in a friendly against the Polish RAF XI at Turf Moor on 2 March 1946. He made his senior debut on the opening day of 1946–47, just five days after celebrating his 32nd birthday.

A tee-totaller and non-smoker, Brown absorbed all he could from Britton, and during his stay at Turf Moor he attended FA coaching schools. He described himself as a 'centre full-back' rather than a centre-half and was a key component in Britton's 'Iron Curtain' defence. The manager immediately recognised the organisational qualities that Brown possessed and made him his captain. He proved to be an influential personality and encouraged all around him.

Brown played a pivotal role in guiding the Clarets back into the First Division and in reaching the FA Cup Final in 1946–47. Indeed, during that memorable campaign Burnley conceded a meagre 29 League goals thanks to a defence that he organised with meticulous precision on the pitch.

His contribution to the rise of the Clarets brought him personal recognition in October 1947 when he was selected to captain the Football League team that faced the Irish League in Belfast. The result, however, a 4–3 victory for the Football League, was not the type of goalscoring bonanza that he was synonymous with. Another of the 'Iron Curtain' defence, Arthur Woodruff, also featured in the Football League defence that day.

Twelve months after his appearance for the Football League, Brown suddenly left Turf Moor to join Notts County. The fee of £12,500 was too good an offer to refuse for a 34-year-old defender. Unfortunately, the style of football that he faced in the Third Division North was not to his liking, and he asked to be placed on the transfer list before being released in 1949. He then embarked on a long and successful career as a coach and manager that was to bring him back to Turf Moor in August 1954. He succeeded Frank Hill as manager at Burnley and enjoyed relative success, taking the Clarets to 10th place and two seventh-place finishes in the First Division. It was under his stewardship that a string of promising young players were blooded and Gawthorpe began his development. However, it was for his initial planning of a successful youth set-up that the club had most reason to be grateful to him. The players he introduced formed the nucleus of the Championship-winning side, but Brown didn't stay long enough to see his endeavours completely fulfilled.

In July 1957, Brown returned to his native North East to accept the position of manager of Sunderland and then moved to Sheffield Wednesday, in a similar capacity, in August 1964. He took Wednesday to the 1966 FA Cup Final and then returned to Sunderland for another spell as manager. He also coached in Norway before ending his coaching career at Plymouth Argyle in the mid-1970s.

Frank Casper

Date of birth: 9 December 1944, Barnsley

Burnley record:
Appearances: League 230+7, FA Cup 11, League Cup 22, others 5
Goals: League 74, FA Cup 5, League Cup 9, others 1
Debut: League, 19 August 1967 v Coventry City (h) won 2–1
Manager: January 1983–June 1983 (caretaker); January 1989–October 1991

Also played for: Rotherham United, Football League (1 appearance)

In Frank Casper's Testimonial programme, the following tribute was paid by Bob Lord: 'He was a rather quiet type of individual, of mild temperament, but nevertheless an excellent player, one who could score goals out of the blue, one who could read the game in a manner which allowed him to be in the correct position at the right time. During his career at Burnley he scored many fine goals, and in doing so must have surprised many goalkeepers in the manner he got them. His positional sense was excellent, he could shoot equally well with both feet, and best of all he was a player who never descended to employing dirty, unsportsmanlike tactics to gain position or possession. He played the game in a manner which endows him with full credit.' Certainly these are sentiments with which those Clarets fans who were fortunate enough to see him in his prime would heartily agree. Casper was a fine servant to Burnley Football Club and one who was hugely popular with the paying public. Yet, with all the goodwill of the Burnley faithful behind him, he couldn't quite achieve the success that he gained as a player when he tried his hand at management at Turf Moor.

When Casper arrived at Turf Moor in June 1967, he was already a veteran of 102 League games for Rotherham United. He'd made his debut for Rotherham against Derby County in 1962, just before his 17th birthday, and had marked his senior bow with a goal in a 1–1 draw. He was fortunate to be blessed with perfect balance and the ability to retain complete control over the ball when moving at speed. He wasn't a robust, battling type of forward but adopted a more elegant style that was remarkably deadly in and around the penalty area.

In each of his first two seasons at the club Casper was the leading marksman, and in March 1969 he was selected to represent the Football League against the Scottish League at Hampden Park. Naturally enough, he marked this representative honour with a goal in a 3–1 win.

However, the club was about to embark on a period of transition, with Jimmy Adamson stepping up to succeed Harry Potts as manager. Like so many of his colleagues, Casper struggled to find his best form in 1970–71, with four goals in 21 League outings proving a disappointing return as the Clarets lost their First Division status. The following season he was back on

form and developed a fine understanding with Paul Fletcher, which enabled him to score 18 League goals. Although he only grabbed a dozen goals in 1972–73, he and Fletcher spearheaded the Clarets push for the Second Division Championship and a return to top-flight football.

Casper was at the peak of his powers when he was cruelly cut down by injury in September 1973. As a result, he was out of action for five months. Unfortunately, after just six appearances on his return, he was the victim of a robust challenge from the Leeds United defender Norman Hunter. He managed to play in the FA Cup semi-final against Newcastle United, with his injury heavily strapped, but he then missed the rest of the season and the entire 1974–75 campaign.

Casper made a valiant effort at a comeback in 1975–76 and scored his 100th goal for the club against Queen's Park Rangers in October 1975. However, this proved to be his last goal for the Clarets as he was forced to hang up his boots and turn to coaching the youth players at the club. He then joined the backroom staff and was appointed assistant to Brian Miller in 1979.

In January 1983 Casper was suddenly thrust into the spotlight when Miller was relieved of his duties on the morning of a League Cup quarter-final against Tottenham Hotspur at White Hart Lane. It proved a baptism of fire for Casper, but he managed to inspire the players to pull off an unlikely 4–1 victory. Although the Clarets lost the first leg of the semi-final to Liverpool, he was able to pull off another shock when his Burnley team enjoyed a narrow 1–0 win over them at Turf Moor in the second leg. Although it was insufficient to take the club to the Final, it had shown that he was a highly-capable coach. Unfortunately, the club's League plight was desperate, and relegation to the Third Division ended his hopes of getting the manager's job on a permanent basis.

As John Bond moved in, Casper left to enjoy a spell at Bury as coach and then assistant manager. In January 1989 he returned to Turf Moor as manager. However, by this time the Clarets were a Fourth Division outfit, and Casper, despite taking them to the Play-offs, was unable to lift the club out of the doldrums. After a disappointing start to the 1991–92 campaign, he resigned and turned his back on football to become involved in a successful business venture.

Albert Cheesebrough

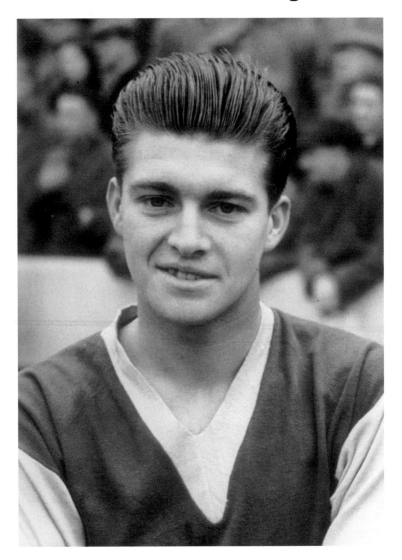

Date of birth: 17 January 1935, Burnley

Burnley record:

Appearances: League 142, FA Cup 16
Goals: League 35, FA Cup 5
Debut: League, 11 April 1952 v Manchester United (h) drew 1–1

Also played for: Leicester City, Port Vale, Mansfield Town, England Under-23
(1 cap)

When Albert Cheesebrough lined up alongside Billy Morris in the Burnley team that faced Manchester United at Turf Moor in April 1952, he fulfilled a dream that most schoolboys have – that of playing for their local club. The fact that he was playing alongside Morris, a player whom he greatly admired, made it all the more special. 'In those days it was the be-all and end-all to play for your home-town team. I was brought up on Billy Morris and Peter Kippax, who were our heroes...'

'Cheesy', as he became known to the Turf Moor faithful, would go on to become one of those heroes that Burnley schoolboys of the 50s worshipped, and yet, with the club on the brink of greatness, he was superseded by Jimmy Robson. As a result, he was allowed to join Leicester City in January 1959, not that he has any regrets about missing out on a golden time in Burnley's history:

'The club always worked on the lines, in those days, of raising good, young players, getting a few years out of them and, if they're surplus to requirements, getting a nice fee for them,' he explained in later life, 'there's nothing wrong with that, and going to Leicester turned out to be a good bet for me. It was a marvellous move really. I was there for five years, and we got to two Cup Finals.'

A Wembley Final seemed a distant dream for the 15-year-old, who joined the Burnley office staff in the summer of 1950. Two years later he had joined the professional ranks at the club, but despite his early senior debut he had to bide his time before he made his big breakthrough at Turf Moor. After appearing in the final five games of 1952–53, he featured in the opening game of the following campaign. However, he had to wait until December 1954 for his next opportunity to play League football, and it wasn't until 1955–56 that he was able to win a regular place at inside-forward. He had originally begun his Turf Moor career as a winger, and it was in this role that his early appearances for the Clarets were made. However, during the period of obscurity in the Central League, he had developed into a skilful inside-forward. Stocky and powerfully built, he packed a venomous shot but, strangely, was never a prolific goalscorer. Nonetheless, he scored a number of vital goals for the club and formed an impressive left-wing partnership with Brian Pilkington.

The three seasons that Cheesebrough was a regular in the inside-left berth brought two seventh-place finishes and one sixth-place spot for the club. In October 1956 he won an England Under-23 cap when he was selected to play against France at Ashton Gate, Bristol.

Inexplicably, Cheesebrough's career at Burnley began to stutter during the 1958–59 campaign. From being the automatic choice at inside-left, he suddenly found himself in and out of the team due to the emergence of Robson. It was at this point that the Clarets decided to allow him to join Leicester City in June 1959 for £19,755.

A rejuvenated Cheesebrough found life at Filbert Street to his liking and scored 15 goals in 41 League games during 1959–60 – his best tally for a single season. During the following season he was utilised in his old position on the left wing, and it was in this position that he featured for Leicester at Wembley in the 1961 FA Cup Final. Sadly, he was on the losing side, as Tottenham Hotspur claimed a League and Cup double. Unfortunately, when Leicester reached Wembley again in 1963, he was no longer a member of the first team.

The summer of 1963 found him on the move to Port Vale, and Cheesebrough began to make plans for a life outside football. His father-in-law was a butcher, and Cheesebrough bought a shop in Southport that would become his business when he finally hung up his boots. He learnt the trade of butchery while still playing with Port Vale, spending a couple of hours working for a master butcher before training each day.

After a couple of seasons in the Potteries, Cheesebrough linked up with former Burnley colleague Tommy Cummings, who was manager of Mansfield Town. Sadly, a broken leg ended his career in the game, and he concentrated on his business interests instead.

Cheesebrough's own sporting pastimes turned away from football and towards the golf course, while his daughter Susan, one of three daughters, represented Great Britain as an Olympic gymnast. During his time at Burnley he was also a well-known member of the Lowerhouse Cricket Club.

Jackie Chew

Date of birth: 13 May 1920, Blackburn
Died: 19 October 2002, Blackburn

Burnley record:
Appearances: League 225, FA Cup 23, Wartime 25
Goals: League 39, FA Cup 2, Wartime 2
Debut: League, 31 August 1946 v Coventry City (h) drew 1–1

Also played for: Blackburn Rovers, (wartime guest for Leeds United, Luton
                  Town), Bradford City, Darwen

Jackie Chew had just signed amateur forms for Blackburn Rovers on 24 May 1939 when the ominous clouds of war began to gather. The outbreak of war and the suspension of the Football League put his career in limbo for the duration of the hostilities. With the constant ebb and flow of players that ensued, he got an early opportunity to show his ability when he was selected to play on the left wing for Blackburn's opening game in the North West Regional League against Blackpool at Ewood Park in October 1939. It proved to be the first of 23 appearances for Blackburn in wartime football, prior to acting as a wartime guest player for a variety of clubs, including Burnley.

Chew, who served in the RAF during the war, first appeared for the Clarets on 8 September 1945 in the Football League North match against Bolton Wanderers at Burnden Park. He went on to appear in 25 games for the club during that final season of wartime football, during the course of which he turned professional with the Clarets in March 1946. Although he made his wartime debut for the club on the left wing, he was quickly switched to the opposite flank to enable Peter Kippax to play on the left.

When the Football League was restored for 1946–47, he made his 'official' debut in the opening match of the season at outside-right, with Kippax on the opposite flank. For the remainder of that campaign, the pair dashing down the wings at Turf Moor was a familiar sight. Illness kept Kippax out of the closing stages of the League season and undermined his effectiveness in the FA Cup Final. However, he struck up a fine understanding with Billy Morris, the regular inside-right, and the pair played a major part in pushing the Clarets towards the First Division. 'I have lots of fond memories of Jackie, how I used to try and mimic his Lancashire accent, and he used to sing comic songs. We had a good understanding down the right, and we got on well from the first time we met,' reminisced Morris on hearing of Chew's death in October 2002. While

defeat in the FA Cup Final proved a disappointment, Chew celebrated the climax to his first season of League football with promotion to the top flight.

Affectionately known as 'Cowboy' because of his bandy legs, he quickly acclimatised to life in the top Division. He was more than just an orthodox wingman who beat the full-back and crossed the ball from the dead-ball line; while he possessed those facets to his game, he also had the ability to cut inside and then unleash the fiercest of shots. Indeed, he was so dangerous when he did this that he finished the 1948–49 campaign as the club's top marksman, with 11 goals being scored in 40 League appearances. 'He was a really good striker of the ball, and if he got in a shooting position he would finish it off,' explained Jimmy McIlroy, who figured alongside Chew and Morris in the early 50s.

In what may be remembered as some of the halcyon days of Burnley Football Club, Chew was at the forefront of the attack. Hugely popular with supporters, he remained the automatic choice on the right wing until the arrival of Billy Gray in August 1953.

In June 1954, having made just three appearances during the previous campaign, Chew left Turf Moor to join Bradford City. He spent his final season in League football operating in the Third Division North alongside Reg Attwell, who joined him at Bradford in October 1954. Released by Bradford, the pair then spent the 1955–56 season together with Darwen in the Lancashire Combination.

Chew was still a familiar figure around Turf Moor long after he had hung up his football boots. As a talented middle-order batsman and captain of Rishton Cricket Club, he was seen on the adjoining cricket ground at Turf Moor, churning out runs in the Lancashire League with the same type of consistency that made him so popular on the football field. Ironically, Peter Kippax, his original ally on the wing, was often opposing him on the cricket field as skipper of Burnley Cricket Club.

Ralph Coates

Date of birth: 26 April 1946, Hetton-le-Hole

Burnley record:
Appearances: League 214+2, FA Cup 12, League Cup 22+2, Europe 7
Goals: League 26, FA Cup 1, League Cup 2, Europe 3
Debut: League, 19 December 1964 v Sheffield United (h) won 3–1

Also played for: Eppleton Colliery Welfare, Tottenham Hotspur, St George's (Australia), Orient, Hertford Heath, Ware FC, Nazeing FC, England (4 caps), England Under-23 (8 caps), Football League (4 appearances)

Although it is 35 years since Ralph Coates was last seen in the Claret and Blue of Burnley, he still finds that the Clarets are close to his heart: 'I played some of my best football at Burnley. Their's is the first result I look for.' Considering that after leaving Turf Moor he went on to appear in two UEFA Cup Finals (winning one of them) and lift the Football League Cup, as well as make 248 senior appearances for Tottenham Hotspur, it is a testimony to his love of Burnley Football Club.

Coates went through the full spectrum of a career during his time at Turf Moor. 'I remember going into the side at a very young age, 18 or 19, and playing alongside people like Ray Pointer, Brian Miller, Andy Lochhead and Willie Irvine. Playing with people like that gave me a good education at an early age. Gradually these older players started to retire, and Jimmy Adamson brought through the younger men like Leighton James, Steve Kindon and Dave Thomas. Suddenly, from being the younger player, I was the senior pro,' reflected Coates on his Burnley career. He was one of the outstanding players at the heart of the last truly great Burnley team that distinguished itself in the First Division. For a generation of Burnley fans, the thinning thatch of Coates was a familiar sight as he orchestrated the Burnley attack like the conductor of an orchestra.

He originally signed amateur forms and then moved through the apprentice ranks to turn professional in May 1963. In those days he was regarded as a forward and was a consistent goalscorer in the youth and reserve teams. He made his first-team debut in December 1964 when he was called up to replace the injured Lochhead. With Willie Morgan on the right wing, Andy Lochhead and Gordon Harris at inside-forward and Willie Irvine at centre-forward, there was little scope for him to make much headway. The only problematic position in 1964–65 was at outside-left, where Ian Towers and Johnny Price had both been used at different times during the season. Indeed, he was called upon on five occasions to fill the number-11 shirt as the season neared its end.

The 1965–66 campaign was his big breakthrough at Turf Moor, and Coates spent most of the season occupying the wide midfield role on the left wing. At first glance he didn't quite fit the picture of the fleet-footed winger. Stockily built, with long trailing wisps of thinning hair, he hardly conjured up a picture of athleticism, and yet he was one of the fittest players that the club had ever had. Combined with his pace and power was his uncanny knack of being able to deliver teasing crosses with the tightest of angles.

Coates's special qualities were soon recognised when he was selected for the England Under-23 team that beat Wales 8–0 at Molineux in October 1966. He celebrated his Under-23 debut with a goal and went on to win a total of eight Under-23 caps. His first full England cap came in April 1970 when he figured in the 3–1 win over Northern Ireland at Wembley. He was selected in the provisional England squad for the World Cup in Mexico but, sadly, was one of six players who didn't make the final cut. He made four appearances for England, and he was also chosen to represent the Football League on four occasions between 1968 and 1971.

By the early 70s, Coates had graduated to be one of the senior players at the club and was certainly the most sellable asset at that time. It was, therefore, no great surprise when Tottenham Hotspur stepped in to sign him. He revealed, 'It was a bit of a cloak and dagger affair with Jimmy Adamson arranging for me to meet Spurs boss Bill Nicholson. When he told me they wanted to pay £190,000 for me, I told him that no player was worth that; at the time it was a crazy amount. I had been determined to stay at Burnley and help them come straight back up, but the chairman Bob Lord realised the financial implications and so I left, although I was delighted that they got promotion without me. But it was still a very sad day for me when I left because I had enjoyed every moment at Burnley.'

Coates enjoyed great success at White Hart Lane. As a member of the team that won the UEFA Cup in 1972 and reached the Final of the same competition in 1974, he also came off the bench in the 1973 League Cup Final to hit the winning goal against Norwich City. In the summer of 1978 he spent some time in Australia, on loan to the St George's club in Sydney, before bringing the curtain down on his League career in England with a stint at Orient, where he also undertook some coaching. He later moved into non-League football and worked as a leisure complex manager in Hertfordshire.

Doug Collins

Date of birth: 28 August 1945, Newton, near Doncaster

Burnley record:
Appearances: League 172+15, FA Cup 9, League Cup 12+1, others 7+1
Goals: League 18, others 1
Debut: League, 28 September 1968 v Chelsea (h) won 2–1

Also played for: Rotherham United, Grimsby Town, Plymouth Argyle, Sunderland, Tulsa Roughnecks, Rochdale
Managed: Rochdale

Doug Collins was a busy, combative midfield player who was at the hub of the engine room when the Clarets last won promotion to the top flight of English football. He played in 37 games in 1972-73, when Jimmy Adamson restored the club to its rightful place among England's elite.

Collins took his first steps in professional football on the groundstaff of Rotherham United. It was while at Millmoor that he first met Frank Casper. 'He was a couple of years older than I was and one of my chores was to clean his boots,' he recalled. In March 1963 he followed his former manager at Millmoor, Tom Johnston, to Grimsby Town as an amateur player. In June 1963 he turned professional and made his League debut at outside-left against Cardiff City in October 1963.

At Blundell Park Collins earned a reputation as an industrious player, despite his slight build, and was a creator of goals while covering every blade of grass in pursuit of the ball. It was while playing for Grimsby that he caught the eye of Harry Potts in September 1968. The Burnley manager saw at close quarters how effective Collins could be when he performed heroically in Grimsby's 1-1 draw with the Clarets in the second round of the Football League Cup competition. Although Grimsby slumped to a 6-0 defeat in the replay, Potts had seen enough of his potential to snap him up in a £30,000 deal. As well as potential, Potts was also buying a player who had already amassed over 100 League appearances for his former club.

Collins quickly made the adjustment from playing in the Fourth Division to rubbing shoulders with the elite of English football. During the 1968-69 campaign, he started 23 League games and also popped up as a substitute on four occasions. He also proved he could be dangerous in front of the goal and finished the season as the club's second leading goalscorer. 'I got some terrific notices. Everything seemed to go right for me. It wasn't until the following season that I started to struggle,' he said.

A difference of opinion with Harry Potts and a subsequent loss of form led to Collins being axed from the team. 'I found it very difficult to make any impression,' he explained. 'I simply couldn't get a place, let alone keep one. I was really worried, and when we finally got relegated I started wondering whether it had all been a mistake to move there.'

As the Clarets slipped to a mid-table position in the Second Division, following relegation in 1970-71, Collins continued to struggle to find his feet. Then, with his career at Turf Moor at its lowest ebb, he was recalled for the second game of the 1972-73 campaign and suddenly his fortunes were revived. Collins became a vital cog in Jimmy Adamson's team that won the Second Division Championship that season. His busy approach complemented the silky skills of Martin Dobson perfectly in the midfield area.

The next two seasons in the First Division resulted in him playing some of the best football of his career. Fair-haired, yet slightly-built, Collins proved to be an industrious worker whose contribution often went unnoticed. Nonetheless, his tigerish approach was valued by his colleagues and manager alike, and the fans began to warm to his wholehearted approach to the game.

Ultimately, ageing legs began to blunt his effectiveness, and it was during the 1975-76 campaign that Collins lost his place in the team, as the Clarets again lost their way and hurtled towards relegation. He left Turf Moor in May 1976 to spend a short spell with Plymouth Argyle before linking up again with Jimmy Adamson, who was now the Sunderland manager, at Roker Park. However, he was reaching the end of his playing career, and after just seven appearances for Sunderland he moved to the United States to join Tulsa Roughnecks.

When Collins returned to England he spent some time on the coaching staff at Derby County before accepting the player-manager's role at Rochdale in January 1979. He left Spotland in November of that year, and in 1981 he emigrated to Australia to join Sydney Olympic as coach.

John Connelly

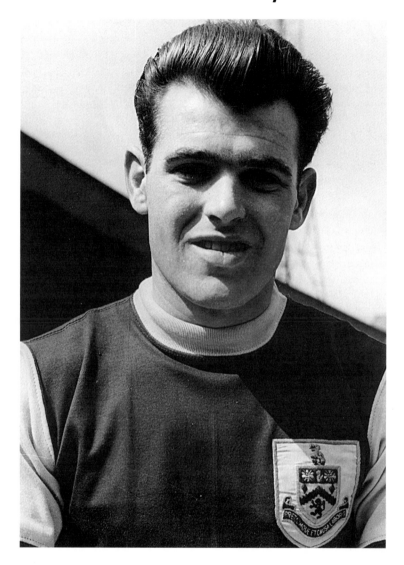

Date of birth: 18 July 1938, St Helens

Burnley record:
Appearances: League 215, FA Cup 38, League Cup 7, Europe 4, others 1
Goals: League 86, FA Cup 15, League Cup 2, Europe 1, others 1
Debut: League, 11 March 1957 v Leeds United (a) drew 1–1

Also played for: St Theresa's School Old Boys, St Helens Town, Manchester
United, Blackburn Rovers, Bury, England (20 caps), England
Under-23 (1 cap), Football League (8 appearances)

For a generation of Burnley fans there was no finer sight than that of John Connelly straining every sinew and muscle to race past an opposing full-back before centring the ball with radar-like accuracy. He was the very essence of the orthodox winger, a man whose precision crosses were his stock in trade but one who was also a deadly predator in his own right. Indeed, only Louis Page, in the 1920s and early 1930s, scored more goals for Burnley from a wing position than him.

Born and brought up in Rugby League territory, Connelly came to the notice of the Clarets while he was playing for St Helens Town in the Lancashire Combination. At the time of his arrival at Turf Moor in November 1956, he was still serving his time as a joiner, a trade that he continued to work in during his early days of professional football. Indeed, he was working at the local colliery when he was told that he had been awarded his first England international cap in October 1959.

Billy Gray and Doug Newlands were competing for the outside-right slot when Connelly joined the Clarets, and as a result it wasn't until the 1958–59 season that he was able to win a regular first-team place. He scored 12 goals in 32 League outings that season and established himself as the undisputed first choice on the right-wing.

However, it was the Championship-winning campaign of 1959–60 that catapulted Connelly onto a national stage. His performances for the Clarets were truly electrifying, and he netted 20 goals in 34 League games from his berth on the right wing. He caught the eye of the England selectors when he was chosen to face Wales at Ninian Park, Cardiff, in October 1959. It proved to be the first of 20 England caps, which involved him in both the 1962 World Cup Finals in Chile and, of course, the successful World Cup campaign in 1966, when he appeared in the opening game of the tournament.

Connelly continued to excel in the Burnley attack and picked up an FA Cup-finalists' medal in 1962. During his final season at the club, he was switched to the left flank to allow the blossoming talent of Willie Morgan to emerge on the right wing. It made no difference to Connelly's level of performance and merely underlined his versatility – a fact that had not gone unnoticed by other clubs.

In April 1964 he left Turf Moor to join Manchester United for a fee of £56,000. At that time he had appeared for England on 10 occasions, making him second only to Bob Kelly as the most capped Englishman

to represent the Clarets. He readily adapted to life at Old Trafford and scored 15 goals in 42 League outings, as United won the First Division Championship in his first season at the club. Connelly, who had made his last appearance for England in February 1963, was also restored to the international team in October 1965. The move to Manchester couldn't have gone any better for him, and he appeared to take on a new lease of life in the free-flowing, attacking football that Matt Busby encouraged at Old Trafford. While with United, he appeared in two FA Cup semi-finals as well as a European Cup semi-final and notched 35 goals in 113 senior appearances.

In the opening game of the 1966 World Cup Finals, Connelly hit the post in a somewhat disappointing 0–0 draw with Uruguay at Wembley. He was desperately unlucky to lose his place when Martin Peters was drafted in on the left flank for the next game. When Alf Ramsey opted to use Alan Ball and Martin Peters in the third game of the competition, the 'Wingless Wonders' were born, and Connelly had to settle for watching the rest of the tournament from the sidelines.

In September 1966 Connelly left Old Trafford to join Blackburn Rovers, who had just been relegated to the Second Division. He had the opportunity to return to Turf Moor but felt that it wouldn't have been the same as his earlier spell with the club. Thus, he opted to move to Ewood Park. He spent four years at Blackburn and was a huge favourite with the supporters, who, like the Turf Moor fans, warmed to his dashing runs down the wing and his poacher's eye for goal.

Connelly ended his career with three seasons at Bury before retiring in May 1973 to concentrate on his fish and chip shop. In recent years he has had both his knees replaced due to the wear and tear of a life in football. He has finally retired from running 'Connelly's Place', his successful shop in Brierfield.

Andy Cooke

Date of birth: 20 January 1974, Shrewsbury

Burnley record:
Appearances: League 134+37, FA Cup 7+3, League Cup 8+2, others 9+2
Goals: League 52, FA Cup 2, League Cup 6, others 2
Debut: League, 29 August 1995 v Bristol Rovers (a) lost 0–1

Also played for: Telford United, Newtown, Stoke City, Busan Icons (South Korea), Bradford City, Darlington, Shrewsbury Town

When Andy Cooke joined Burnley in May 1995 it was the culmination of a long-held dream to play professional football. He had previously played part-time football with Welsh League outfit Newtown, which meant long hours working by day and then training in the evenings with his club. However, it was a background that made him all the more appreciative of the life of a professional footballer. It also made him critical of those youngsters who tossed away opportunities through sheer lack of application. 'I have come across players who I don't think appreciate just what they have got... I've seen young lads who have had the ability and then have thrown it all away. Now, they are probably working in a factory somewhere and it's such a waste,' he reflected.

Lack of application was certainly one accusation that could never be levelled at Cooke. He readily admitted that it was his willingness to perspire rather than inspire that had always been his strength. He was a workhorse, a player who could not only score goals but who was prepared to work for the good of the team.

Cooke, who was brought up on his family's farm in Market Drayton, always harboured dreams of becoming a professional footballer. As a teenager, he signed apprentice forms with Shrewsbury Town before spending three years with Telford United in the Nationwide Conference. However, it wasn't until he joined Newtown that his career began to take an upward direction. Financially, of course, there was little money to be had in the Welsh League, which meant that he had to supplement his income by working as an agricultural labourer. It was this working environment which taught him the values that enabled him to make the most of his talents on the football field.

Initially, he was somewhat overawed by his move to Burnley. 'It did play on my mind a bit to begin with. I think one of my first games was against Sheffield Wednesday in a pre-season friendly, and some of the players I played against that day I had watched on TV the week before,' he recalled.

During his first season at the club, Cooke seemed the ideal foil for the more skilful Kurt Nogan. He was frequently used as a substitute but gradually proved he had an eye for goal. The departure of Nogan provided him with the opportunity to establish himself, and he became a big favourite with the crowd because of his non-stop running and the sheer effort he put into his game. He was also a fine goalscorer, and his two goals against Plymouth Argyle on the final day of the 1997–98 season helped save the Clarets from relegation to Division Three.

The arrival of Andy Payton meant that Cooke found himself somewhat overshadowed. He became a supporting player to Payton, and suddenly he looked a little lethargic and unable to recapture his previous scoring touch. A hamstring injury hampered his effectiveness during 1999–2000, but, nonetheless, he proved a willing chaser and useful support act to Payton.

In December 2000 the Clarets made a huge profit on him when he was sold to Stoke City for £300,000. The arrival of Ian Moore and the improved form of Graham Branch meant that he lost his place in the pecking order at Turf Moor. With Cooke no longer an automatic choice for the first team, manager Stan Ternent believed the time was right to allow him to leave Turf Moor: 'Andy hasn't been getting regular first-team football and is out of contract at the end of the season, so really the time was right.'

Cooke continued to score goals following his move to Stoke City and his wholehearted commitment made him popular with the fans. However, in July 2003 he left the Britannia Stadium to try his luck abroad with a move to Busan Icons in South Korea. He remained in Korea until joining Bradford City in January 2005. Sadly, the move to the Yorkshire club wasn't the success that he had hoped for, and he spent the latter stages of the 2005–06 campaign on loan with Darlington.

Released by Bradford in the summer of 2006, Cooke completed a successful trial with Shrewsbury Town and signed a contract with the Gay Meadow club in July 2006.

Steve Cotterill

Date of birth:	20 July 1964, Cheltenham

Burnley record:

Manager:	2004–present
Played for:	Cheltenham Town, Alvechurch, Burton Albion, Wimbledon, Brighton & Hove Albion, AFC Bournemouth, Dorchester Town, Salisbury City, Cirencester Town
Also managed:	Sligo Rovers, Cheltenham Town, Stoke City

Although Steve Cotterill's playing career was largely spent in the lower Divisions and non-League football, he went on to become one of England's top young coaches. Curiously, his management career began in Ireland with Sligo Rovers in the mid-1990s before entering English football as manager of Cheltenham Town in February 1997. He enjoyed tremendous success at Whaddon Road and guided Cheltenham from the Southern League to Division Three of the Football League in a matter of five years. Three promotions were also accompanied by success in the FA Trophy Final at Wembley in 1998.

In May 2002 Cotterill was enticed away from Whaddon Road to become manager of Stoke City. However, after just 13 games with the Potteries club he left to become assistant manager to Howard Wilkinson at Sunderland. Unfortunately, his non-stop success came to an end in the North-East, and he was sacked, along with Wilkinson, as Sunderland slid towards relegation from the Premiership. He had lasted just five months at the Stadium of Light, but his enthusiasm for the game remained undiminished.

Cotterill spent the latter part of 2003–04 coaching at Leicester City before agreeing to become manager of Burnley in June 2004. In taking control at Turf Moor, the 39-year-old found himself in charge of a team that had struggled to avoid relegation and was handicapped by financial restraints. This was a fact he readily acknowledged: 'I'll be looking at free agents and the loan market. We won't be buying anybody, not unless I, or the chairman, win the lottery.'

Cotterill, the holder of the prestigious UEFA Pro licence, appointed Dave Kevan as his assistant, while former Burnley player Mark Yates, a UEFA A licence coach, was given the position of first-team coach. Cotterill indicated that he wanted his Burnley team to play a high-tempo, passing style of football.

His early moves in the transfer market brought experienced campaigners like John McGreal and Frank Sinclair to Turf Moor, while later in the season he snapped up Gary Cahill, Aston Villa's immensely talented young defender, on loan. On the down side, the financial problems meant that the Clarets had to allow Richard Chaplow, one of the club's brightest young players, to move to West Bromwich Albion in January 2005 for £1,500,000. At the same time the club lost the services of Robbie Blake, who after becoming unsettled by overtures from Wigan Athletic, left to join Birmingham City. However, the departures allowed him to fund the transfer of Ade Akinbiyi from Stoke City for £600,000 to lead the Burnley attack.

The Clarets finished in a respectable 13th position at the end of Cotterill's first season in charge. However, the financial problems meant that once again he had little room to manoeuvre in the transfer market during the summer. Wayne Thomas and Gifton Noel-Williams both arrived on free transfers from Stoke City, while Garreth O'Connor was another free transfer from AFC Bournemouth.

Burnley began the 2005–06 campaign with one of the smallest pools of players in the Championship. Nonetheless, after a disappointing start, Cotterill worked miracles to guide the club into the top half of the table. Indeed, by November 2005 the club had reached the Play-off places. Sadly, it didn't last as the threadbare nature of the Burnley squad began to cause him problems.

In January 2006 Mark Yates left to manage Kidderminster Harriers, while Steve Davis stepped up from the scouting staff to replace him. During the same month the club lost the services of Ade Akinbiyi, the club's leading goalscorer, who moved to Sheffield United. In his place, Cotterill had to gamble on bringing Michael Ricketts on loan from Leeds United for the remainder of the campaign. Sadly, Ricketts, who had lost his way since leaving Bolton Wanderers, was unable to provide the goals that the Clarets required.

Results began to fall away, but Barry Kilby, the Burnley chairman, was anxious to tie Cotterill to the club with a new long-term deal. After protracted negotiations, he signed a new contract in March 2006 that will keep him at the club until the summer of 2010. In the same month, he brought three new players to the club on loan. Phil Bardsley came from Manchester United, Alan Mahon from Wigan Athletic and Andy Gray from Sunderland, while young Kyle Lafferty appeared on a few occasions towards the season's end. Cotterill finished his second season at Turf Moor with the Clarets in 17th position in the Championship. Reflecting on a disappointing season, he commented 'It has been a difficult season – chopping and changing, and when you're not stable, it's very difficult.'

The summer of 2006 brought the permanent signings of Alan Mahon and Andy Gray at Turf Moor, as Cotterill once again faced a season in which he would have to compete against clubs with more financial muscle. However, while the club might not be able to compete on the transfer front, in Cotterill the Clarets are blessed with one of the best young coaches in English football and one who continues to defy the odds by keeping Burnley competitive in the Championship.

Benny Cross

Date of birth: 1898, Birkenhead
Died: June 1984, Blackpool

Burnley record:
Appearances: League 237, FA Cup 17, others 1
Goals: League 57, FA Cup 4
Debut: League, 6 September 1920 v Huddersfield Town (h) won 3–0

Also played for: Runcorn, Football League (1 appearance)

At the heart of any successful team is a playmaker: a schemer who can open up the tightest of defences, a player whose control of the ball is mesmeric and whose main function is to create goalscoring opportunities for his colleagues. In Burnley's 1920–21 Championship-winning side that player was Benny Cross.

Cross joined the club in April 1920 from Runcorn and was drafted into the first team after the opening three games of 1920–21 were all lost. He replaced the legendary Bert Freeman, a task which would have daunted many a more experienced man than Cross. Unperturbed, he made his debut in the home game against Huddersfield Town and helped the Clarets to a 3–0 win. It was the start of a 30-match unbeaten run, which took the club to the brink of the Championship. Cross was at the heart of the Burnley attack, probing the opposition defences for weaknesses and then feeding his colleagues with precision passes. Indeed, his search for the perfect pass often led to him being accused of retaining possession when a pass was required.

The correspondent of the *Lancashire Daily Post Football Annual* observed at the start of 1924–25, that Cross was 'A rare schemer who is apt to hang on to the ball too long. When he remedies his weakness for pattern-weaving par excellence, the club's playing stock should begin to soar...' However, he refused to compromise and hit long hopeful balls into the opposition area. He was a master craftsman and would retain possession in the hope of creating a better opening for the natural goalscorers in the team.

Although a playmaker by choice, Cross was not averse to popping up and chipping in with a goal or two of his own. Indeed, when the title was secured at Goodison Park on 23 April 1921, it was Cross who scored the goal that gave the Clarets a point and the Championship. During the title-winning campaign he scored 14 goals, his best tally for a single season

throughout his time at Turf Moor, and during his career with the club he topped a half century of goals.

However, it was as a playmaker that Cross will be primarily remembered at Burnley. Even when the heady days of the Championship success had waned, he still delivered the goods on a regular basis. Indeed, in 1924–25, when the Clarets narrowly escaped relegation, it was Cross who provided the main inspiration to an ailing forward line. His successful right-wing partnership with Bob Kelly that season proved to be a telling factor in retaining First Division status.

The following season the Clarets slipped even closer to the Second Division, but Cross proved he was still capable of virtuoso performances. Thus, when Louis Page netted six goals in the 7–1 victory at Birmingham on 10 April 1926, it was Cross who pulled the strings and completely destroyed the home defence with his incisive passing.

Curiously, apart from a couple of Schoolboy caps, international honours eluded him. In the summer of 1926 he travelled to Canada with an FA tour party, but he was continually overlooked by the England selectors. His sole senior representative honour came in March 1927 when he was selected to play for the Football League against the Scottish League at Filbert Street, Leicester.

Sadly, by this time Cross's career was coming to an end. In November 1926 he had suffered a bad injury when he stepped on the ball and badly twisted his knee. This injury was to mark the beginning of the end for him, as injuries and ill health took their toll and kept him out of the Burnley team with increasing frequency.

Cross made his final appearance for the Clarets on 5 May 1927, the last match of the season and his only senior outing during that entire campaign. In 1929 he left the game for good.

Tommy Cummings

Date of birth: 12 September 1928, Sunderland

Burnley record:
Appearances: League 434, FA Cup 38, League Cup 6, others 1
Goals: League 3
Debut: League, 18 December 1948 v Manchester City (a) drew 2–2

Also played for: Hilton Colliery Juniors, Stanley United, Mansfield Town, England B (3 caps), Football League (1 appearance)
Managed: Mansfield Town, Aston Villa, Great Harwood

It was somewhat ironic that two of the club's greatest post-war stars should leave Turf Moor within days of each other. However, while Jimmy McIlroy's departure was emblazoned across the front page of local newspapers, amid an outcry by supporters, Tommy Cummings slipped quietly away almost unnoticed. In truth, he had dropped out of the first team months before his departure, while McIlroy was still at the heart of the Burnley team.

Although his father was a miner, it was the Sunderland shipyards that first provided Cummings with employment. He was spotted while playing for Stanley United and following a successful trial was signed in October 1947, with Burnley making a donation of £25 to his previous club. With an eye to the future, his dad insisted that his son should learn a trade, and so he only played part-time in his early years with the club, while working as an apprentice engineer at the Bank Hall Pit. It was a tough regime for young Cummings, working down the pit by day and training at night.

After a handful of Central League games, Cummings made his senior debut against Manchester City at Maine Road in December 1948. He returned to the team in mid-January 1949 and remained the automatic choice at centre-half until the latter stages of 1955–56, when he was switched to right-back. He appeared to be on the verge of international honours in October 1950 when he was selected as a reserve for the England team that travelled to Belfast to face Northern Ireland. It was during this month that he was selected to represent the Football League against the Irish League at Bloomfield Road, Blackpool. In March 1953 Cummings made his debut for the England B team in the 2–2 draw with Scotland B at Edinburgh. However, he had to wait until February 1956 for his second cap, when he played at right-back in another 2–2 draw with Scotland B. The following month he was again chosen to represent the B team against Switzerland B. Sadly, his international prospects came to an abrupt end when an injury to his right knee kept him out of action for almost two seasons.

Those who felt inclined to write off his career underestimated Cummings's powers of recovery and his desire to return to action. He made 39 League appearances in 1958–59 and, although no longer a regular, contributed 23 appearances in 1959–60 to win a Championship medal. He also featured in the team that shared the FA Charity Shield after a 2–2 draw with Wolverhampton Wanderers and appeared in the 1962 FA Cup Final defeat by Tottenham Hotspur. Indeed, as Burnley chased a League and Cup double in 1961–62, he played at centre-half in 39 League games and missed just one match of the FA Cup run. However, this was to be his swansong at Turf Moor as the following season he was replaced by John Talbut after the opening two games.

Although he is fondly remembered as a first-class defender at Burnley, Cummings is also remembered for a goal that many regard as one of the finest ever seen at Turf Moor. It came after 84 minutes in a First Division clash with Newcastle United, which looked destined for a 1–1 draw. Having won the ball on the edge of his own area, he ran towards the opposition goal looking in vain for a colleague to whom he could pass. When he was some 18 yards from the Newcastle goal, he decided to let fly and hit the most perfectly struck left-foot shot that screamed into the Newcastle net and secured a 2–1 win for the Clarets.

Cummings was held in high regard within the game and followed Jimmy Hill into the chairmanship of the Professional Footballers' Association. With his playing career approaching its end, he met with officials of Bath City with a view to becoming manager at the Southern League club. He was still in negotiations with Bath officials when the offer to take control of Mansfield Town was made. Preferring to begin his managerial career in the Football League, he accepted the player-manager's job at Field Mill but was restricted to just 11 appearances before injury finally brought an end to his playing career.

Cummings spent four and a half years at Mansfield and endured some turbulent times before being appointed as manager of Aston Villa. He spent a couple of seasons at Villa Park before the arrival of a new consortium, led by Doug Ellis, brought an end to his managerial career.

Cummings returned to the Burnley area and spent a short time in charge of non-League Great Harwood. However, his future lay away from football, and he spent many years in the pub trade but has retained his links with the Turf Moor club as a popular match-day host.

Steve Davis

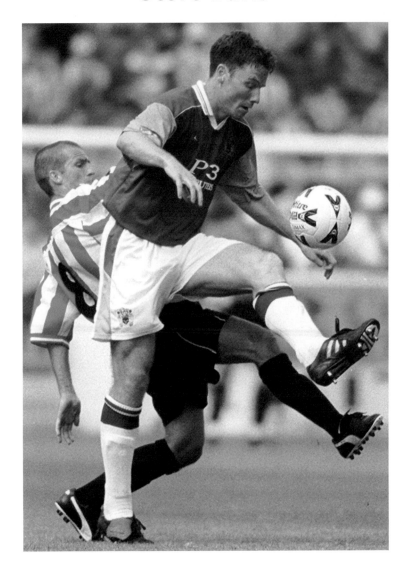

Date of birth: 30 October 1968, Hexham

Burnley record:
Appearances: League 321+6, FA Cup 24+1, League Cup 19, others 14
Goals: League 42, FA Cup 1, League Cup 4
Debut: League, 25 November 1989 v Lincoln City (a) lost 0–1 (substitute)

Also played for: Montague Boys Club, Southampton, Notts County (on loan), Luton Town, Blackpool, York City

The 1990s was the time when Burnley finally began to climb the Divisions after the disasters of the previous decade. Between 1989 and 2003 Steve Davis enjoyed three spells with the Clarets and many would argue that he was the club's most proficient performer during that period.

Initially, Davis came on a month's loan from Southampton and made his debut as a substitute in a Fourth Division match at Lincoln City. The following week he lined up in the centre of defence with another Steve Davis, to form a central-defensive partnership that was a reporter's nightmare. The confusion didn't last long as Davis returned to Southampton after making nine League appearances for the Clarets. Nonetheless, he had made a favourable impression on the fans at Turf Moor with his ability to play in defence or midfield. There was no doubt that this young man was going be a quality footballer, and many fans rued the fact that it wasn't likely to happen at Turf Moor.

A native of the North East, Davis was one of many young recruits from that region who made their way to The Dell. It was there that he came under the guidance of Dave Merrington, the former Burnley player, who was youth coach for the south-coast club. He turned professional in July 1987, and after spending some time playing for the reserves he arrived at Turf Moor to make his bow in League football.

On his return to The Dell Davis made his League debut for the Saints in a home match against Norwich City in February 1990. In total he made six League appearances for Southampton and also made two substitute appearances for Notts County during a loan spell at Meadow Lane in April 1991.

In July 1991, after having failed to gain promotion via the Play-offs, Steve Peter Davis opted to leave Turf Moor and was transferred to Barnsley for £180,000. However, the blow of that departure was softened the following month with the announcement that Southampton's Steve Mark Davis had signed for the Clarets in a deal worth £60,000. Davis was installed into the defence alongside John Pender, and they formed the solid central-defensive partnership, upon which the Fourth Division Championship was won in 1991–92.

Davis and Pender continued to provide the club with a solid defence, and in 1993–94 they celebrated a second promotion when Stockport County were beaten in the Second Division Play-off Final at Wembley.

Restored to the new First Division, Pender was replaced by Mark Winstanley and Davis was given the captaincy. It was a fitting reward for a player who offered the club more than just his defensive qualities. He was comfortable in possession and liked to make lung-bursting runs from the midfield into the heart of opposition territory. He was also a threat in front of the goal at set pieces.

Unfortunately, Burnley's stay in the First Division was brief, and relegation after just one season brought another parting of ways for Davis and the Clarets. Out of contract, he opted to join Luton Town, and the Clarets picked up a fee of £750,000 – a record transfer fee at the time.

During his time at Kenilworth Road, Davis appeared in 138 League games for Luton, but at the end of his first season at the club the Hatters were relegated and joined Burnley in the Second Division. He always received a warm welcome when he visited Turf Moor with Luton, and in December 1998 he returned to Burnley for a third time when Stan Ternent paid £800,000 for him. Although past 30 and clearly not quite the player he had been, his arrival was warmly greeted by the fans.

Initially, Davis operated in a back five alongside Mitchell Thomas and Ian Cox in the centre of defence. At the end of his first season back at the club, the Clarets only just missed out on the Play-offs. However, in 1999–2000 the Clarets finally regained their place back in the First Division, although Davis was, perhaps, a little more circumspect in terms of his surging runs from the back. However, he again proved a threat from set pieces, and when Gordon Armstrong lost his place Davis was again given the captaincy. His consistency earned him a place in the Professional Footballers' Association's award-winning Second Division side.

He proved to be a colossus at the heart of the defence on the club's return to the First Division. A steady performer on the ground and combative in the air, he remained a fixture in the Burnley defence until injuries began to take their toll. He was released by Burnley at the end of 2002–03 and spent a season at Blackpool before ending his playing career with a move to York City in June 2004. In October 2005 he joined the scouting staff at Turf Moor before being appointed first-team coach in January 2006.

Jerry Dawson

Date of birth:	18 March 1888, Holme-in-Cliviger near Burnley
Died:	8 August 1970, Cliviger near Burnley

Burnley record:

Appearances:	League 522, FA Cup 46, others 1, Wartime 78
Debut:	League, 13 April 1907 v Stockport County (h) won 3–0

Also played for: Portsmouth Rovers, England (2 caps), Football League (4 caps)

A playing career that stretched over 20 years was sufficient in itself to achieve legendary status for Jerry Dawson at Burnley. During that time he featured in a record-breaking 533 League games and played in well over 700 first-team games for the Clarets. Yet, there is more to his claim to legendary status than just the sheer longevity of his reign between the posts at Turf Moor. Unquestionably one of the finest goalkeepers in the history of the club, he is remembered at Turf Moor for, among other things, the selfless act he made of missing the 1914 FA Cup Final for the good of the club.

Born and bred in the village of Cliviger, it remained his home for his entire life, and, if not for football, Dawson might well have become a blacksmith there. It was while serving his apprenticeship in that trade that he was spotted by Burnley when playing junior football. He was whisked away to Turf Moor and signed professional forms just before his 20th birthday in February 1907. At that time the goalkeeping position was in the capable hands of Billy Green, but just four games into the 1907–08 season he was handed the opportunity to make the position his own.

The Clarets were languishing in Division Two, but a gradual improvement resulted in promotion in 1912–13. This improvement was, in no small part, due to Dawson's consistency. He missed just eight League games during the promotion campaign, and the following season he was as imperious as ever between the posts, as the Clarets not only adapted to life in the top flight but also embarked upon a successful run in the FA Cup.

Dawson was at the peak of his powers when he was injured in the semi-final meeting with Sheffield United at Old Trafford in March 1914. An injured thigh muscle kept him out of the replay that was played at Goodison Park four days later, when Tommy Boyle scored the only goal of the game. With the FA Cup Final still a few weeks away, a race began to get Dawson fit to face Liverpool at Crystal Palace. The week before the Final, he returned to first-team action for a meeting with Manchester City at Maine Road. It was hoped that the match would enable him to gain valuable match practice before the meeting with Liverpool. Unfortunately, he received another injury, this time to the ribs, as Burnley crashed to a 4–1 defeat.

The week prior to the Final was filled with rumour and speculation with regard to the fitness of Dawson.

Ultimately, it was he himself who made the decision that he shouldn't play and that Ronnie Sewell, his understudy, should take his place. Unsure of his fitness and not wanting to let his colleagues down on their big day, he sacrificed his chance of FA Cup glory. Sewell kept a clean sheet and a goal by Bert Freeman gave the Clarets a 1–0 win. The club had a special medal struck for him, but the chance to appear in an FA Cup Final again never came for the long-serving custodian.

Like so many players of his generation, the outbreak of World War One robbed Dawson of a sizeable chunk of his playing career. He continued to feature for the club during the wartime games, but his appearances became increasingly spasmodic.

Fortunately, the restoration of the Football League in 1919–20 found him back to first-team duty on a regular basis. The Clarets ended the season in second place in the First Division, and Dawson proved as reliable as ever. The following season he missed just three games as the Clarets lifted the First Division Championship for the first time in the club's history.

Despite his heroics for Burnley, international recognition came somewhat belatedly to Dawson. In February 1910 he had been selected to represent the Football League against the Scottish League at Ewood Park, Blackburn, and then went on to appear for the Football League on a further three occasions. However, his first England cap wasn't awarded until October 1921, when he kept goal in a 1–1 draw against Ireland in Belfast. His second, and final, England cap came in April 1922 in a defeat against Scotland at Villa Park.

Dawson made his 400th League appearance for the club on 2 December 1922, when the Clarets crashed to a 4–1 defeat at Middlesbrough. Undaunted, he continued as the first-choice custodian until the end of the 1925–26 campaign. The arrival of George Sommerville in the summer of 1926 meant that Dawson, now aged 38, had to settle for a back-up role. His final appearance for Burnley came on Christmas Day 1928, some nine months after he had celebrated his 40th birthday. After hanging up his boots, he continued to serve the club in a backroom role.

As well as an outstanding goalkeeper, Dawson was also a familiar sight at the crease at Burnley Cricket Club, serving as a distinguished batsman for many years. A lifelong bachelor, he passed away at his Cliviger home in August 1970 at the age of 82.

Ray Deakin

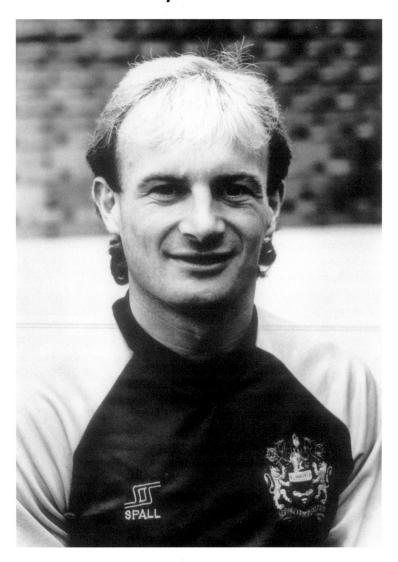

Date of birth: 19 June 1959, Liverpool

Burnley record:
Appearances: League 212+1, FA Cup 7, League Cup 15, others 17
Goals: League 6
Debut: League, 17 August 1985 v Northampton Town (h) won 3–2

Also played for: Everton, Port Vale, Bolton Wanderers

'He led by example and experience' were the words of legendary full-back Alex Elder when he presented the Man of the Match award to Ray Deakin after the great escape against Orient in May 1987. Local journalist Keith McNee commented that, 'Nobody made a bigger contribution than Deakin, courageous at the heart of the defence... Cometh the hour, cometh the man,' and when the chips were down the Clarets found an unlikely hero in the shape of their skipper. A player who had spent his career in the shadows of more illustrious colleagues finally gained the credit his career so richly deserved.

A former England Schoolboy international, Deakin had a good grounding in the game having served his apprenticeship at Everton's 'School of Science' at Goodison Park. He turned professional with Everton but failed to progress beyond Central League football on Merseyside. He dropped into football's basement in search of a first-team spot and joined Port Vale in August 1981. He was 22 years old when he made his League bow at left-back against Halifax Town on 29 August 1981. He made 23 appearances for Vale that season, mostly at left-back, and scored six goals, four of which came from the penalty spot.

The summer of 1982 brought another move when Deakin joined Bolton Wanderers on a free transfer. He made his debut for Bolton in the home win over Crystal Palace on 2 October 1982 and held down the left-back spot for the remainder of the season. Sadly, it was not a happy campaign at Burnden Park, with Bolton being relegated alongside Burnley into the Third Division. Nonetheless, he had finally established himself as a first-team regular, although during the 1984–85 campaign he switched to a role in the centre of the defence.

In the summer of 1985 Deakin moved to Turf Moor on a free transfer, while Derek Scott made the trip in the opposite direction in exchange for £20,000. Deakin's first competitive game for the club came in the pre-season Lancashire Manx Trophy, when he played in the centre of defence alongside Vince Overson in the 3–1 home defeat by Bury. However, two convincing wins over Rochdale and Bolton Wanderers took the Clarets to a meeting with Blackburn Rovers in the Final. Although the Clarets were beaten 1–0, Deakin had made a good impression and was included in the team that faced Northampton at Turf Moor on the opening day of 1985–86, thus making his 'official' senior debut for the club.

In his first two seasons at Turf Moor Deakin was an ever present in the Burnley defence. He could operate in a normal back four in either the centre or at left-back and was also utilised by the Clarets as a sweeper. His intelligent reading of the game enabled him to position himself where the danger arose, and he had a calming influence on his colleagues. He proved an inspirational captain, and 12 months after leading the team to victory against Orient he led them out at Wembley in the Sherpa Van Trophy Final against Wolverhampton Wanderers.

Deakin spent much of 1988–89 on the sidelines because of injury. However, the following season he reclaimed his left-back role and remained as the first choice for that position until being ousted by Ian Bray in 1991. Having amassed over 200 League appearances for the Clarets, he was released by the club in May 1991.

Deakin settled in the Burnley area at the end of his playing days and is still fondly remembered by the Turf Moor faithful. He endured some of the darkest days in the history of the club, and perhaps that is why his contribution can sometimes be easily overlooked. However, the Burnley faithful know his true value to the club and never was it better exemplified than on that day in May 1987 when Burnley almost dropped out of the Football League.

Martin Dobson

Date of birth:	14 February 1948, Rishton, Lancashire

Burnley record:

Appearances:	League 406+4, FA Cup 31, League Cup 34, others 2
Goals:	League 63, FA Cup 7, League Cup 4
Debut:	League, 23 September 1967 v Wolverhampton Wanderers (a) lost 2–3
Also played for:	Bolton Wanderers, Everton, Bury, England (5 caps), England Under-23 (1 cap), Football League (1 appearance)
Managed:	Bury, Northwich Victoria, Bristol Rovers, Abob (Cyprus)

Martin Dobson was released by Bolton Wanderers in May 1967 as it was deemed he was unlikely to make the grade by the Second Division club. At Burnden Park he had been used as a traditional type of centre-forward, but the hurly-burly of chasing long balls from defence was never going to be his strong point. However, after being shown the door at Burnden Park, Dobson was quickly snapped up by the Clarets following a short trial. Within four months of being released by Bolton he had made his debut in the top Division and was on his way to a glittering career that brought him five England caps.

Harry Potts had seen the potential that Dobson possessed and for a time he vied with Willie Irvine and Andy Lochhead for an attacking role at Turf Moor. Despite his early debut at Wolverhampton in September 1967, Dobson only made spasmodic appearances during 1967–68. However, it was Potts who discovered that he, while a naturally elegant midfielder, was sufficiently versatile to operate in defence. Thus, when Colin Waldron suffered a dip in form midway through the 1969–70 campaign, it was Dobson who was chosen to fill the gap in the centre of defence. Indeed, he was impressive enough as a central-defender to be capped by England Under-23 in that position.

Sadly, a broken leg suffered in a friendly against Middlesbrough kept Dobson out of action until November 1970. When he returned, he found the Clarets in a relegation battle that was ultimately lost. The 1971–72 season proved to be one of rebuilding as Jimmy Adamson looked to fulfil his prophecy that Burnley would be the 'team of the 70s'. In 1972–73, Dobson proved an inspirational figure in the Burnley midfield as he captained the team to the Second Division Championship. He possessed all the skills required for a top-class midfield player. His versatility meant that he could defend as well as get forward and score goals. His timing of the tackle was an art form in itself and allowed him to win possession cleanly in the fierce environment of a crowded midfield. Once in possession, he had an elegant style of running with the ball, always keeping it under control, before sweeping passes to all points of the field. Rarely did he give the ball away, and whenever he was in range he was never afraid to have a pop at goal.

Dobson's outstanding form brought him his first England cap in April 1974, and by October of that year he had represented his country on five occasions. However, by the time he made the last of these international appearances he was no longer a Burnley player. In August 1974 he became the subject of a new British transfer record when Everton signed him for £300,000. It was a blow for the Burnley fans, who felt that he had been sacrificed to finance the building of the new Bob Lord Stand.

Dobson's cultured style of play ought to have flourished at Everton's 'School of Science', and yet some felt that his time on Merseyside was not quite as successful as it might have been. Nonetheless, the fluent distribution and impeccable control that had been a feature of his play at Burnley enabled him to feature in some 230 League and Cup games for Everton. In 1976–77 he picked up a League Cup-finalists' medal when Everton were beaten by Aston Villa in a Final that went to three matches. He also enjoyed two successful campaigns in the League, with Everton finishing in third place in 1977–78 and fourth place in 1978–79 in the top Division.

Dobson returned to Burnley, then in the Second Division, in August 1979 for a fee of £100,000. It was a surprise move and initially it was not a happy one. The Clarets were relegated to the Third Division at the end of 1979–80, and sadly he was sidelined by injury during the closing months of that campaign.

In 1981–82 Dobson undertook a new role when he was asked to use his vast experience to guide the younger players by operating as a sweeper. He once again skippered the team and led them to the Third Division Championship, his second title as a captain at Turf Moor.

Sadly, immediate relegation followed in 1982–83, and the summer of 1983 brought the entry of John Bond into Turf Moor. The new manager left Dobson out of the opening day defeat at Hull City but was quickly forced to recall him. However, Bond was never really taken with him, and in March 1983 he allowed him to move to Bury as player-manager.

Dobson enjoyed a successful stint at Gigg Lane, winning promotion from the Fourth Division in 1984–85. Unfortunately, a spell in charge of Bristol Rovers wasn't quite as happy. He also managed in non-League football and in Cyprus. In May 1996 he was appointed youth development officer at Bolton Wanderers and remained in charge of the youth set up at the club until June 2000.

Alex Elder

Date of birth: 25 April 1941, Glentoran, Northern Ireland

Burnley record:

Appearances: League 271, FA Cup 39, League Cup 11, Europe 8, others 1
Goals: League 15, FA Cup 2
Debut: League, 15 September 1959 v Preston North End (a) lost 0–1

Also played for: Altona FC, Glentoran, Stoke City, Leek Town, Northern Ireland (40 caps), Northern Ireland B (1 cap), Northern Ireland Under-23 (1 cap)

An Irish schoolboy international, Alex Elder had played as a part-time professional with Glentoran while working as a costing clerk for a firm of car distributors. Originally a half-back, he was converted to full-back while playing junior football in Ireland. He was just 17 when Potts paid £5,000 to bring him to England in January 1959 as the final piece of his Championship-winning team.

Elder was groomed in the Central League team for the remainder of his first season at the club but got his senior chance at Deepdale in September 1959. Although Burnley lost, the 18-year-old left-back made his mark and retained his place for the remainder of that memorable season. Indeed, the only match he missed after his debut during the Championship triumph was due to international duty. He was awarded his first full cap when Northern Ireland lost 3–2 to Wales at Wrexham in April 1960 and went on to make 40 appearances for his country, 34 of which were made while still at Turf Moor.

Elder proved to be the ideal counterpart to John Angus on the opposite flank. He was a rugged competitor whose strong tackling was combined with a mature positional sense. Like Angus, he could also set up attacking moves with a series of accurate long passes from defence. However, he also had the ability to embark upon electrifying runs down the wing and attack opposing defences. Like so many players of his era, he paid tribute to the encouragement and help he received from the long-serving George Bray.

During the 1961–62 season, when the Clarets challenged for a League and Cup double, Elder missed just one game. Despite his youth, he had become a fixture at Turf Moor due to his amazing consistency in terms of performance.

Sadly, Elder received a major blow during pre-season training in August 1963 when he suffered a broken ankle. It was an injury that would keep him out of action until December. It also robbed him of the opportunity to play for the Rest of the World team that was to face England in the FA Centenary Match at Wembley. The fact that he had been selected to line up alongside the likes of Lev Yashin, Djalma Santos, Eusebio, Di Stefano, Pele and Puskas perhaps illustrates just how good he was in his position. In many ways he was perhaps the most underrated player in the Championship-winning team.

Fortunately, he recovered from the injury and continued to give excellent service to the club at a time when the team was in transition. In July 1965 Elder was made club captain, and that season he helped Burnley reach third place in the First Division and qualify for the Inter-Cities Fairs' Cup. Indeed, but for a bizarre own-goal by Elder at Leeds in the penultimate game of the season, the Clarets might well have snatched the runners'-up spot.

In August 1967, Elder became part of the changes that had become a feature of life at Turf Moor in the mid-60s. Although only 26, and after making over 300 senior appearances for the Clarets, he was sold to Stoke City for a fee in the region of £50,000.

Sadly, Elder didn't enjoy the best of fortune in the Potteries. A knee injury, picked up in pre-season training, was to plague him for the rest of his career. He made just 83 appearances for Stoke during his six years at the Victoria Ground before bringing his career to an end with a short stint at Leek Town. He then embarked upon a life outside of football and ran his own company, which supplied equipment to the licensed trade. He continues to reside in the Burnley area, which has become his adopted home.

David Eyres

Date of birth: 26 February 1964, Liverpool

Burnley record:
Appearances: League 171+4, FA Cup 14, League Cup 17, others 9
Goals: League 37, FA Cup 8, League Cup 7, others 3
Debut: League, 14 August 1993 v Port Vale (h) won 2–1

Also played for: Rhyl, Blackpool, Preston North End, Oldham Athletic, Bury (trial), Hyde United

On 18 August 2006 the Clarets travelled to Gigg Lane for a pre-season friendly. Sitting on the substitutes' bench for Bury was a 42-year-old midfield player who was on trial and hoping to win a contract for yet another season of League football. Certainly Chris Casper, son of Frank and the Bury manager, had no hesitation in using such an ageing figure: 'For a 42-year-old, he is still very fit, it's quite amazing how fit he is.' Sadly, David Eyres didn't get called into action, but if he had he would have received a rapturous reception from all Clarets fans, for Eyres remains one of the modern-day heroes to many of the Turf Moor faithful.

At the start of 2006–07, Eyres was about to embark on his 17th season as a professional footballer, and yet, despite being held in such high esteem at Burnley, he only spent a little over four seasons with the Clarets. What, then, made him such a cult figure with the fans at Turf Moor? Was it the fact that he became the first Burnley player in 32 years to score a goal for the club at Wembley? Was it the fact that this goal set the Clarets on the way to winning promotion for the second time in three years? Or was it his exciting style of play on the left flank that endeared him to the supporters? In truth, it was perhaps that he reminded supporters of an earlier era, when a winger with pace and skill could enlighten the darkest of afternoons. In many ways he was an old fashioned type of winger, a player who would work the ball into a position from where he could float almost inch-perfect crosses into the opposing goalmouth. Another trick was to feign a cross before dragging the ball inside to alter the angle for the cross, and, of course, he also had the ability to fire in shots from all angles.

Eyres's career had started at Rhyl before he joined Blackpool in August 1989 for £10,000. He spent four seasons with the Seasiders and gained promotion from the Fourth Division in 1991–92. Jimmy Mullen, for whom he had played briefly at Bloomfield Road, paid £90,000 to bring him to Burnley in July 1993 and immediately installed him on the left flank of the Burnley midfield. He scored 19 goals in 45 League appearances that season and established himself as a firm favourite with the fans.

His goals were a major factor in the Clarets

reaching the Play-off Final against Stockport County, and, of course, he got his name on the score sheet as the Clarets won promotion to the Second Division. In a higher League, his goals were not quite as frequent, but his contribution was no less important. Indeed, his versatility in being able to play at left-back meant that he became an invaluable member of Mullen's squad. The manager even asked him to lead the attack on occasions during 1994–95 when both the players and team suffered a difficult season which resulted in relegation, just one year after celebrating promotion.

In 1995–96 the Clarets almost slipped straight through the Second Division, but Eyres proved an inspiration over the closing weeks of the campaign, and the club retained its status by the narrowest of margins.

Adrian Heath converted him into a left-sided wing-back for the 1996–97 season. While it reduced his effectiveness in terms of goals, Eyres enjoyed the position, as he explained at the time of his move to Preston in October 1997: 'I felt happy with my performances last season, and I think I played the best football of my career at wing-back.'

The appointment of Chris Waddle to the manager's position at Turf Moor brought a return to 4-4-2, but Eyres found his form dipping as he tried to adapt to the new manager's methods. In October 1997 the Burnley directors accepted a bid of £80,000 from Preston North End, and he departed to spend the next three years at Deepdale.

In 1999–2000 Eyres helped Preston win the Second Division title, while the Clarets finished in the runners'-up spot. He made over 100 League appearances for Preston before joining Oldham Athletic on a free transfer in October 2000. He was 36 at that point and many believed his move to Boundary Park would be little more than a brief swansong to the Football League. However, Eyres had other ideas, and by the time he was released by the Latics in the summer of 2006 he had clocked up over 200 senior appearances for the club and scored some 44 League and Cup goals.

After failing to win a contract at Bury, Eyres began the 2006–07 season in non-League football with Hyde United.

Andy Farrell

Date of birth: 7 October 1965, Colchester

Burnley record:
Appearances: League 237+20, FA Cup 19+2, League Cup 17+4, others 27+3
Goals: League 19, League Cup 1, others 3
Debut: League, 15 August 1987 v Colchester United (h) lost 0–3

Also played for: Colchester United, Wigan Athletic, Rochdale, Morecambe,
Leigh RMI, Halifax Town, Harrogate Town, Halifax Town, Leek
Town, Ramsbottom United

Andy Farrell was just 21 years of age when he joined Burnley in August 1987 for a fee of £5,000. Despite his tender years, he was already a veteran of 128 League and Cup games for Colchester United. At Layer Road he had operated in either defence or midfield, and it was his versatility that proved to be his trademark during his stay at Turf Moor.

When Farrell arrived at Burnley, the club was still recovering from the aftermath of its near relegation from the Football League. In the wake of the Orient game, Brian Miller had undertaken a major rebuilding programme during the summer of 1987. It resulted in Farrell being one of eight debutants who opened the 1987–88 campaign. Ironically, Colchester United were the visitors to Turf Moor on the opening day of the new season, and he must have felt a little disappointed when his former club romped to a 3–0 win. While a crowd of just 5,419 watched the opening day debacle, he ended the season playing in front of 80,841 at Wembley in the Sherpa Van Trophy Final. Unfortunately, Farrell finished on the losing side again, as Wolverhampton Wanderers inflicted a 2–0 defeat on the Clarets. Nonetheless, he had impressed everyone with his steady displays during his first season with the club.

Fortunately, there followed a period of gradual improvement in the fortunes of Burnley. During this time, he enjoyed spells at left-back and centre-half as well as in midfield. In truth, he could play in any position for the good of the team. Indeed, he even filled in between the posts when Chris Pearce was given his marching orders in a match against Stockport County at Turf Moor.

Farrell played a prominent role in the team that captured the Fourth Division Championship trophy in 1991–92. His impressive performances in midfield that season made him a popular figure with the supporters. The previous campaign, he had become the first Burnley substitute to score twice in a game when he left the bench to help the Clarets beat Carlisle United at Turf Moor in March 1991. He also holds another record in that he is the only Burnley player to play for the club twice at Wembley. In 1994 he came onto the pitch as a substitute when the Clarets beat Stockport County in the Second Division Play-off Final. Sadly, this was to be something of a swansong for him at Burnley. Apart from a couple of pre-season games, this was to be his final game for

the club as he was off-loaded to Wigan Athletic in September 1994.

Farrell again showed his versatility at Springfield Park and operated in both midfield and defence during his two seasons at Wigan. In July 1996 he was on the move again when he signed for Graham Barrow at Rochdale. He featured in 135 League and Cup games for Rochdale before embarking on a series of moves to non-League clubs.

Farrell returned to Turf Moor to become part of the club's Football in the Community team. Although he spent his entire career in the bottom two Divisions of English football, he continues to be fondly remembered by supporters of Burnley as a player whose commitment to the cause at Turf Moor never wavered during 257 League appearances for the club.

Paul Fletcher

Date of birth: 13 January 1951, Bolton

Burnley record:
Appearances: League 291+2, FA Cup 16+1, League Cup 18, others 24
Goals: League 71, FA Cup 7, League Cup 1, others 7
Debut: League, 6 March 1971 v Southampton (h) lost 0–1

Also played for: Bolton Wanderers, Blackpool, England Under-23 (4 caps)

Paul Fletcher belongs to that rare breed of professional footballer who graduates from the field to the boardroom. When injury brought his playing career to a premature end, he spent a brief period away from the game before returning to pursue a career not in management or coaching, but in the commercial and business side of the game. His business acumen proved to be just as successful as his predatory instincts as a goalscorer. However, he is quick to point out that his time at Burnley stood him in good stead for his future in the business world, 'I learnt about the importance of team ethic. At Burnley we had a wonderful side in the 70s and everything was so professional. In order to play well as an individual, you needed guys around who you could rely on. Everybody functioning like a well-oiled machine. I brought this concept into other aspects of my life.'

Fletcher began his football career with Bolton Wanderers, who he joined as an apprentice prior to signing professional forms in November 1968. He was just 17 when he made his League debut for Wanderers, scoring in a 2–1 defeat at Crystal Palace on 2 November 1968. It wasn't until the 1970–71 campaign that he got a prolonged run in the first team at Burnden Park, but sadly this was to be the season that the Wanderers dropped into the Third Division for the first time in the club's history. He left one relegation battle at Burnden Park to join another when he signed for Burnley in March 1971 for £60,000. It was, perhaps, too much to expect a young player of limited experience to rescue the Clarets. At the time of his transfer, he had only started 38 senior games and made four substitute appearances, which brought seven goals. While he couldn't save the Clarets from dropping into the Second Division, Jimmy Adamson felt he had the potential to help raise the club to its former status.

Fletcher featured in every game in 1971–72 and scored 10 goals, but it was the following campaign that proved a memorable one for supporters at Turf Moor. The Clarets won the Second Division Championship as Adamson wove a successful team together. 'He didn't want skill, he wanted balance, and suddenly we had great balance. We had a great goalkeeper in Alan Stevenson, a solid defence, good midfield, and we were scoring goals. The most unusual thing was, most of us

played every single game that season. We were very together,' explained Fletcher. It was also a personal triumph for him as he finished as leading goalscorer with 15 League goals.

In November 1973 Fletcher was one of three Burnley players to play for England Under-23 against Denmark at Fratton Park. He and Dave Thomas appeared as substitutes, while Alan Stevenson kept goal. It was the first of four Under-23 caps that he won.

Unfortunately, Fletcher's career was severely disrupted by a serious knee injury that he received at Upton Park in March 1975. It was to keep him out of action for over eight months, and when he returned the Clarets were again on the brink of relegation to the Second Division. Undoubtedly, his absence was a factor in the club's demise that season.

Although Fletcher continued to score goals in the Second Division, he was not as prolific as in the period before his injury. He helped the club to win the Anglo-Scottish Cup in 1978, yet his game lacked some of the drive that had been so prominent earlier in his career. The early stages of 1979–80 proved particularly disappointing for Fletcher, who failed to find the net in any of his 13 League appearances that season. His lack of form, coupled with the arrival of Billy Hamilton, led to him joining Blackpool in February 1980 for £30,000.

At Bloomfield Road, Fletcher found himself in the company of former Burnley colleagues Peter Noble and Terry Pashley. Unfortunately, in September 1980 he broke his leg and suffered knee ligament damage that brought his playing career to an end.

Released by Blackpool in 1982, he had a spell out of the game before becoming the commercial manager at Colne Dynamoes. In 1991 he was appointed chief executive of Huddersfield Town and oversaw the club's relocation from Leeds Road to a new stadium. He then moved to Bolton Wanderers where he was again responsible for taking a club into a new stadium.

After leaving Bolton, Fletcher spent 18 months as commercial director at Wembley before returning to club football with Coventry City. Once again, he was involved in the development of a new stadium for the club and today remains as Coventry's managing director.

Brian Flynn

Date of birth: 12 October 1955, Port Talbot, Glamorgan

Burnley record:

Appearances: League 193+9, FA Cup 18, League Cup 18+2, others 10
Goals: League 19, FA Cup 2, League Cup 4, others 2
Debut: League, 2 February 1974 v Arsenal (a) drew 1–1

Also played for: Neath Boys, Afan Lido, Leeds United, Cardiff City, Doncaster
                        Rovers, Bury, Limerick, Doncaster Rovers, Wrexham, Wales (66
                        caps), Wales Under-23 (2 caps)
Managed: Wrexham, Swansea City

Although short in stature at 5ft 4in, Brian Flynn had the heart of a lion and was a combative midfielder throughout his career. His tenacious approach was accompanied by a constructive passing game that made him a popular figure during his three spells at Turf Moor.

A Welsh Schoolboy international, Flynn began his career as a junior with Burnley before turning professional in October 1972. He made his senior bow against Arsenal in February 1974, but, despite a particularly successful debut at Highbury, he had to bide his time before sampling League football on a regular basis. The departure of Martin Dobson provided him with increased opportunities to hone his skills in the cut and thrust of the First Division. He featured in 26 League games during 1974–75 as the Clarets finished 10th in the top flight, and he became a recognised member of the senior team.

Flynn made his debut for Wales in November 1974 when making a substitute appearance against Luxembourg at the Vetch Field, Swansea. Although he was just 19 at the time, he quickly became a fixture in the Welsh team and went on to win 66 caps for his country.

One of the more consistent performers during the relegation campaign of 1975–76, the following season found Flynn in outstanding form, and it soon became clear that his talents would become hunted by clubs in the top flight. In November 1977 he moved to Leeds United in a deal that was said to be worth £175,000. At Elland Road he formed a successful partnership with Tony Currie in a Leeds team that was in the midst of transition following the success of the Don Revie years.

In October 1978, Flynn was reunited with his former Burnley manager when Jimmy Adamson took the helm at Elland Road. He only missed one game during that season, as Adamson used Flynn's talents to the full in the Leeds midfield. Hard work, neat control and accurate passing were attributes that the Leeds crowd fully appreciated.

Flynn's appearances at Leeds became more infrequent during 1981–82, and in March 1982 he returned to Turf Moor on loan. The Clarets were in the throes of a promotion battle, and Brian Miller wanted to use Flynn to supplement his attacking options. Thus, he was utilised as a second striker in a 1–1 draw against Fulham and occupied the same role four days later at Chester. Unfortunately, the robust nature of the Chester defending meant that he didn't complete the match, and he returned to Leeds.

However, in November 1982, with his immediate future uncertain, Flynn opted to rejoin Burnley on a permanent basis in a £60,000 deal. It was a season of mixed fortunes for the Clarets, with the club being relegated to the Third Division and yet reaching the sixth round of the FA Cup and the semi-final of the League Cup. He remained at the heart of the Burnley midfield throughout it all. The following season brought John Bond to Turf Moor, and Flynn maintained his place in the midfield. Indeed, he seemed to do well under Bond and combined well with Tommy Hutchinson and Kevin Reeves, two of Bond's signings from Manchester City.

Of course, these were turbulent times at Turf Moor, and the departure of Bond brought further upheaval, which included Flynn's departure from the club for the final time. In November 1984 he returned to his native Wales to join Cardiff City for £15,000. Ironically, he had signed schoolboy forms for Cardiff before an administrative error had allowed Burnley to nip in and sign him as a junior. The move to Cardiff signalled the beginning of a nomadic period in his career, with spells at Doncaster Rovers, Bury and Limerick, a return to Doncaster and finally a move to Wrexham, all occurring within the space of less than four years. It was at Wrexham where he finally brought his playing days to an end and entered the world of football management. He served briefly as caretaker manager of the Welsh club before being appointed manager in November 1989. One of his first actions was to appoint Kevin Reeves, his former Burnley teammate, as his assistant. For a time he combined his work at Wrexham with the managership of the Welsh Under-21 squad, before ending his spell at Wrexham in October 2001. A year after leaving, he returned to management at Swansea City, with Reeves again acting as his assistant, and he remained with the club until the closing stages of 2003–04.

Following the appointment of John Toshack as the Welsh international manager, Flynn was appointed as manager of the intermediate national teams, ranging from the Welsh Under-17 team to the Welsh Under-21 team.

John Francis

Date of birth: 21 November 1963, Dewsbury

Burnley record:
Appearances: League 143+34, FA Cup 12+2, League Cup 9+4, others 15+5
Goals: League 37, FA Cup 1, League Cup 1, others 6
Debut: League, 10 February 1990 v Gillingham (h) lost 1–2

Also played for: Emley, Halifax Town, Emley, Sheffield United, Cambridge United, Scunthorpe United, Halifax Town, Lancaster City

Exponents of exciting wing play are always popular at Turf Moor, and Burnley have certainly had their fair share of maestro's on the wing; indeed, the pages of this book contain a good many of them. In the early 1990s it fell to John Francis to try and pick up the baton and continue the traditions of the flying winger at Turf Moor. If he lacked some of the skill and technique of those who passed before him, no one could fault his enthusiasm or eye for goal, and at a time when the club languished in football's basement he provided a ray of hope for something better. In April 1992 it was Francis who nipped in with an injury-time winning goal at York's Bootham Crescent, which captured the Fourth Division Championship and so began Burnley's long awaited climb up the Divisions.

A native of Dewsbury, Francis's early career in the game was spent with non-League Emley in the Northern Counties East League. In April 1988 he played at Wembley in the FA Vase Final against Colne Dynamoes. However, attempts to break into League football with Halifax Town in February 1985 proved unsuccessful.

Continued success with Emley earned him a second crack at League football when Sheffield United paid £10,000 for him in September 1988. At the end of that season he had played his part in helping the Blades to win promotion from Division Three. Yet of his 22 League appearances that season, no fewer than 19 were made as a substitute – a role with which he became familiar during his career.

Francis enjoyed a second promotion season in 1989–90, making 11 starts and nine substitute appearances as Sheffield finished runners-up to Leeds United in the Second Division. However, long before the celebrations had begun at Bramall Lane, he had departed to join the Clarets for £90,000. The transfer was carried out under the media spotlight, as Sheffield United were the subject of a documentary television series at that time.

Francis's electrifying pace soon captured the imagination of the fans at Turf Moor, and he quickly became an extremely popular figure with supporters. Initially he played as a striker, and in 1990–91 he scored 15 League goals, second only to Ron Futcher's 18. The following season he was moved to the wing. His goal tally fell to eight in the League, but, nonetheless, he continued to tear defences apart and set up numerous chances for Mike Conway and Roger Eli in particular.

At times, Francis's blistering pace proved too much even for himself, and on more than one occasion he literally lost control of the ball as he increased his momentum. However, when he got everything in sync he was a delight to watch.

In August 1992 he was sold to Cambridge United for £95,000, but when the move didn't work out Francis returned to Turf Moor in March 1993. He continued to operate on the flank until he was relegated to the substitutes' bench during the latter stages of 1993–94. However, he returned for the Play-off semi-final against Plymouth Argyle and rescued a seemingly desperate position with two goals in three minutes, which sent the Clarets to a Wembley date with Stockport County. Sadly, the Play-off Final ended in disappointment for him as a knee injury ended his big day before it had really begun. Unfortunately, it proved to be an injury that would hamper the remainder of his career.

The next two seasons were disappointing ones for Francis as he was largely confined to a peripheral role as substitute. In May 1996 he was released by the Clarets and tried, unsuccessfully, to resurrect his League career with Scunthorpe before playing in the Vauxhall Conference with Halifax Town. In December 1997 he moved further down the ladder when he joined Lancaster City.

While his career might well have faded after that fateful day at Wembley, there is no doubting the fact that Francis continues to remain a popular character among the Turf Moor faithful. During some of the darkest days in the club's history, he illuminated the ground with some of his sparkling runs down the wings and brought back memories of happier times when the likes of Brian Pilkington, John Connelly and Willie Morgan were the wizards on the wing at Turf Moor.

Bert Freeman

Date of birth:	10 October 1895, Handsworth, Birmingham
Died:	11 August 1955, Birmingham

Burnley record:

Appearances:	League 166, FA Cup 23, Wartime 76
Goals:	League 103, FA Cup 12, Wartime 39
Debut:	League, 15 April 1911 v Wolverhampton Wanderers (h) drew 1–1

Also played for: Gower Street Council School, Gower Street Old Boys, Aston Manor, Aston Villa, Woolwich Arsenal, Everton, Wigan Borough, Kettering Town, England (5 caps), Football League (4 appearances)

Between 1905 and the outbreak of World War One, Bert Freeman achieved almost legendary status within English football. By the time he joined Burnley in April 1911 he was already an English international and one of the First Division's leading goalscorers. However, it was at Turf Moor where he finally won club honours to go with his international caps.

Freeman's career began in Birmingham's youth football with Gower Street Old Boys and Aston Manor, before he graduated to Aston Villa in April 1904. However, during his 18 months at Villa Park he failed to break into the first team, and in November 1905 he moved to the capital to join Woolwich Arsenal. It was during his first season at the Manor Ground that he showed his goalscoring prowess. He scored on his debut at Nottingham Forest on 25 November 1905 and went on to score nine goals in 17 appearances that season. Unfortunately, this proved to be his most successful period with the London club. In April 1906 Peter Kyle was signed from Tottenham Hotspur to fill the centre-forward berth, and as a result Freeman found himself relegated to a bit-part role during the remainder of his time at Arsenal. Nonetheless, by the time he moved to Everton in April 1908 he had notched up 21 goals in 44 League outings.

Freeman made an immediate impact at Goodison Park in 1908–09 with 38 goals being scored in 37 League appearances. It made him the first Evertonian to reach 30 goals in a League campaign. A tenacious front runner, he was blessed with quick feet that enabled him to bring the ball under instant control, while he also possessed a fierce shot. Although not the tallest of men, he was excellent in the air and his timing enabled him to make up for his lack of inches. He was the complete centre-forward.

Freeman was awarded his first international cap by England on 15 March 1909, and he scored one of the goals in a 2–0 victory over Wales at the City Ground, Nottingham. He retained his place the following month for the meeting with Scotland at Crystal Palace but was then absent from the international scene until his switch to Burnley in April 1911.

After the success of his initial campaign at

Goodison Park, Freeman followed it up with another 22 League goals in 1909–10. The following season his form wavered, yet it still came as something of a shock when Everton agreed to allow him to join the Clarets.

In stepping down a Division, he accepted the role of spearheading Burnley's return to the top flight, a task that was completed in 1912–13 when his 31 League goals clinched the runners'-up spot in the Second Division. This came in the wake of 32 League goals the previous campaign, and the correspondent of the *Lancashire Daily Post Annual* described Freeman as 'a leading centre forward of the day.' He went on to describe him as 'Sturdily built, wonderfully quick off the mark, and exceedingly resourceful in beating backs and goalkeeper.'

Freeman's successful stint at Turf Moor brought another three England caps and two goals in 1912. He and Teddy Hodgson developed a formidable understanding as they powered the Clarets to the 1914 FA Cup Final. It was at Crystal Palace on 25 April 1914 that he secured his place in the annals of Burnley Football Club, when he took advantage of Hodgson's headed knock-down to beat Kenny Campbell in the Liverpool goal and score the only goal of the match. It remains the only time in the club's history that the FA Cup has been won by Burnley.

Freeman's career was at its peak when the clouds of war gathered over Europe and led to the suspension of the Football League. Four years of meaningless regional football followed, in which he continued to shine, scoring 39 goals in 76 Regional League games.

When the Football League was restored in 1919–20, Freeman was nearing his 34th birthday. He still featured prominently during that first campaign of peacetime football – 28 League appearances and 12 goals – but it was clear that his age was beginning to affect his game. Although he played in the opening three games of the Championship-winning season of 1920–21, he was axed in the wake of three defeats and didn't feature again for the club.

In September 1921 Freeman joined Wigan Borough and later played for Kettering Town before bringing his career to an end in 1924.

Billy Gray

Date of birth: 24 May 1927, Dinnington, Co. Durham

Burnley record:
Appearances: League 120, FA Cup 10
Goals: League 30, FA Cup 2
Debut: League, 19 August 1953 v Wolverhampton Wanderers (h) won 4–1

Also played for: Dinnington Colliery, Wolverhampton Wanderers, Gateshead,
Leyton Orient, Chelsea, Nottingham Forest, Millwall
Managed: Millwall, Brentford, Notts County

When Jack Hill was able to entice Billy Gray to leave Chelsea and join Burnley in August 1953, it was viewed as something of a coup for the Turf Moor club. The fee of £16,000 reflected the esteem in which Gray was held at Stamford Bridge. He was a player who could operate on either wing and was already the holder of an England B cap.

Gray began his football career in his native North East, playing for Dinnington Colliery in the Newcastle and District League. However, his attempts to break into League football floundered after abortive trials with Wolverhampton Wanderers and Gateshead. Fortunately, he fared rather better in London when he went to Leyton Orient as a 20-year-old in May 1947. During his early days with Orient, he was known by his middle name of 'Patrick' and showed great promise with his scintillating style of wing play. He marked his League debut for Orient against Newport County in September 1947 with a goal, but this proved to be the only one that he would score while at Brisbane Road. On 27 December 1948 he enjoyed the unique experience of playing two games for Orient on the same day! He featured for the reserves at Chelsea in the morning and then turned out for the first team against Port Vale in the afternoon.

After just 19 League appearances for the Brisbane Road club, Gray left Leyton Orient to join Chelsea in March 1949. He appeared in two League games for Chelsea during the closing stages of the 1948–49 campaign, but the following season he quickly established himself as a first-team regular, initially on the left wing and then later at outside-right. Indeed, during his first full season at Stamford Bridge he helped Chelsea to reach an FA Cup semi-final. His impact there was sufficiently impressive for him to be selected for the England B team that beat Switzerland 5–0 at Hillsborough in January 1950, and, as in his Orient debut, he celebrated his call up by scoring one of the goals.

Gray became an automatic choice in one or the other of the wide positions at Stamford Bridge, and in 1951–52 he again helped the club reach the semi-final of the FA Cup where, as two years earlier, they were beaten by Arsenal. He was extremely popular with the Chelsea supporters, who appreciated his fast and clever style of wing play. Therefore, it came as a major surprise when the Clarets were able to prise him away from Stamford Bridge in August 1953.

Gray was immediately installed on the right wing of the Burnley attack, and, such was his consistency, he only missed two games between making his debut and February 1956. However, at that point he came under pressure from Doug Newlands, and his appearances became increasingly spasmodic.

During his first season with the Clarets Gray proved that he was not only a creative winger (one who could fashion openings and chances for his colleagues), but that he was also a steady goalscorer. Indeed, he finished the 1953–54 campaign as the leading marksman with 19 League goals and another in the FA Cup. Although not quite as prolific the following campaign, his eight goals were a tidy return from a player whose primary function was to supply the ammunition for others to fire.

The 1956–57 campaign found Gray on the sidelines, as Newlands claimed the outside-right position at Turf Moor. After making just seven League appearances that season, he agreed to join newly promoted Nottingham Forest in June 1957. At the City Ground he was used mainly as a winger or inside-forward, and it was in this latter position that he appeared in the 1959 FA Cup Final when Forest beat Luton Town. In the latter stages of the 1960–61 campaign, he was used at full-back on a couple of occasions, and it was at left-back that he spent the remainder of his time with Forest. He made a total of 201 League appearances for the Nottingham club before moving to Millwall in November 1963 as player-manager.

Gray suffered a traumatic introduction to management, with Millwall being relegated to the Fourth Division at the end of his first season with the club. However, he quickly turned things around and led Millwall to an immediate return to the Third Division. He followed this up with a second successive promotion in 1965–66, when Millwall gained a place in the Second Division for the first time in 18 years. At the same time, he looked to the future of the club by instigating a youth scheme that would later pay dividends for the London club.

Gray didn't stay to guide Millwall in the Second Division but left to become manager of Brentford in May 1966. He also managed Notts County during the 1967–68 campaign before becoming groundsman at Forest's City Ground for many years.

Neil Grewcock

Date of birth: 26 April 1962, Leicester

Burnley record:
Appearances: League 180+22, FA Cup 10, League Cup 12+1, others 16
Goals: League 27, FA Cup 1, League Cup 2, others 2
Debut: League, 25 August 1984 v Plymouth Argyle (h) drew 1–1

Also played for: Leicester Beavers, Leicester City, Gillingham Kettering Town,
Shepshed Charterhouse, Burnley Bank Hall

Neil Grewcock arrived at Turf Moor during the summer of 1984, as John Bond reflected on his first season in charge of Burnley. The flamboyant Bond had spent a sizeable sum assembling a team that finished its first season mid-table in the Third Division. Grewcock was signed as another bout of rebuilding was about to begin, but before he could make his debut Bond had left and been replaced by John Benson. Thus, he was left with the task of trying to convince Bond's former assistant that he was good enough for a place in the first team.

Although he had been signed from non-League Shepshed Charterhouse, Grewcock already had experience of League football with Leicester City. As a 16-year-old apprentice, he had made his League bow against Cardiff City at Filbert Street in March 1979. He made a total of nine senior appearances for Leicester before playing in 40 games for Gillingham prior to entering the world of non-League football. He was, therefore, still something of an unknown quantity to the Clarets fans when he made his League debut on the opening day of the 1984–85 campaign.

Benson's faith in Grewcock was soon rewarded, and he quickly won over the fans with his energetic displays on the right-hand side of the midfield. Short and stockily built, he was not everyone's picture of the ideal winger. However, on his day he possessed the trickery required to extricate himself from the tightest of spots, and his ability to cross the ball was as good as many of the so-called more traditional wingmen.

Sadly, at the end of Grewcock's first season at Burnley the Clarets found themselves relegated to the Fourth Division for the first time in the club's history. As the turnover of players increased and managers came and went, he provided some much needed consistency on the field and was a virtual ever present during his first three years at the club.

However, despite Grewcock's contribution at a time when fortunes were at a low ebb at Turf Moor, he might well have passed into the pages of history almost unnoticed but for the events of 9 May 1987. On that day he drove home Ian Britton's pass to give the Clarets the lead in the most crucial match that the club had played. When he floated over a free-kick for Britton to head home, three minutes into the second half, Grewcock had guaranteed his place among the legends of Turf Moor. The match against Orient was won, and Burnley retained their place in the Football League that they had helped to found in 1888. Of course, if Orient had come back and won the game then it is open to conjecture as to the importance supporters might have put on his overall contribution to Burnley Football Club.

The following campaign was a happier one at Turf Moor, with the Clarets in a comfortable mid-table place in the Fourth Division. The Clarets also reached Wembley that season in the Sherpa Van Trophy Final, but, sadly, Grewcock missed the game through injury.

Although he returned to action the following season, Grewcock was never quite the same player again. In 1988–89 he was restricted to just 13 League appearances, while the following campaign brought seven League games. In 1990–91 he helped the Clarets reach the Fourth Division Play-offs but didn't appear in either of the legs against Torquay United that condemned the club to yet another season in football's basement.

Grewcock was released by the club in the summer of 1991 but continued to live in the area and play in local non-League football.

George Halley

Date of birth:	29 October 1887, Cronberry
Died:	18 December 1941, Burnley

Burnley record:

Appearances:	League 137, FA Cup 16, Wartime 5
Goals:	League 4, FA Cup 1, Wartime 5
Debut:	League, 15 March 1913 v Bury (h) won 3–1

Also played for: Glenbuck Cherrypickers, Kilmarnock, Bradford Park Avenue, Southend United, Bacup Borough, Scottish League (1 appearance)

George Halley was the final player that John Haworth signed for the team that would win the FA Cup in 1914. With his arrival, the legendary half-back line of Halley, Boyle and Watson was born. It was the rock on which the FA Cup and League Championship glories were built.

Halley had graduated, via Scottish junior football and Kilmarnock, into English football at Bradford. He missed just one game in 1911–12, his first season in English football, as Bradford finished mid-table in the Second Division. Ironically, his first goal for Bradford came in their 2–1 home win over Burnley in October 1911.

The energetic young half-back continued to impress at Bradford, making 68 League appearances and eight in the FA Cup until Haworth stepped in and brought him to Turf Moor in March 1913. Halley was immediately drafted into the team over the closing stages of the season to fill the right-half berth. It was a position that had become something of a problem, with no fewer than five men being utilised in the role prior to his arrival. He made eight appearances for the Clarets during the remainder of that campaign as the club clinched promotion to the First Division.

The following season Halley was the automatic choice at right-half, as the Clarets established themselves in the top flight with a 12th-place finish. However, it was the FA Cup that caught the imagination in 1913–14, with the Clarets winning the trophy for the first time in the club's history. The half-back line of Halley, Boyle and Watson reigned supreme as Burnley lifted the trophy at the Crystal Palace, courtesy of a 1–0 win over Liverpool, in front of 72,778 spectators.

However, despite his stylish performances, Halley found himself under pressure to retain his place the following season due to the form of Levy Thorpe. Indeed, he was restricted to just 10 League appearances in the final season of peacetime football. The suspension of the Football League for the duration of the war hindered his attempts to win back his place in the team. He made only five wartime appearances for the club, curiously scoring five goals, before embarking upon another battle with Thorpe in 1919–20. For a time, he was used at left-back as the Clarets finished in the runners'-up spot in the First Division.

Halley was at the peak of his Turf Moor career during the Championship-winning season of 1920–21. Thorpe had been sold to Blackburn Rovers in February 1920, and Halley was now the undisputed right-half for the first team. He was in commanding form as the Clarets moved

into gear and embarked upon a 30-match unbeaten run. Sadly, illness prevented him from completing that run and playing a part in the final stages of the Championship success. Nonetheless, the 26 appearances he made that season helped the club to win the title for the first time in its history.

Strangely, international honours eluded Halley throughout his career. He represented the Scottish League against the Football League at Blackburn in 1910 and assisted the Anglo-Scots against the Home Scots in international trials in 1913 and 1914. However, that was as far as his international career progressed until he was selected to face Ireland in Belfast in February 1921. Unfortunately, his illness meant that he had to pull out of the fixture and the call to his national colours never came again.

Halley was back on form the following season and appeared in 34 League games as the Clarets finished in third position in the First Division. It was, therefore, something of a surprise when he rejected the opportunity to extend his stay at Turf Moor at the end of the 1921–22 campaign. Eventually, he joined Southend United in November 1922 and made his debut at Plymouth Argyle in a Third Division South match. He made a total of 21 League appearances for Southend as well as appearing in two FA Cup ties.

Halley returned to the locality in 1924 to join Bacup Borough as a coach before retiring from the game. A plasterer by trade, he continued to live in Burnley until his death in 1941.

Billy Hamilton

Date of birth: 9 May 1957, Belfast

Burnley record:
Appearances: League 200, FA Cup 23, League Cup 16, others 9
Goals: League 58, FA Cup 10, League Cup 5, others 3
Debut: League, 1 December 1979 v Bristol Rovers (a) drew 0–0

Also played for: Linfield, Queen's Park Rangers, Oxford United, Limerick, Northern Ireland (41 caps), Northern Ireland Under-21 (1 cap)
Managed: Limerick, Distillery

Something of an enigma to most of those on the terraces, Billy Hamilton signed for the Clarets in November 1979. He had joined Queen's Park Rangers from Linfield for £25,000 in April 1978 but had only made a handful of appearances for the Loftus Road club, despite having gained his first Northern Ireland cap during his brief stay in London. When Brian Miller paid £38,000 to bring him to Lancashire, he was very much an unknown quantity.

He arrived at a time when the club found itself involved in a desperate struggle against relegation. Sadly, it was a battle that was lost, and although he finished as leading goalscorer, with just seven League goals, he couldn't prevent the Clarets fans having to endure a miserable end to the season. Not one of the final 16 matches was won as Burnley slipped into the Third Division for the first time in the club's history.

In truth, Hamilton always impressed more as a target man than a prolific goalscorer. Although not the quickest of athletes, he was an industrious worker whose build made him the perfect man to hold up play and keep possession while others joined him in attack. A powerful figure, he was excellent in the air and quickly became a firm favourite with the supporters.

In 1980–81 Hamilton formed a new attacking partnership with Steve Taylor, who had been signed from Mansfield Town in the close season. The two struck up an immediate understanding, with Taylor feeding off the flicks that Hamilton provided. Taylor ended the season with 16 goals, many of which were a direct result of picking up passes from his Irish partner, while Hamilton netted nine League goals.

It was the following season when Hamilton came into his own as he struck up two successful partnerships. In the early part of the season he continued to work well with Taylor, while the final months of the campaign found him linking up with Paul McGee. McGee, a Republic of Ireland international, joined Burnley from Preston North End in March 1982 after spending a successful loan spell with the club earlier in the season. Hamilton finished the season as leading goalscorer with 11 goals as the Clarets won the Third Division Championship. Having secured promotion, he jetted off to Spain as part of Northern Ireland's World Cup squad. He played a leading role in their successful World Cup campaign, creating the goal chance for Gerry Armstrong that gave his country a remarkable win over Spain. Hamilton also got on the score sheet himself when he scored both goals in the 2–2 draw with Austria in the quarter-finals.

Hamilton returned to Burnley for the 1982–83 campaign and endured a traumatic time at Turf Moor. A place in the League Cup semi-final and a quarter-final place in the FA Cup was poor consolation for losing Second Division status after only one season at the higher level. He was again top scorer in the League with 13 goals and found the back of the net twice in the League Cup quarter-final with Tottenham Hotspur at White Hart Lane. His second goal was an absolute screamer, a 20–yard drive that left England's Ray Clemence helpless in the Tottenham goal as Burnley enjoyed a shock 4–1 win.

The 1983–84 campaign brought Third Division football and John Bond to Turf Moor. It was not a happy combination, although he enjoyed his best campaign with the club in terms of goals scored as he struck up an immediate understanding with Kevin Reeves, Bond's big money signing from Manchester City. Sadly, Reeves received an injury at the turn of the year that was to end his career, and unfortunately this also had a detrimental effect on Hamilton. Nonetheless, 18 League goals made him the top scorer and the target of other clubs.

In the summer of 1984 Hamilton moved to newly-promoted Oxford United, having won the Third Division Championship in 1983–84, in exchange for £95,000 and Neil Whatmore. Hamilton led Oxford's charge to the Second Division Championship and the top flight, while Burnley dropped into football's basement.

Unfortunately, injury limited Hamilton's appearances in the First Division and also caused him to miss Oxford's League Cup Final victory over QPR at Wembley in April 1986. Plagued by injury, he joined Limerick in the Republic of Ireland and became player-manager. He then took a similar role north of the border when he took charge of Distillery.

Hamilton later opened a sports shop in Banger. However, he still kept an eye open for young talent for the Clarets and was instrumental in the arrival of Glen Little at the club.

Ray Hankin

Date of birth: 2 February 1956, Wallsend

Burnley record:
Appearances: League 110+2, FA Cup 6, League Cup 12, others 9
Goals: League 37, FA Cup 2, League Cup 4, others 4
Debut: League, 24 April 1973 v Luton Town (h) won 3–0 (substitute)

Also played for: Leeds United, Vancouver Whitecaps, Arsenal, Shamrock Rovers, Vancouver Whitecaps, Middlesbrough, Peterborough United, Wolverhampton Wanderers, Whitby Town, Blue Star FC, Guisborough Town, Hamrun Spartans (Malta), England Under-23 (3 caps)
Managed: Northallerton Town

Ray Hankin had the perfect build to play the traditional centre-forward role, and it was one that he undertook with gusto. Physically strong, good in the air and with a powerful shot, he seemed destined for a successful career from a very early age. However, despite an impressive record, many felt that Hankin didn't quite fulfil his potential at Turf Moor before embarking upon a somewhat nomadic career.

Hankin, the son of a ship-yard worker, was yet another youngster who followed that well-trodden path from the North East to Turf Moor. He came to Burnley with an excellent pedigree, and within months of signing as a professional for the club in February 1973 he was part of the England Youth team that won the Little World Cup in Italy. The goals he scored in that tournament merely underlined the potential that he possessed as a traditional type of centre-forward.

Hankin had been given a taste of first-team football at Turf Moor prior to his trip to Italy when he appeared in the penultimate game of the Second Division Championship-winning campaign of 1972–73. An early season injury to Frank Casper ensured that he was given a chance to make his mark in the First Division, as he formed a twin spearhead with Paul Fletcher. Despite their relative inexperience, Hankin and Fletcher did sufficiently well for the Clarets to end the season in sixth place in the top flight. The club also reached the semi-final of the FA Cup, but Hankin missed out as Casper was patched up to play against Newcastle United. However, Casper missed the newly introduced third-place Play-off in the FA Cup at Filbert Street against Leicester City, and Hankin, who'd returned to action after the semi-final, clinched the match with the only goal of the game.

Having proved his worth against some of the best defenders in the country, Hankin graduated to the England Under-23 team in October 1974 when he won the first of his three caps at that level.

Hankin finished two goals behind leading scorer Leighton James in 1974–75 with 14 League goals, and the following season he finished joint leading goalscorer with Peter Noble, both players scoring 13 times each. Sadly, the goals proved insufficient to prevent the club from slipping into the Second Division at the end of 1975–76. A tremendous competitor, his somewhat fiery temperament sometimes let him down, but at his best he was capable of scoring great goals and led the attack in a robust style that made him popular with the supporters.

Hankin was clearly better than Second Division football, and it wasn't long before he attracted the attention of top-flight clubs. In September 1976 he agreed to move to Elland Road after Leeds United's bid of £172,000 had been accepted by the Burnley directors.

Unfortunately, the move to Yorkshire produced mixed results for Hankin. Injuries prevented him from making an initial impact at Elland Road and restricted him to just four League games in 1976–77. His second season at Leeds was a much more successful affair, with Hankin scoring 20 goals in 33 First Division games, making him easily the Yorkshire club's top scorer. That proved to be the highpoint of his time at Leeds, as Terry Connor edged ahead of him in the race for the number-nine shirt at Elland Road.

Although only 24, Hankin turned his back on English football and joined Vancouver Whitecaps in March 1980. He spent 18 successful months in the North American Soccer League before spending a couple of months with Arsenal as a non-contract player. He returned to Vancouver in March 1982 before signing for Middlesbrough in September 1982. He ended his League career with short spells at Peterborough United with nine goals in 38 games and Wolves with a solitary goal from 10 appearances, before drifting into non-League football. He later enjoyed a stint at Newcastle United, where he was the football in the community officer at St James' Park.

Gordon Harris

Date of birth: 2 June 1940, Langold near Worksop

Burnley record:
Appearances: League 258, FA Cup 30, League Cup 16, others 9
Goals: League 69, FA Cup 5, League Cup 5, others 2
Debut: League, 3 January 1959 v Leeds United (h) won 3–1

Also played for: Firbeck Colliery, Sunderland, South Shields, England (1 cap),
                    England Under-23 (2 caps), Football League (2 appearances)

'His ability to carry the ball 50 and 60 yards in the heaviest conditions was remarkable, and he was capable of long, accurate crossfield passes that some others would never attempt. The sheer power of the man attracted attention,' wrote one local scribe when Gordon Harris left Turf Moor in January 1968 for a club record fee of £70,000. When he was 'in the mood' he was a joy to watch as he was exceptionally strong and skilful and had a superb left-foot shot, which earned him the nickname of 'Bomber'.

Harris came from the tiny village of Langold near Worksop, and as a boy he idolised the late Tommy Lawton (a former Burnley protégé) when he was at Notts County. The Herculean Harris, a pit worker, was spotted while playing for the Firbeck Colliery team against Anston in the Worksop and District League.

Harris arrived in Burnley with the club on the verge of greatness, but he missed out on a Championship medal as he made just two League appearances during 1959–60. His senior debut had been in January 1959, but at that stage in his career he was regarded as merely an understudy to Brian Pilkington.

It was during the first half of 1960–61 that things began to change, and Harris found himself being given an increasing number of first-team opportunities. Indeed, his form was sufficiently impressive for the Burnley directors to sell Pilkington to Bolton Wanderers in March 1961 and install Harris on the left wing. He was the only member of the 1962 FA Cup Final team who was not a regular in the Championship-winning side, a reflection of the consistency of the Burnley players at that time.

A stocky, powerfully built winger, he was to later become an even more effective midfield dynamo. Perhaps because of his build, he was not regarded as the quickest of wingers, and yet his deceptive turn of pace caught out many an unsuspecting full-back. Harris was a winger who possessed a trick or two, and his superb ball control and willingness to run at defenders made him a dangerous opponent. He also possessed the added threat of a thunderous shot, which he was more than willing to unleash whenever he got sight of goal. He was also a reliable penalty taker.

International honours were bestowed on him fairly early in his career. In May 1961 he was selected for a Young England team that was to play an England side on the eve of the FA Cup Final. Then, in November 1961, he was selected alongside Brian Miller and John Connelly to represent the Football League against the Irish League at Windsor Park, Belfast. Harris and Miller both marked their call up with a goal each in a 6–1 victory. Eight days later, Harris was a member of the England Under-23 team that enjoyed a 7–1 win over Israel Under-23 at Elland Road, Leeds.

Harris's final Under-23 cap came in March 1963 against Yugoslavia Under-23 at Old Trafford. His international career stalled at that point, and it wasn't until January 1966 that he made his full England debut, when he featured in a match against Poland at Goodison Park. Alf Ramsey selected him in his provisional squad of 40 players for the following summer's World Cup. However, he was one of the players who didn't quite make it into the final group of 22.

During 1966–67 Harris featured prominently in the Clarets run in the Inter-Cities Fairs Cup, and the following season he was appointed club captain at Turf Moor. Unfortunately, this proved to be his last season at the club. He suddenly resigned the captaincy on 12 December 1968, and three days later he was dropped for disciplinary reasons. He was to play just one more game for the club before moving to Roker Park to join Sunderland. 'I am very happy to be joining a club with such a fine reputation. I don't want to start any controversy about the last few weeks. Generally, I have been very happy at Turf Moor for 10 years, but I am looking forward to this change,' was the diplomatic way in which Harris announced his departure.

Widely recognised as a skilful midfield general, Harris quickly settled into his new surroundings and proved to be the long-term replacement for former Rangers and Scottish legend Jim Baxter. Despite his best efforts, he couldn't prevent Sunderland from slipping into the Second Division at the end of 1969–70. He drew his own career in League football to a close in the summer of 1972, after 135 senior appearances for Sunderland.

Harris entered the world of non-League football with a stint at South Shields and later worked as a driver in the coal industry.

John Haworth

Date of birth: 1876, Accrington
Died: 4 December 1924, Burnley

Burnley record:
Manager: July 1910–December 1924

The role of manager in the early 20th century was totally different from that held by today's managerial icons. Many of the early managers came from an administrative background and often held the title of secretary-manager. More often than not, they would employ a trainer to run the day-to-day coaching of the players, while they looked after the administrative work required to run a professional football club. So it was with John Haworth, the fourth man to be appointed into the position of manager of Burnley Football Club.

Haworth's own playing career had been limited to that of a full-back with Meadow Bank Rovers in Accrington. However, he did have sporting blood within his veins as his uncle was none other than George Haworth, the former England international half-back who played for the original Accrington club and won an FA Cup-winners' medal with Blackburn Rovers.

Haworth quickly hung up his boots to become involved in administrative matters at Meadow Bank Rovers. When that club disbanded in 1897, he took his players to Accrington Stanley and became a member of the club's committee. Within months of joining the club he had become secretary and was also given responsibility for playing affairs. Under Haworth's stewardship, Accrington Stanley went from strength to strength. The North East Lancashire League title was won in 1897–98, and in 1902–03 he led Stanley to the Lancashire Combination title, a feat he repeated in 1905–06.

Following the tragic death of Spen Whittaker in April 1910, the managership at Turf Moor had been undertaken on a temporary basis by R.H. Wadge, the club secretary. However, in July 1910 the Burnley directors appointed Haworth, who was still aged only 34, as manager. The correspondent of the *Burnley Express* noted that 'In the Accrington district, he was respected as a man of tact and talent, for he can manage players with the velvet gloves and conceal a will of iron.'

It was a far-from-ideal time to take charge of the club as the directors had announced a loss of £1,974, which had meant a reduction in the players' wages. Nonetheless, Haworth proved an excellent appointment, and during his tenure of office the club won promotion from the Second Division, won the FA Cup Final and finally lifted the First Division Championship. It was also Haworth who, very early during his spell at the club, changed the colours of the shirt from green to the now famous claret and blue.

Haworth's first season at the club was fairly unspectacular, with the team finishing in eighth place in the Second Division. Early in the season he introduced Billy Watson into the left-half position, while the campaign ended with a major transfer coup when Bert Freeman was prised away from Everton. The following season found Burnley closer to promotion with a third-place finish, while the arrival of Tommy Boyle from Barnsley for a club-record fee proved an astute piece of business on behalf of the young manager.

Haworth took the club to promotion in his third season at Turf Moor and found the ideal trainer for his team in Charlie Bates, a man who he had actually signed as a player shortly after his arrival at the club. His third season at Turf Moor also resulted in an FA Cup semi-final appearance, with the Clarets losing to Sunderland by the odd goal in five in a replay. The 1912–13 season also brought George Halley to play alongside Boyle and Watson in what was to become a famous half-back line.

In November 1913 Haworth made another telling swoop in the transfer market when he snapped up Bob Kelly from St Helens Town. By the end of the season the Clarets had finished a very respectable 12th in the League, while a Bert Freeman goal had enabled the club to win the FA Cup for the first time in their history.

The steady progress that Haworth had made in rebuilding the fortunes of the club was threatened by the outbreak of World War One. By the time the Football League was restored in 1919–20, a question mark remained over the future of the Turf Moor squad. However, any doubts about the players were quickly dispelled when the team ended the campaign in second place in the First Division. Twelve months later the Championship was won for the first time in the club's history. He had assembled a team of real quality and knew how to get the best out of each and every one of them. His man-management skills were beyond reproach, and he gave the club the greatest decade in its history.

Alas, as with all footballing dynasties, fortunes began to wane, and sadly, before he could set about the task of rebuilding the club, Haworth was struck down with a bout of pneumonia. On 4 December 1924 he tragically died, but his place in the history of Burnley Football Club will live forever.

Adrian Heath

Date of birth: 17 January 1961, Knutton, Stoke-on-Trent

Burnley record:
Appearances: League 110+10, FA Cup 12, League Cup 8+1, others 7
Goals: League 29, FA Cup 6
Debut: League, 22 August 1992 v Stockport County (a) lost 1–2
Manager: March 1996–June 1997

Also played for: Stoke City, Everton, Espanyol (Spain), Aston Villa, Manchester
     City, Stoke City, Sheffield United, England Under-21 (8 caps)
Also managed: Sheffield United

Adrian Heath had two spells at Turf Moor, firstly as a player between August 1992 and December 1995 and then as the club's first player-manager between March 1996 and June 1997. On both occasions he enjoyed a good rapport with the supporters and provided a touch of quality as the Clarets won promotion via the Play-offs in 1994. Indeed, both spells with the club might have been longer but for the emotional pull of working with his former mentor Howard Kendall.

Heath, known as 'Inchy' due to his size, began his career in the Potteries with Stoke City. He made his debut at the age of 17 and went on to score 16 goals in 95 League appearances. However, it was in January 1982 that his career really took off when Howard Kendall, who he had been with at Stoke, paid a record fee of £700,000 to take him to Goodison Park. Initially, Kendall used him in both attack and midfield, and as a result it took Heath time to settle on Merseyside.

Despite his lack of inches, at 5ft 6in Heath was a skilful, hardworking player – a real midfield dynamo. His scurrying feet seemed to take him away from defenders, and he was strong enough to withstand the most robust of challenges. Indeed, his amazing stamina left many an opponent in awe. Despite the speed at which he worked, he always seemed to have the ball under his control, and when used in attack he specialised in making darting runs between defenders which completely unnerved them.

Heath was at the peak of his powers in 1983–84 when Everton challenged for domestic and European honours. However, a wrenched knee in December 1983 kept him out of action for the remainder of the campaign as Everton won the First Division Championship, reached the FA Cup Final and won the European Cup-winners' Cup. Fortunately, he had made sufficient appearances to add a Championship medal to the FA Cup-winners' medal he had won during the previous campaign.

A fully recovered Heath picked up a finalists' medal from the Merseyside FA Cup Final of 1986, and in 1986–87, when Everton recaptured the First Division Championship, he missed only one League game. However, the following season was a disappointing one for him, and in 1988 he moved to Spain to join Espanyol. It was the start of a series of moves that ended in his arrival at Turf Moor in August 1992.

Jimmy Mullen used Heath as one of his strike force at Turf Moor, and he ended his first season at the club with 20 League goals. In 1993–94 he was an influential figure in the Clarets' promotion to the First Division via the Play-offs. Sadly, the following season resulted in the club's immediate relegation with Heath struggling with injury. He became a fringe figure following relegation, and the club didn't stand in his way when he opted to join Howard Kendall as assistant manager at Sheffield United.

Heath, however, left with many fond memories of his time at Turf Moor: 'Although I've had a difficult last six months, through injury and limited first-team opportunities, I will never forget the letters and words of encouragement from Burnley fans. I've had a great three years, and it is one of the most enjoyable spells I've had in football. I like to think that one day I might come back to Burnley.' The last sentence proved to be prophetic.

In March 1996 Heath left Sheffield United and returned to Turf Moor as player-manager at a time when the club was once again involved in a relegation battle. It was a double celebration for him, as he was named Burnley manager just 24 hours after watching his son being born. The fans were delighted with his appointment and even more so when he guided the Clarets to safety. The following season he narrowly missed out on the Play-offs as he turned the club around.

Unfortunately, Heath's term of office at Turf Moor was cut short when Howard Kendall offered him the opportunity to return to Everton as assistant manager. Not that it was an easy decision to make, as he readily admitted: 'I've such tremendous feeling for Burnley and that will always remain with me for the rest of my life. In fact leaving Burnley was the hardest decision I've ever had to make.'

Unfortunately, Kendall and Heath were unable to restore Everton to its former glories, and in June 1999 he became a manager in his own right when he took over at Sheffield United. He followed this with a spell as coach at Sunderland, under Peter Reid, and then followed Reid to Coventry City. Following Reid's departure from Coventry, he remained there and is now assistant manager to Micky Adams at the Ricoh Arena.

Jack Hillman

Date of birth: 1871, Tavistock, Devon
Died: 1 August 1955, Burnley

Burnley record:
Appearances: League 175, FA Cup 9, others 4
Debut: League, 5 September 1891 v Accrington (a) lost 0–1

Also played for: Everton, Dundee, Manchester City, Millwall, England (1 cap)

Undoubtedly one of the great characters of the 19th-century game, and without question one of Burnley's more colourful and controversial personalities, at 6ft 4in and weighing over 16st Jack Hillman was not exactly unnoticeable at the best of times. Throughout his career, he seemed to court controversy and scandal. He was suspended by one club for allegedly not trying, banned by the Football Association for 12 months after trying to fix the outcome of a game, and finally embroiled in a financial scandal at Manchester City. Little wonder that he enjoyed a reputation for notoriety as well as brilliance between the posts as an international goalkeeper.

Although a native of Devon, Hillman's family moved to Burnley when he was just a child. He was spotted by the club while playing in local junior football and made his first appearance for Burnley Reserves in 1890. At that time Archibald Kaye was the undisputed first-choice custodian at Turf Moor, and Hillman had to wait until Kaye left in the summer of 1891 before he got his chance. However, from making his debut in September 1891 until he left to join Everton in February 1895, he missed only six League matches. Whatever misdemeanours he may have been guilty of later in his career, there is no doubt that he was one of the great exponents of goalkeeping during the Victorian period. He had a natural ability and athleticism that was not always found in goalkeepers of that era. It was because of this talent that Everton were forced to pay £200 to take him away from Turf Moor.

Once again, Hillman proved his reliability at Goodison Park and missed just one game during 1895–96 as Everton claimed third place in the First Division. However, he was unable to settle on Merseyside, despite his success, and in June 1896 he opted to try his luck north of the border with a move to Dundee. Unfortunately, Scotland proved not to be to his liking either, and at one point during the 1897–98 campaign he was suspended by his employers amid allegations that he wasn't giving total commitment to the cause. However, the financial plight of the club led to a counter allegation that there wasn't the money to pay his wages!

A fee of £225 ended Hillman's exile in Scotland and brought him back to Turf Moor. Once again, he impressed with his natural goalkeeping skills. Indeed, in February 1899 he was rewarded with his one and only England cap when he appeared in the 13–2 win over Ireland at Roker Park. However, Jack Robinson was the undisputed first-choice 'keeper for England, and any aspirations that he might have had with regard to international football disintegrated during the 1899–1900 season.

The Clarets were embroiled in a desperate battle against relegation as they approached the final week of the season. The final match was a visit to Nottingham Forest and a win was essential if First Division status was to be retained. The game was lost 4–0, but allegations were made that Hillman had tried to bribe the Forest skipper, Archie McPherson, to throw the game. He strenuously denied the allegations when he was hauled before the Football Association. He tried to pass the incident off as a jocular remark that had been misunderstood. Sadly for Hillman, the FA officials also misunderstood his sense of humour and banned him from the game for 12 months. Indeed, it was pointed out to him that but for his previous good conduct, he would have faced an even longer ban. It was a costly error of judgement for him as he not only missed out on a year's wages but also had to forgo a £300 benefit. To rub salt into the wound, two days after the defeat at Nottingham Preston North End went to Blackburn and gained a 2–0 win that lifted them into safety and sent the Clarets into the Second Division.

Hillman returned to action at the start of 1901–02 and was immediately installed as Burnley's first-choice 'keeper. He performed as peerlessly as ever, and in January 1902 Manchester City stepped in to sign him. He helped City win promotion to the First Division and won an FA Cup-winners' medal with them in 1903–04. However, the following season brought allegations that City had circumvented the rules regarding wages and bonus payments, and, as a result, he was one of the players that the club was ordered to sell.

In January 1907 Hillman made his final move when he joined Millwall of the Southern League. Unfortunately, an elbow injury brought his career to an end after just a couple of appearances for his new club. He retired from the game to run his confectionery shop in Burnley. He later returned to Turf Moor to join the training staff, working at various levels for the club well into the 1920s. After his retirement from the game he continued to live in Burnley and ran his shop for a number of years.

Bill Holden

Date of birth: 1 April 1928, Bolton

Burnley record:
Appearances: League 187, FA Cup 12
Goals: League 75, FA Cup 4
Debut: League, 2 September 1950 v Middlesbrough (h) won 3–1

Also played for: Lomax's FC, Sunderland, Stockport County, Bury, Halifax Town,
Rugby Town, Hereford United, England B (1 cap)

'His career with Burnley has been varied and interesting,' was the somewhat ambiguous comment by the correspondent of the *Burnley Express* when Bill Holden left Turf Moor to join Sunderland in December 1955. At the time, the fee was not disclosed but merely described as 'substantial.' Many commentators believed it to be in the region of £12,000, which was not a bad profit on a player who didn't cost the club a penny when he arrived from Bolton junior football in September 1949.

Holden had attended the same Bolton school as Tommy Lawton, another great centre-forward who began his football career with the Clarets. It was Jack Marshall, another former Claret, who spotted him playing for his works' team in Bolton and recommended him to Turf Moor. A trial with Everton had already come to nothing, but he happily joined the amateur ranks at Burnley in September 1949. He turned professional the following August and made his debut in the 3–1 win over Middlesbrough at Turf Moor in September 1950. Indeed, such was the impression he made that Holden retained his place for the rest of the campaign.

Holden possessed many of the attributes that make a classical centre-forward. His strong build made him a robust leader of the attack, yet there was more to his game than just brute strength. He was an intelligent footballer, who was blessed with good ball control as well as a powerful shot. Add to this his aerial ability, and it is easy to see why he made such a big impression at the club. His first goals for Burnley came at Turf Moor in the 5–1 demolition of Charlton Athletic, just over a month after his debut. He finished his debut season with a dozen League goals, sufficient to make him the club's leading goalscorer that season.

Holden remained the automatic choice at centre-forward until he suffered a broken leg at Villa Park in March 1952. Fortunately, he recovered quickly, and in 1952–53 he featured in every game and again finished the season as the club's leading goalscorer with 22 League goals. His largest haul in a game came on 11 April 1953, when he scored four times in the 5–1 victory over Sunderland. A month earlier his goalscoring exploits had won him international recognition when he was asked to lead the England B forward line against Scotland B. He was in good company when he travelled to Easter Road, Edinburgh, for both Jimmy Adamson and Tommy Cummings also represented England that day. He took to international football with ease and scored both of England's goals in a 2–2 draw. Yet, as so often happened with players at Turf Moor, he was then overlooked for international honours for the remainder of his career.

Although Holden slipped to third leading goalscorer in 1953–54 with 14 goals, he again led the goalscorers the following season with 15 League goals. At that point he had been the automatic choice at centre-forward for five seasons and seemed likely to be so for the foreseeable future. However, after a 2–0 home defeat by Blackpool in the second game of the 1955–56 campaign, he found himself out of favour. Within weeks Peter McKay, who had been a prolific goalscorer in the Central League for Burnley, had ousted Holden from the team. Unhappy at being unable to regain his place, he requested a transfer which was duly granted. In December 1955 he moved to Roker Park where he joined Billy Elliott, a former colleague at Turf Moor.

The switch to Roker Park was not the success that Holden had hoped for. Although he scored on his debut in a local derby with Newcastle United at St James' Park he never really settled in the North East. When he left to join Stockport County in October 1956 his career began a downward spiral. There was to be one more flirtation with success for him, when he helped Bury lift the Third Division Championship in 1960–61. To many, Holden's was a talent that remained unfulfilled, but, nonetheless, during the five seasons he led the line at Turf Moor he was fondly remembered as a goalscoring centre-forward who made a major contribution to the club.

Willie Irvine

Date of birth:	18 June 1943, Carrickfergus

Burnley record:

Appearances:	League 124+2, FA Cup 9+1, League Cup 8+1, Europe 3
Goals:	League 78, FA Cup 9, League Cup 8, Europe 2
Debut:	League, 11 May 1963 v Arsenal (a) won 3–2

Also played for: Preston North End, Brighton & Hove Albion, Halifax Town, Great Harwood, Northern Ireland (23 caps), Northern Ireland Under-23 (3 caps)

As a Northern Ireland Schoolboy international, Willie Irvine had no shortage of offers when the time came to take his first steps in the world of professional football. A host of top clubs all expressed interest in young Irvine's future. However, he came to Turf Moor on trial and was taken on as a groundstaff boy in 1959 before turning professional in June 1960.

'I started as a midfield player and maybe I wasn't suited to being a midfielder. I was mediocre, then Burnley put me up to centre-forward against Liverpool's C team, and I got a hat-trick. They kept me there then, and I just carried on. I seemed to score goals as I went along,' he recalled.

The young Irishman found he had natural predatory instincts in and around the penalty area, and in one season he notched up 66 goals for the junior teams and the reserves. Indeed, when he had been asked to step up to Central League football he immediately served notice of his potential with a hat-trick against Barnsley Reserves at Turf Moor in October 1961.

Despite his explosive debut, Irvine was unable to claim a regular place in the team that won the Central League Championship in 1961–62. However, the following season, when the title was retained, it was he who led the forward line. His form in the reserves was impressive enough to warrant a call up by the Northern Ireland Under-23 selectors, and in April 1963 he made his full international debut when he played in the Northern Ireland team that was beaten by Wales in Belfast. The Irish team that day featured his brother Bobby, who kept goal for Stoke City, as well as Jimmy McIlroy and Alex Elder from Turf Moor.

Shortly after his international debut, Irvine was given his chance in the Burnley first team. He made his senior debut in the penultimate game of the season, when he scored in the 3–2 win over Arsenal at Highbury. Three days later he made his bow at Turf Moor in a League game and notched a hat-trick in a 3–1 win over Birmingham City. However, he had to bide his time as both Andy Lochhead and Jimmy Robson were ahead of him in the pecking order, and it wasn't until the closing stages of 1963–64 that Irvine won a regular first-team place.

In 1964–65 Irvine formed a wonderful strike partnership with Andy Lochhead. He notched 22 goals and Lochhead 21, as they complemented each other perfectly. The following season, when the Clarets finished third in the First Division, he struck 29 League goals while Lochhead chipped in with 15. He relished his role at the cutting edge of the Burnley attack.

'Scoring goals is instinctive,' he recalled, 'It's the best feeling in the world for a centre-forward, and I never got tired of it. I always said I was deadly from two yards. I could lose a defender and worked hard on getting away from him. Andy and I used to work on our game during training and talk about whatever positions we would have on the park during a game....an awful lot of it is anticipation. You think you know where the ball is going to drop and you go for it. It doesn't always drop there, but when it does, it's up to you then.'

Irvine's career at Turf Moor took a turn for the worse when he broke his leg in an FA Cup tie at Everton in January 1967. He was a player who was always prepared to put himself in situations where he could get hurt for the sake of a goal. Sadly, the broken leg proved to be the beginning of the end for him at Burnley, and the arrival of Frank Casper merely added to the pressure. Suddenly, Irvine seemed to have lost the spark that made him the player he had been in his prime, and in March 1968 he moved to Preston North End for £45,000.

Irvine's time at Deepdale was not the best, despite a respectable 27 goals from 81 appearances in League games. At the end of 1969–70 North End slipped into the Third Division, and although they made an immediate return, Irvine, no longer a regular in the first team, had departed for Brighton & Hove Albion before the season was over. In 1971–72 he helped the Goldstone club win promotion from the Third Division as runners-up to Aston Villa. He rediscovered his scoring touch and netted on 16 occasions as he formed an impressive strike partnership with Kit Napier.

However, Brighton struggled in the higher Division and Irvine, again suffering indifferent form, returned north to join Halifax Town in December 1972. When the Shaymen refused permission for him to play in the John Angus testimonial, Irvine turned out in the game and then promptly announced his retirement.

Joe Jakub

Date of birth: 7 December 1956, Falkirk

Burnley record:
Appearances: League 203+2, FA Cup 19, League Cup 11, others 16
Goals: League 8, others 1
Debut: League, 24 April 1976 v Coventry City (h) lost 1–3

Also played for: Airdrieonians, Bury, AZ67 Alkmaar (Holland), Chester City, Colwyn Bay, Wigan Athletic

Joe Jakub had been a junior at Airdrieonians prior to joining Burnley as an apprentice in 1973. He became a professional in December of the same year and spent two spells at Burnley, which spanned three decades and a range of Divisions. During that time, he proved himself to be a player who could operate in midfield or defence with equal aplomb.

When Jakub made his debut for the Clarets at Coventry City on the final day of the 1975–76 campaign, Burnley were still a First Division club, albeit one that was headed for relegation. He enjoyed a run of five League games early in the following season, but for the remainder of that campaign and the whole of the following one he had to settle for Central League football. Indeed, it wasn't until March 1979 that Harry Potts gave him an extended run in the first team.

The 1979–80 campaign found Jakub a fully-fledged member of the first-team squad, making 23 League appearances as the Clarets slipped into the Third Division for the first time in the club's history. Having made just 42 League appearances since his debut, he was allowed to leave Turf Moor to join Bury in October 1980.

Jim Iley, the Bury manager, immediately installed Jakub into his midfield, and he went on to make 33 League appearances for the Shakers that season. He remained a fixture in the Bury team, and in March 1984 he found himself under new management with the arrival of Martin Dobson at Gigg Lane. The 1984–85 season at Bury contained a heavy Turf Moor influence, with Frank Casper being appointed Dobson's assistant and Ray Pointer also added to the coaching staff. The playing staff also included three former Burnley favourites in Jakub, Terry Pashley and Leighton James. The conglomeration of Turf Moor old boys certainly proved successful, as Bury won promotion to the Third Division during that season. Jakub, who had been appointed club captain in 1982, made 40 League appearances that campaign.

Jakub made a total of 308 League and Cup appearances for Bury before sampling life on the continent, with a move to AZ67 Alkmaar in Holland. He spent almost two years with the Dutch club before joining Chester City in August 1988. However, after just one season with Chester, he returned to Burnley for his second (and most profitable) period with the Clarets.

Initially, Jakub lined up alongside John Deary in the centre of the Burnley midfield. He was a tenacious

competitor who proved adept at the defensive aspects of midfield play. After two seasons propping up the central midfield at Turf Moor, he was switched to left-back at the start of the 1991–92 season. It proved a significant move as he played a prominent role in the capture of the Fourth Division Championship, which brought the club's seven-year stint in the bottom Division to an end.

Jakub continued to be a key figure in the Burnley team in the years that followed, and in January 1993 he clocked up his 500th Football League appearance when he turned out for the Clarets at Mansfield Town. Unfortunately, it was not a happy occasion for him as his big day was ruined when he was sent off for the first time in his career. In April of that year he played his final match for Burnley after losing his regular berth in the side to Paul Wilson. In July 1993 he returned to Chester and spent another season with them before ending his playing career with a short stay at Wigan Athletic.

Jakub then turned his attention to coaching, and after a brief period with Preston North End he became youth development officer with Stockport County. He later turned to a journalistic career and worked for PA Sports, as well as undertaking some scouting work for Preston North End in North Wales.

Leighton James

Date of birth: 16 February 1953, Llwchwyr, Swansea

Burnley record:
Appearances: League 331+5, FA Cup 17, League Cup 22, others 22+1
Goals: League 66, FA Cup 2, League Cup 8, others 5
Debut: League, 21 November 1970 v Nottingham Forest (h) won 2–1

Also played for: Gowerton, Penyrheol, Neath Boys' Club, Derby County, Queen's Park Rangers, Swansea City, Sunderland, Bury, Newport County, Wales (54 Caps), Wales Under-23 (7 caps)
Managed: Gainsborough Trinity, Morecambe, Netherfield, Darwen, Ilkeston Town, Accrington Stanley, Llanelli

Turf Moor proved something of a magnet to Leighton James, during what can only be described as a nomadic career in professional football. Clubs queued up to employ this multi-talented Welshman and 'Have boots will travel' was always ready to undertake a new challenge. However, throughout his playing career, although he travelled far and wide, the lure of Turf Moor was never far away, and each of his returns to the club were warmly greeted by the supporters.

The son of a steelworker, James first left his native South Wales to become an apprentice at Turf Moor in October 1968. He was already a Welsh Schoolboy international by the time he came to Lancashire and quickly graduated through the youth and reserve teams at Turf Moor. He signed professional forms in February 1970, and the following November he made his senior debut when he featured in the 2–1 win over Nottingham Forest.

James played very little part in the relegation campaign of 1970–71, starting three games and appearing as a substitute in another. However, in 1971–72 Jimmy Adamson gave him the chance to establish himself on the left wing. The following season the Clarets romped to the Second Division Championship, with James featuring in every game, notching 10 goals. It seemed that Burnley were on the brink of another successful period, as he explained 'We won the Second Division Championship in 1973 and then in the following season finished just outside a European place. Exciting times.'

Unfortunately the success was short lived, and in 1975–76 the club slipped back into the Second Division. The flow of exciting youngsters through the youth scheme stopped, as James observed, '...there seemed to be a reversal in the club's policy, and the signings of Mike Summerbee and Willie Morgan illustrated it. Before, it was all about producing your own. There was always some young kid from the reserves or youth team who would come into the side and the team didn't suffer.'

James had been just one of a number of exciting youngsters that Burnley had produced. In his prime, he was one of the most talented players in the game. He was naturally gifted with pace and balance and in full flight was a sight to behold. He loved to skip past defenders before picking out the perfect pass or a teasing cross, and, of course, he could also shoot with power and accuracy. He also had a fiercely combative side to his nature that landed him in trouble with opponents and officials alike. But the Burnley fans loved him!

James left Turf Moor for the first time in November 1975 when Derby County paid £310,000 for his services. He had been signed by Dave Mackay and enjoyed a successful time at the Baseball Ground until the arrival of Tommy Docherty signalled his exit to Queen's Park Rangers, in an exchange deal that took Don Masson to the Midlands.

James's stay at Loftus Road was brief, as Harry Potts brought him back to Burnley in September 1978 for a fee of £165,000. Steve Kindon had also returned to the club and the two of them helped the Clarets win the Anglo-Scottish Cup in December 1978. With Burnley heading for the Third Division, James opted to return to his native South Wales to join Swansea City in May 1980.

James's time at the Vetch Field proved to be one of the most successful periods in his career. He celebrated his first season with John Toshack's team by helping them win promotion to the First Division, as he explained: 'We got into the top Division to finish sixth, and with seven of that team in the Welsh squad it was like playing League matches for your country.'

Sadly for James, the bubble burst and relegation followed. Financial problems brought the break up of the Swansea team, and he left to join Sunderland in January 1983. He helped Sunderland avoid relegation before moving to Martin Dobson's Bury. He gained promotion to the Third Division during his season at Gigg Lane, before returning to South Wales to join Newport County as player-coach.

In July 1986 James returned to Turf Moor for a third time, just as the Clarets embarked upon one of the most dramatic seasons in the club's history. He scored 10 goals in 42 League outings that season, and, of course, he played in the nail-biting finale against Orient. With Football League status retained, he featured rather more spasmodically in the team as he became more involved with coaching duties.

On leaving Burnley in May 1989, James embarked upon a career in coaching and management that has taken him the length and breadth of the country. He has also undertaken media work, and, in 2004, he was appointed director of the academy at the League of Wales side Port Talbot.

Bob Kelly

Date of birth:	16 November 1893, Ashton-in-Makerfield
Died:	22 September 1969, Fylde area of Lancashire

Burnley record:

Appearances:	League 277, FA Cup 21, Wartime 72, other 1
Goals:	League 88, FA Cup 9, Wartime 26
Debut:	League, 15 November 1913 v Aston Villa (h) won 4–0
Also played for:	Ashton White Star, Ashton Central, Earlestown Rovers, St Helens Town, Sunderland, Huddersfield Town, Preston North End, Carlisle United, England (14 caps), Football League (7 appearances)
Managed:	Carlisle United, Stockport County, Barry Town

Bob Kelly was not only a Burnley legend, but he was also one of the finest players of his generation. Twice during his career he was at the centre of record transfer deals: firstly, and more modestly, when he joined Burnley from St Helens Town in October 1913 at a cost of £275, which created a new record fee for a player coming out of the Lancashire Combination, then, in December 1925, Sunderland had to pay a record fee of £6,550 to acquire his services as the replacement for the legendary Charles Buchan. In between these two transfers, he won the hearts of the Burnley faithful with his pure creative genius. A vision in passing, with skilful and instant control of the football and deadly finishing, Kelly possessed all the attributes required of a great player.

When Burnley first spotted Kelly playing in the Lancashire Combination, he was already attracting a horde of scouts from various clubs. Fortunately, while others dithered, Burnley took the plunge and made the sizeable investment required to bring him to Turf Moor. One local wordsmith drew attention to the fact that although he had cost a sizeable sum, his game still needed improvement: 'The new capture is not a robust player, but with proper training he should develop. He is a fine dribbler, and has even been spoken of as "a second Buchan." He has rather a tendency to individualism... Kelly has played centre-forward, but scarcely seems robust enough to fill such a position in first-class football.' Nonetheless, it appeared money well spent when he scored a goal on his debut against Aston Villa. However, he was unable to win a regular place until he was drafted in at outside-right a year after his debut. He immediately struck up a good understanding with Bert Freeman and Teddy Hodgson, as the Clarets ended the 1914–15 campaign in fourth place in the First Division.

Kelly seemed destined for a bright future until the assassination of Archduke Franz Ferdinand, the crown prince of the Austrian Empire, sent Europe spinning towards conflict. The suspension of the Football League brought the introduction of a fairly meaningless regional game. Although he featured prominently in wartime football it wasn't until the 1919–20 campaign, and the return of the Football League, that Kelly was seen at his best.

The end of the war brought a glorious period in the history of Burnley Football Club with second place, first place and third place finishes to the first three seasons of peacetime football. In a team that was rightly regarded as the best in the country, Kelly was hailed far and wide as the best man in the team. By the time of the Championship campaign of 1920–21, he had been transformed into an inside-right. Billy Nesbitt, the man who occupied the flank position, had an instinctive understanding of his style and, as a result, was able to provide him with the kind of service on which he thrived.

Kelly's brilliance soon caught the eye of the England selectors, and on 10 April 1920 he made a spectacular England debut when he scored twice in the 5–4 win over Scotland at Sheffield. It was the first of 14 international caps, and he was also chosen to represent the Football League on seven occasions. Eleven of those caps were won while he was still a Burnley player, and he continues to hold the record as the most capped English international for the Clarets.

Sadly, the good times didn't last, and as the 1920s went on so the club's fortunes began to wane. Financial difficulties were reported by the *Burnley Express* just one week before Kelly's departure: 'Unless help comes quickly, the directors state they will be reluctantly compelled to take steps to reduce the very big overdraft at the bank.' Ultimately, in December 1925, force of circumstances compelled them to part with Kelly. It was Sunderland, looking for a replacement for Charlie Buchan (the man who he had been so favourably compared with in the past), who paid an unprecedented fee of £6,500 to Burnley. The size of the fee is all the more remarkable when it is remembered that he had already turned 32 years of age at this point.

After 50 League games and 10 goals, Kelly moved to Huddersfield Town for £3,500 before returning to Lancashire in July 1932 to join Preston North End. Despite his advancing years, he still remained the complete inside-forward. At 39, the *Lancashire Daily Post Football Annual* described him as 'an effective schemer, seldom putting a foot wrong.'

Kelly entered the world of football management when he hung up his boots and had spells with Carlisle United and Stockport County in the years before World War Two. He later coached in Switzerland and the Channel Islands before settling and working as a publican in Blackpool. He died in September 1969 at the age of 74, and with his passing the Clarets lost the man who many regard as the greatest player to wear the Burnley shirt.

Steve Kindon

Date of birth: 17 December 1950, Warrington

Burnley record:
Appearances: League 175+10, FA Cup 10+1, League Cup 14+2, others 13
Goals: League 46, FA Cup 2, League Cup 2, others 8
Debut: League, 26 August 1968 v West Ham United (a) lost 0–5

Also played for: Wolverhampton Wanderers, Huddersfield Town

Tall and well built, Steve Kindon cut an unlikely figure sprinting down the wing. He was blessed with the most extraordinary turn of pace, which he used to devastating effect. 'Skippy' or 'Tank', as he was often called, combined both pace and power; these were attributes that made Steve a dangerous opponent, particularly when he was bearing down on the goal. A member of the successful FA Youth Cup-winning team of 1967–68, he was also selected for the England youth team on three occasions. However, his senior debut was hardly an auspicious affair, with the Clarets slumping to a 5–0 defeat at West Ham United.

Fortunately, Kindon was undeterred by this early setback and established himself on the left wing during the middle part of 1968–69. Ironically, his Turf Moor debut on 8 October 1968 was also against West Ham United, but, on this occasion, he enjoyed a happier result. The Clarets enjoyed a 3–1 win, and Kindon managed to net his first senior goal for the club. The victory over the Hammers marked the beginning of a sequence of eight successive wins for the Clarets, as Harry Potts gradually began to rebuild his Burnley team.

Kindon was an ever present during 1969–70, finishing the season as top goalscorer with 17 League goals. The following campaign brought relegation to the Second Division, and Kindon never quite found his goalscoring touch again. Somehow, he appeared to lose his way as the Clarets embarked upon the task of winning back their pace in the top flight. He found himself on the bench all too often, and in July 1972 he moved to Wolverhampton Wanderers for a fee of £100,000.

Kindon marked his debut for Wolves with a goal against Newcastle United on the opening day of 1972–73. However, his time at Molineux found him in and out of the side, with his best season being in 1974–75, when he scored 10 goals in 29 League outings, as Wolves finished in 12th position in the First Division. The following season proved disastrous for Wolves as the club slipped into the Second Division, and Kindon, who netted on just five occasions in the League, found his place in jeopardy. He helped the Molineux club to make an immediate return to the top flight by clinching the Second Division Championship, but spent the latter part of the campaign out of the team. As the 1977–78 season began, his future at Wolves seemed uncertain.

Fortunately, Harry Potts, Kindon's former mentor at Turf Moor, offered him an escape route and re-signed him for Burnley in November 1977, a deal worth £80,000. Potts hoped that his former protégé would help lift Burnley's ailing fortunes. Just one win from the opening 14 League matches had found the Clarets entrenched at the bottom of the Second Division and facing relegation.

Kindon immediately set about the task of reviving his former club's fortunes with a flourish. His return to the Claret and Blue brought a 3–1 home win over Notts County and a homecoming goal for him. His pace and power remained intact, and by the end of the season he helped lift the club to a respectable mid-table position.

The 1978–79 campaign brought success for the Clarets in the form of winning the Anglo-Scottish Cup. Kindon notched two goals in a 4–1 win at Oldham Athletic in the first leg of the Final, to ensure the Clarets lifted the trophy despite a 1–0 reversal in the second leg. It was a much livelier affair in the quarter-final meeting with Celtic, with Kindon at the heart of a near riot at Turf Moor. He scored the only goal of the first-leg meeting and sparked an outbreak of violence among the visiting fans. Both teams left the field, only for Billy McNeil, the Celtic manager, and Kindon to be asked to go out arm in arm and quell the visiting hordes. Peace was restored and the game completed. However, Kindon rubbed further salt into Celtic wounds when he scored one of the two goals that helped the Clarets enjoy a 2–1 win at Celtic Park a fortnight later.

Kindon left Burnley for a second time in December 1979 to join Huddersfield Town. He enjoyed an 'Indian Summer' to his career at Leeds Road and helped the club to win the Fourth Division Championship in 1979–80. In football's basement his unique qualities made him an instant hit, and he scored 14 goals in just 22 starts and one substitute appearance as Huddersfield lifted the title. The following season was even more successful for him when he notched 18 goals as Huddersfield almost clinched a second successive promotion, finishing in fourth place in Division Three.

Sadly, a serious knee injury brought an end to his playing career, and he joined the staff at Huddersfield as promotions manager, a position he kept for five years before departing from football for good.

Brian Laws

Date of birth: 14 October 1961, Wallsend

Burnley record:
Appearances: League 125, FA Cup 15, League Cup 14, others 3
Goals: League 12, FA Cup 1, League Cup 2
Debut: League, 3 May 1980 v Watford (a) lost 0–4

Also played for: Huddersfield Town, Middlesbrough, Nottingham Forest, Grimsby Town, Darlington, Scunthorpe United, England B (1 cap)
Managed: Grimsby Town, Scunthorpe United

All managers make mistakes when it comes to releasing players, particularly young players. However, when John Bond decided that Lee Dixon and Brian Laws were two full-backs who were surplus to requirements, it proved to be a particularly embarrassing decision. In Dixon's case, the young full-back had only made four League appearances, and so, to a certain extent, was still an unknown quantity. However, Laws was already a veteran of 125 League games and had only missed two games during the 1981–82 Third Division Championship-winning campaign. The Burnley faithful had no doubts about his quality, even if the new manager remained unconvinced. The fact that Laws went on to enjoy great success in his career, particularly under Brian Clough at Nottingham Forest, would suggest that his popularity at Turf Moor was well founded.

Laws had arrived at Burnley as an apprentice in 1978, after representing Wallsend and Northumberland schoolboys. He signed professional forms when he turned 18 and made rapid progress through the youth and reserve ranks. Indeed, his development was so rapid that he received a first-team call up on the final day of the 1979–80 season, when he played at right-back in the 4–0 defeat at Watford.

With the Clarets relegated to the Third Division, coupled with the arrival of Ian Wood, Oldham Athletic's veteran full-back, prospects for an immediate breakthrough for Laws seemed bleak. However, after the opening three League games of 1980–81 brought just one win, he was installed at right-back. He quickly impressed with his sound defensive work and figured in 42 League games that season, as the Clarets finished in eighth place in the Third Division.

The following season the Clarets won the Third Division Championship, and Laws, who only missed two League games, was voted the Young Player of the Year. Unfortunately, the 1982–83 campaign ended with Burnley losing their newly-won Second Division status. Nonetheless, he featured prominently in both the League and two successful Cup campaigns that season. Despite relegation, Laws was regarded as the automatic choice for the right-back spot and a bright future seemed to be ahead of him at Turf Moor.

Sadly, the arrival of John Bond changed all that, and clearly he didn't want Laws to be part of the future he had planned for Burnley. In August 1983 he accepted a bid of £50,000 from Huddersfield Town to take him to Leeds Road. It was to be the start of a successful career for him, although his stay at Huddersfield proved to be relatively brief, making just 56 League appearances for the Terriers.

In March 1985 a fee of £30,000 took him to Ayresome Park to join Middlesbrough. It was here that he blossomed into a fine attacking full-back, despite enduring some difficult times as Middlesbrough hit financial problems. He suffered his own injury problems with a cruciate knee-ligament injury in February 1987. For a time he was successfully converted into a midfield player, and during his stay at Ayresome Park he helped the club to win promotion to the First Division in 1987–88.

After appearing in 108 League games for Middlesbrough, Laws became embroiled in a contract dispute in the summer of 1988, which resulted in a transfer to Nottingham Forest in exchange for £180,000. He enjoyed great success at the City Ground and won the League Cup with Forest in 1989 and 1990, and the Simod Cup in 1989. He also appeared for Forest as a substitute in both the 1991 FA Cup and 1992 League Cup Final defeats by Tottenham Hotspur and Manchester United respectively. In 1993–94 he also helped them win promotion to the Premiership, having suffered relegation from that Division the previous season. While with Forest he also picked up an England B cap.

During his time at Forest, Laws was regarded as one of the finest and safest full-backs in the game. A tough tackler, he had the speed to recover well in difficult situations and his steady consistency meant he was a valued member of the team.

In November 1994 Laws entered management when he became player-manager at Grimsby Town. A short spell as a non-contract player with Darlington in November 1995 was followed by a similar spell at Scunthorpe United in January 1997. However, the following month he was appointed manager at Scunthorpe and led them to promotion into the Second Division in 1999. Sadly, the club suffered immediate relegation, but in 2004–05 he again won promotion when he took Scunthorpe into the newly formed First Division of the restructured Football League.

Tommy Lawton

Date of birth: 6 October 1919, Bolton, Lancashire
Died: 6 November 1996, Nottingham

Burnley record:
Appearances: League 25
Goals: League 16
Debut: League, 28 March 1936 v Doncaster Rovers (h) drew 1–1

Also played for: Everton, Arsenal, Chelsea, Notts County, Brentford, England (23 caps)
Managed: Brentford, Kettering Town

Tommy Lawton is one of the legendary centre-forwards in English football. His exploits with Everton, Chelsea and Notts County in particular are well documented. On either side of World War Two he was a goalscorer supreme and the holder of 23 England caps. Unfortunately, his exploits as a teenage sensation at Turf Moor are often overshadowed by the success he enjoyed later in his career. However, there can be no doubt that for a brief period in the mid-1930s he appeared from nowhere and dominated the headlines in Burnley. At Turf Moor he was a legend in the making.

There was little interest in the story that the pages of the *Burnley Express* carried in February 1935, announcing that the club had signed Tommy Lawton. After all, he was simply a Bolton schoolboy who had trained with Bolton Wanderers once or twice and had featured in one game with Rossendale United in the Lancashire Combination. When Burnley signed the 15-year-old on amateur forms and gave him a job in the office, it was not the sort of signing that captured the headlines or caused eyebrows to be raised.

Lawton appeared for the A team on 23 February 1935 and scored two goals against Lancaster. Before the end of the season he had featured in three more A team games and notched seven goals. As a result, although he began the 1935–36 campaign in the A team, he was almost immediately promoted to reserve-team football while still only 15 years of age. During the season he was utilised for both the A team and the reserves, and his goalscoring exploits were sufficiently impressive to earn him a call up to the first team in March 1936.

When Lawton made his debut for the Clarets against Doncaster Rovers on 28 March 1936 he was just 16 years and 174 days old, making him Burnley's youngest-ever player. A week later he retained his place for the trip to Swansea and scored his first two goals for the club in a 3–1 win. His opener was a typical Lawton effort when he met a cross from Ronnie Hornby and headed it into the net. He grabbed a second goal after half-time as the Clarets clinched two vital points

in their fight against relegation from the Second Division. Thus, within a season Lawton had risen from A team to first team and had scored goals at all levels in so doing.

Lawton began the 1936–37 season at centre-forward and scored three goals in the opening two fixtures, before an injury kept him out of action for several weeks. He signed professional forms when he turned 17, and four days after his 17th birthday he celebrated with a hat-trick in a 3–1 win over Tottenham Hotspur at Turf Moor. Indeed, his opening goal came in the first minute of the match when he nodded down a cross from Jack Gastall for Jimmy Stein. The latter returned the ball to Lawton, who seemed to hit it without breaking stride past Percy Hooper in the Tottenham goal. His second was a familiar far-post header from a Gastall corner, and three minutes into the second half he completed his hat-trick when he ran onto another pass from Gastall, left Arthur Rowe in his wake and crashed an unstoppable drive past Hooper. Rarely can a player have made such an impact on joining the ranks of the professionals. One local correspondent had no doubts as to why Lawton had proved so successful, 'Lawton's remarkable physique for one so youthful has undoubtedly contributed to his meteoric advancement in the football world.'

Of course, with the Clarets in the Second Division, it wasn't long before the top-flight clubs started to show interest in a player who had bagged 11 goals in 18 League appearances during the first half of 1936–37. Ultimately, it was Everton who paid a fee of £6,500 to take Lawton to Goodison Park at the end of December 1936. The rest, as they say, is history. He went on appear in 390 League games for his various clubs and scored an astonishing 231 goals. At international level, he was equally prolific, with 22 goals coming in just 23 appearances for England. It must also be remembered that all this was achieved during a career which was severely interrupted by World War Two. Quite simply, Tommy Lawton was not just a Burnley legend but one of the all time greats of English football.

Glen Little

Date of birth: 15 October 1975, Wimbledon

Burnley record:
Appearances: League 211+35, FA Cup 11+6, League Cup 11+4, others 4
Goals: League 32, FA Cup 3, others 1
Debut: League, 20 December 1996 v Peterborough United (a) lost 2–3

Also played for: Crystal Palace, Glentoran, Reading, Bolton Wanderers, Reading

A seven-and-a-half-year association with Burnley had enabled Glen Little to become firmly entrenched as the fans' favourite at Turf Moor. Yet his arrival was a fairly unheralded event, as he was something of an unknown when he was signed from Glentoran. He had begun his career with Crystal Palace but had failed to make the first team before being loaned out to Glentoran. He made a favourable impression on Tommy Cassidy, the former Claret, who was the Irish club's manager. Thus, when Palace released him, Cassidy was more than happy to sign him on a permanent basis. 'I went back out and signed, and Tommy told me if I did the business for him, he would help to get me back across the water again,' recalled Little.

Little made an immediate impact at Glentoran and was voted the Player of the Year at the club. The English scouts crossed the Irish Sea to keep a close watch on him, but Cassidy was able to steer him in the direction of Turf Moor despite an offer from Notts County. Adrian Heath invited Little to Turf Moor for a couple of days and, after watching the Clarets play Preston North End, Little was impressed by what he saw. 'I instantly thought Burnley was the club for me, and I was proved right,' he said. The fact that Turf Moor was close to Old Trafford might also have had a bearing on his decision, as he was a fervent Manchester United fan in his youth!

Little had few chances to shine during his rare outings in 1996–97, but during the second half of the following season he grabbed the opportunity to become a key player for Burnley. As a right-sided midfielder, he combined speed with the kind of trickery the wing wizards of old would have used. His style, if somewhat unconventional, was hugely popular with the fans. In 1998–99, with the team struggling in general, he produced a series of fine displays. His performances were all the more remarkable as he was hampered by injury, suspension and the need for a hernia operation.

Although primarily a right-sided midfielder, Little was occasionally used in a more forward position, but in 1999–2000 Stan Ternent switched him to play on the left side of the Burnley midfield. At his best, Little was a tormentor of defences, but on the left he looked distinctly uncomfortable. Fortunately, it was an experiment that was not persisted with for too long.

Back on the right, he continued to be a constant thorn in the side of the best defences. His sheer unorthodoxy, as much as his speed, enabled him to get past defenders before whipping in pin-point crosses with unerring accuracy. Andy Payton in particular profited from Little's ability to deliver the perfect centre.

Little was hampered by hamstring problems in 2000–01 and occasionally found himself being used as a wing-back, despite the fact that defence was not exactly a strong point of his game. The following campaign, although plagued by injury, he again reasserted himself as an outstanding exponent of playing wide on the right of midfield. Once again, pace, trickery, and an eye for goal made him a key figure in the Turf Moor set up.

In the light of his tremendous success at the club, the 2002–03 campaign proved a hugely frustrating one for Little. He was seemingly at his best before Christmas but then his form fell away, and in April 2003 he joined Reading on loan, helping them reach the Play-offs and becoming a firm favourite with their supporters.

In September 2003 Little was on his travels again when Sam Allardyce took him on loan to Bolton Wanderers and offered him the chance to prove himself in the Premiership. Sadly, it didn't work out as Little had hoped, and at the end of October he returned to Turf Moor where he enjoyed a solid, if unspectacular, season by his own high standards.

Little became a free agent at the end of 2003–04 but chose to reject the offer of a new contract at Turf Moor. At 28, and in the prime of his career, the Wimbledon-born player opted to return closer to his roots and join Reading. For Burnley fans it was a huge disappointment, as Little was arguably the club's best player in recent times. Indeed, the memory of his winning goal at Scunthorpe that finally clinched promotion back to the First Division will live long in the memories of Clarets supporters.

Ultimately, the move worked out well for Little, and in 2005–06 he helped Reading clinch the Championship title and win promotion to the Premiership. Thus, at the start of 2006–07 Little stood on the threshold of the Premiership stage on which his talents so richly deserved to be paraded.

Andy Lochhead

Date of birth: 9 March 1941, Milngavie, Glasgow

Burnley record:
Appearances: League 225+1, FA Cup 19, League Cup 15, Europe 6
Goals: League 101, FA Cup 12, League Cup 9, Europe 6
Debut: League, 30 August 1960 v Manchester City (h) lost 1–3

Also played for: Renfrew Juniors, Leicester City, Aston Villa, Oldham Athletic,
Denver Dynamo (US)
Managed: Padiham

A native of Glasgow, Andy Lochhead might well have faced a life as a sheet metal worker at John Brown's but for his ability at football. With Partick Thistle and Stirling Albion showing interest in him, Sunderland inexplicably failed to sign him after inviting him to Roker Park for a trial. Fortunately, the powers that be at Turf Moor made no such mistake, and after inviting him to the club for a short trial he was signed as a professional in December 1958. During the next decade he went on to become a prolific goalscorer for the club and became only the sixth Burnley player to complete a century of League goals.

Lochhead was still learning his trade in the Central League team when the Clarets won the Championship, but he was given an early opportunity to taste first team action during 1960–61 as understudy to Ray Pointer. Three goals in five appearances revealed the potential that he possessed. His first goals, a brace, came in the match against Chelsea in March 1961 when Harry Potts made 10 changes from the previous week due to forthcoming Cup ties with Hamburg and Tottenham Hotspur.

Lochhead returned to Central League football in 1961–62 and led the Clarets attack to the Central League Championship. However, his claims for first-team action could no longer be denied, and in September 1962 Potts moved Pointer to inside-right to accommodate Lochhead at centre-forward. It was a decision that reaped instant rewards, with Lochhead finishing the season as top goalscorer with 19 League goals.

His sheer physical power made him a handful for even the best of defenders. A powerful header of the ball, his balding bullet-shaped dome appeared almost granite-like at times. Yet, there was more to his game than just his physical presence. He also had a deceptively good touch on the ball, while his shooting had both power and accuracy. However, Lochhead was also as brave as they come and could never be intimidated by opposition defenders.

The Scottish international selectors spotted his potential and awarded Lochhead with an Under-23 cap in December 1962, when he featured in a 2–0 win over a Welsh Under-23 team at Pittodrie, Aberdeen. Strangely, the selectors overlooked his legitimate claims for a place in the Scottish team, and this Under-23 cap was to remain the sole extent of his international experience.

In 1964–65, Lochhead was switched to inside-right in a new striking partnership that brought in Willie Irvine at centre-forward. Between them, the pair scored 43 League goals with Lochhead hitting the net on 21 occasions. His deadliness in front of goal is supported by the fact that he is the only player to have scored five goals in a game on two occasions for Burnley. He bagged five goals against Chelsea at Turf Moor on the final day of the 1964–65 season and then repeated the feat in January 1966 when Burnley demolished Bournemouth 7–0 in an FA Cup tie. On the final day of the 1967–68 campaign he notched his 100th goal for the club in the 3–0 victory over Leeds United at Turf Moor.

In October 1968 Lochhead was sold to Leicester City for £80,000 to form a strike partnership with Allan Clarke at Filbert Street. Ironically, shortly before this move a transfer to Manchester City had been vetoed by Bob Lord. In 1969 he was a member of the Leicester City team that lost to Manchester City in the FA Cup Final. Unfortunately, his finalists' medal was stolen during a burglary in October 2004, but Steve Cotterill decided to buy a replacement for the former Burnley legend, and the medal was presented to him prior to Burnley's match against Leicester City in November 2005.

Once Leicester had been relegated to the Second Division, Lochhead was allowed to leave Filbert Street, and he joined Aston Villa. Unfortunately, Villa slipped into the Third Division for the first time in their history. However, in 1971 he returned to Wembley and featured in the Villa team that lost a League Cup Final to Tottenham Hotspur. When Villa won the Third Division Championship in 1971–72, Lochhead was top goalscorer with 19 goals from 45 League appearances. In August 1973 he joined Oldham Athletic and ended his first season at the club with yet another Third Division Championship medal in his possession. Although not quite as prolific as in his younger days, Lochhead still managed 10 goals as he struck up a successful partnership with George Jones and then Colin Garwood at Boundary Park. In April 1974 he tried his luck in America with a short loan spell at Denver Dynamo in the flourishing North American Soccer League.

When his career ended, Lochhead spent many years in the licensed trade in the Burnley area and today contributes a column about the club in a local paper. He also renewed his partnership with Willie Irvine, as the two former stars worked at the club on match days looking after the sponsors.

Bob Lord

Date of birth: 19 June 1908, Burnley
Died: 8 December 1981, Burnley

Burnley record:
Chairman: 1955–1981

Bob Lord was not an easy man to like. Popularity was not his style, as he once said 'I've always believed in getting my own way.' It was not a virtue that endeared him to those around him. He was a larger-than-life figure, but a remarkable man nonetheless. Today, a quarter of a century after his death, he still remains the most controversial figure in the club's long history. Indeed, the name Bob Lord can divide opinion among Burnley supporters like no other.

To the modern generation of supporters, the name Bob Lord is largely synonymous with one of the older parts of the ground – the Bob Lord Stand. To a somewhat older generation, that particular edifice is symbolic with the beginning of the decline of a great club. To them, Lord is the man who sold a generation of talented young players as Burnley slid down the Divisions. However, to those supporters who followed the club in the 50s and early 60s, Lord was the man who built a club that could compete with the best in the land. Under his stewardship the Clarets won the First Division Championship, reached an FA Cup Final, almost did the double, and played in European competitions. Furthermore, it was during his term of office that the club produced some of the finest players ever to wear the Claret and Blue shirt of Burnley. Whatever view of the man you take, there can be no denying that for the 26 years he was chairman Bob Lord was Burnley Football Club.

The son of a barber, Lord's character was shaped early in his life as he came from a family that valued hard work and discipline. They were values that he put great store by, as he built up his butcher's business from humble beginnings. Throughout his early life, he had been a supporter of Burnley Football Club, and as his business grew and his chain of shops expanded he became a shareholder at Turf Moor. His early attempts to join the board were rebuffed, but in 1951 he finally gained his seat, and in 1955 he became chairman of the club.

Directors of football clubs were a largely anonymous breed at that time, but Lord soon changed that perception. Within a few years he was known throughout the land, so that Burnley Football Club and Bob Lord were viewed as one and the same.

Diplomacy was not a skill that Lord ever mastered. In truth, it is unlikely he even attempted to master it. He was a man of his time, a blunt speaker who believed in telling people what he thought. In today's world of political correctness, he would have been accused of every 'ism' in the book.

However, for all the controversy that followed in the wake of Lord, there could be no denying his achievements at Turf Moor. The development of a training ground at Gawthorpe and the careful nurturing of a generation of talented young players all came under his watchful eye. He led the club to the summit of English football and for that he will always be remembered.

In March 1963 Lord caused uproar in the town with his decision to sell Jimmy McIlroy to Stoke City. It was the start of a succession of sales that led to the break up of the Championship-winning team and gave his critics ammunition with which to attack him. With the end of the maximum wage, he genuinely believed that Burnley could only survive by developing their own players and then selling them, one at a time, for large sums of money.

Initially, the plan worked and there always seemed an up and coming youngster ready to fill the void left by a departed star. However, cutbacks in the scouting network and Lord's belief that the stadium was in urgent need of attention meant that the plan began to falter.

The club managed to overcome the blow of relegation in 1971 by winning the Second Division Championship just two years later. However, the sale of Martin Dobson to Everton in August 1974 led the more cynical among the Burnley faithful to refer to the newly-constructed Bob Lord Stand as the Martin Dobson Stand.

Instead of talented youngsters emerging through the ranks, the club entered the transfer market and bought veterans like Mike Summerbee and Willie Morgan. The club began to slide and at the end of 1979–80 fell into the Third Division.

Lord, whose own health was failing, sold his shares in the club in October 1981. He undoubtedly stayed too long at the helm, and in a changing world his touch became less sure. Nonetheless, during his time at the helm he rejuvenated Burnley Football Club, while, at the same time, being a tireless worker on behalf of the Football League and the Lancashire Football Association. With his passing in December 1981, Burnley Football Club truly lost one of its great protagonists.

Colin McDonald

Date of birth: 15 October 1930, Tottington, near Bury

Burnley record:
Appearances: League 186, FA Cup 15
Debut: League, 10 April 1954 v Aston Villa (a) lost 1–5

Also played for: Hawkshaw St Mary's, Headington United, England (8 caps),
                   Football League (3 appearances)
Managed: Bury

In the summer of 1958 few could have predicted that Colin McDonald was already at the peak of his football career. McDonald, undisputed number-one choice as goalkeeper for both club and country, appeared to have a long and successful future ahead of him. Burnley had gone from strength to strength in the First Division, while many contemporary critics had acclaimed him as one of the outstanding players of the World Cup Finals, held in Sweden, during that summer.

It was all a far cry from McDonald's debut for the Clarets at Villa Park in April 1954. 'Five goals flew past me that day. I felt so dejected afterwards it would have taken a crane to lift my chin off the floor,' he later reflected on an unforgettable day for him. Yet, within 12 months of making such a hit in Sweden, when he even defied the Brazilian team who eventually won the tournament, his career lay in tatters. A broken leg, suffered playing for the Football League against the League of Ireland in Dublin, forced him into premature retirement.

McDonald began his career as an outside-left with Hawkshaw St Mary's, a Bury Sunday School League side. When they were short of a 'keeper one day, he volunteered to fill the gap and even went on to save a penalty as his team enjoyed a 6–2 victory. As his father had been a goalkeeper with Portsmouth and Bury, it was, perhaps, unsurprising that he should take to the position. It was Jack Marshall, the former Burnley full-back, who arranged for him to have a trial at Turf Moor, and he eventually signed amateur forms in the summer of 1948. He progressed to a part-time professional at the club while following his trade as a plumber.

After his unfortunate debut at Villa Park, McDonald retained his first-team spot for the visit to Burnden Park on Good Friday in 1954. It proved a welcome boost to his confidence as he survived a torrid buffeting from Nat Lofthouse, the England centre-forward, and kept his goal intact. From that point on, he replaced Des Thompson in the Burnley goal on a regular basis.

McDonald had the knack of making goalkeeping look deceptively easy. However, that was down to his temperament, athleticism and perfect positional sense. Tall and sturdily built, he was an imposing figure in the penalty area and was dominant in the air. His handling and judgement were exemplary, and he was able to exude confidence to the defenders in front of him. He also had that rare ability to anticipate danger before it arose, so that he was prepared for every eventuality. Yet he remained a modest individual who was reluctant to emphasise his own part in the success that the team achieved. 'The full backs were Jock Aird and Jock Winton, and with a half-back line of Jimmy Adamson, Tommy Cummings and Bobby Seith my job was made a lot easier,' he later observed during an interview.

A broken ankle, suffered at Chelsea in December 1956, kept McDonald out of action for eight games during 1956–57, but he returned to action with the same level of consistency that had won him so many admirers and finally impressed the England selectors. His international debut came in the final warm-up game prior to the World Cup Finals. In front of over 100,000 spectators, in the Lenin Stadium in Moscow, he made his England debut against the Soviet Union. Less than a month later he was again lining up against the Soviet Union, but this time in Gothenburg in England's opening match of the World Cup. After a sparkling display in Sweden, he retained his place for the opening three international fixtures of the 1958–59 season. Then disaster struck in Dublin.

Although McDonald's leg was set in plaster, complications set in that were wrongly diagnosed as pneumonia. When his condition deteriorated he was taken to hospital and tests revealed that he was suffering from a pulmonary embolism. At the age of 28 his career as a goalkeeper was over.

On leaving Turf Moor, McDonald worked briefly for the Spastics Society before he was invited to join Bury as a youth coach. He then had a spell as chief scout at Gigg Lane before making an abortive comeback as a player with Altrincham. He had a couple of spells with Bury in various scouting and administrative roles and also served Bolton Wanderers, Oldham Athletic and Tranmere Rovers in a backroom capacity.

Jimmy McIlroy

Date of birth: 25 October 1931, Lambeg, near Belfast

Burnley record:
Appearances: League 439, FA Cup 50, League Cup 3, Europe 4, others 1
Goals: League 116, FA Cup 13, League Cup 1, Europe 1
Debut: League, 21 October 1950 v Sunderland (a) drew 1–1

Also played for: Craigavad, Glentoran, Stoke City, Oldham Athletic, Northern Ireland (55 caps), Football League (2 appearances), Great Britain XI (1 appearance)
Managed: Oldham Athletic, Bolton Wanderers

The name of Jimmy McIlroy is always at the forefront of any debate about who was the greatest player to represent the club. Past generations might have argued the merits of Bob Kelly, but for those who were fortunate to witness Jimmy 'Mac' in his prime, there is no doubt that it is he who they regard as the greatest of them all.

McIlroy was still a teenager playing for Glentoran when Frank Hill spotted him and brought him to Turf Moor in March 1950 for a fee of £8,000. The Clarets gained a player who would appear in almost 500 matches and play a leading role in guiding the club to a League Championship, an FA Cup Final and a European Cup adventure. At the same time he would represent Northern Ireland on 51 occasions while at Turf Moor, as well as play a couple of matches for the Football League and appear in a Great Britain XI. Surely, he must have been the bargain of all time!

McIlroy arrived at Turf Moor at a time when the club's fortunes were on an upward curve, and he certainly played his part in establishing Burnley as one of England's leading clubs. It was, perhaps, not surprising that he was destined to become a professional footballer as his father was a part-timer with Distillery while an uncle was a professional with Portadown.

McIlroy progressed from junior club Craigavad to Glentoran, and from there he arrived at Turf Moor. He made his debut for the Clarets at Roker Park just four days short of his 19th birthday. Ironically, he replaced Harry Potts, who had been sold to Everton, and who would later become his manager at Turf Moor.

McIlroy's talent quickly blossomed at Turf Moor under the tutelage of Billy Dougal, the club's trainer. He became the archetypical inside-forward. Always scheming, looking for openings and providing goalscoring opportunities for his colleges. Yet he was more than a playmaker, he was also a taker of chances, and this aspect of his game developed as he got older. In 1952–53 he switched to inside-right, following the retirement of Billy Morris, and this proved to be the first season that he reached double figures in terms of goalscoring.

McIlroy's wizardry was at the heart of the club's Championship challenge in 1959–60. Indeed, on the final day, with the Clarets contemplating a trip to Maine Road, he was nursing a thigh strain. He recalled the moment at which he informed Billy Dougal, and the response with which he was met was 'On the Monday morning I was struggling with a thigh strain, and Billy Dougal, who was the coach, asked me how it was. In such a big game every player wants to be 100 percent fit, but Billy didn't let me finish, he just said "whatever it's feeling like, you're still playing". So I had the thigh strapped and just about got through the game.'

Two years later, the Clarets were embroiled in a bid to win a League and Cup double. However, they ended up second to Ipswich Town in the League and beaten by Tottenham Hotspur in the FA Cup Final of 1962. It was perhaps no coincidence that results fell away at the same time that McIlroy struggled to find his best form.

McIlroy became the most capped player for the club when he picked up no fewer than 51 of his 55 full caps for Northern Ireland with the Clarets. He represented his country in the 1958 World Cup Finals in Sweden. Three years earlier he had been selected for a Great Britain XI that faced the Rest of Europe at Windsor Park.

Rarely can the departure of a player have caused such heated debate as that which occurred when McIlroy left Turf Moor in February 1963. After a dip in form, he was placed on the transfer list after defeat by Liverpool in the FA Cup. The supporters were aghast and the local press was filled with letters of complaint from the fans. McIlroy himself was somewhat taken aback by the speed of events.

Within a week McIlroy had been sold to Stoke City for a fee of £25,000. He appeared in 98 League games for the Potteries club before taking over as manager of Oldham Athletic in January 1966. He returned to Stoke City as coach in August 1968, and 12 months later he left to join Bolton Wanderers as coach and assistant manager to Nat Lofthouse. In November 1970 he was appointed manager at Burnden Park but spent just 18 days in the job.

McIlroy then spent many years as a respected journalist for the *Burnley Express* before retirement. He remains a cult figure at Turf Moor and has had one of the new stands named after him. In a book of legends, he remains the man who many would select as the greatest Burnley legend of them all.

Peter McKay

Date of birth: 23 February 1925, Newburgh

Burnley record:
Appearances: League 60, FA Cup 6
Goals: League 36, FA Cup 2
Debut: League, 31 August 1954 v Chelsea (h) drew 1–1

Also played for: Newburgh FC, Dundee United, St Mirren, Corby Town

In an era when the centre-forward was usually a big, burly type of swashbuckler, blessed with unexpected pace or a potent aerial threat, Peter McKay cut an unlikely figure in the number-nine shirt. Certainly not the quickest of players or the tallest, his somewhat lightweight build made him an unlikely candidate to fill the focal role in attack. Add to this that he was virtually one-footed and showed no inclination to stray too far from the middle, and it is easy to see why eyebrows were raised when he arrived at the club. Yet McKay had one saving grace: he was a natural-born goalscorer. The one thing he was proficient in was finding the back of the net, as his record in Scotland had proved.

During seven seasons with Dundee United, McKay had scored 158 goals in 185 Scottish Second Division matches. He'd proved in Scotland that you didn't need to be a big, burly bustler to succeed. Not surprisingly, his inspiration had been Hughie Gallacher, the diminutive Scottish international goalscorer of the 1920s and 1930s.

'Always you must be looking for the open space and, in addition, must possess a snap shot. But probably the most important thing is that you need to play with colleagues who know how best to blend with your style,' was how McKay explained his success in the mid-1950s.

McKay arrived in English football somewhat late in his career. Not long after celebrating his 29th birthday he left Dundee United to join the Clarets in May 1954. Those who questioned whether his style would work in the English First Division soon gained ample ammunition to back up those doubts. He didn't enjoy a successful introduction to life at Turf Moor. He made just four senior appearances and failed to find the target, as he found it impossible to dislodge Bill Holden from the centre-forward spot. However, in the relative obscurity of Central League football he had begun to make his mark and finished the season with 36 goals at that level.

In 1955–56 McKay was drafted into the first team for the visit of Luton Town on 5 September 1955. At that point the Clarets had won just one of their opening five games and had only scored three goals, all of which had come from Brian Pilkington on the wing. He stepped into the breach and netted a hat-trick as the Clarets romped to a 3–1 win. Five days later he notched one of the goals in a 3–1 win over Birmingham City, and manager Alan Brown kept him in the team for the rest of the campaign.

McKay scored 25 League goals that season – twice as many as Pilkington, his closest rival in the goalscoring stakes. It was also the highest seasonal total in League football since George Beel had scored the same number in 1930–31. He continued to maintain an excellent ratio of goals per game until December 1956, when he lost his place in the team. Initially, McKay lost out when Les Shannan was recalled, and then he found his place under pressure from the challenge of youth in the shape of Ian Lawson and Alan Shackleton.

Brown had shifted the emphasis of McKay's game slightly and expected him to move out to the wings to create space and forage for the ball. This was not his strength. He was at his best near the penalty area, lurking like a predator awaiting its kill. While speed was never his strength, he liked to hover in the danger zone before darting between defenders and unleashing a powerful shot. Strangely, for a man of his build, he had developed the knack of being able to ride even the most robust of challenges in the area of the field were it mattered – the penalty area.

Sadly, McKay found it difficult to adapt to the new demands made upon him and lost his place just before Christmas 1956. Like a shooting star, he had lit up Turf Moor for a brief period before quickly fading. In January 1957, with no likelihood of a return to first-team action, he left Burnley to join St Mirren in search of first-team football. He stressed that while he was happy enough at Turf Moor, he was at an age when he needed first-team football and hence his decision to return to his native Scotland.

Harold Mather

Date of birth:	24 January 1921, Bolton
Died:	1 March 1999, Burnley

Burnley record:

Appearances:	League 301, FA Cup 28, Wartime 132
Debut:	FA Cup, 5 January 1946 v Stoke City (a) lost 1–3
Also played for:	Kendals XI, (wartime guest for Plymouth Argyle, Charlton Athletic, Heart of Midlothian), Nelson
Managed:	Kettering Town, Accrington Stanley, Nelson

Harold Mather was living testimony to the theory that speed of thought remains every bit as important as speed of feet for a professional footballer. No one could pretend that he was the speediest of full-backs. He belonged to an era when the predominant function of the full-back was to defend and not roam downfield to support his attack. Nonetheless, even by the standards of his day he was not the quickest. However, he was blessed with a footballing brain and impeccable timing. These two attributes more than compensated for a lack of pace, so much so that he was rarely bettered by the sprightliest of wingers. Nor did he allow himself to be overawed by an opposing winger's reputation. The more esteemed the opponent, the more he would raise his game to meet the challenge. In short, he was one of the finest full-backs in the history of Burnley Football Club.

Mather received his early football education at Folds Road School, Bolton, the same establishment that produced two other stars who made their initial impact in the game at Turf Moor: Tommy Lawton and Bill Holden. Indeed, it was Mather's desire to follow in the path of Lawton that led to him turning down the opportunity to join Bolton Wanderers and opt for Burnley instead. He joined the Clarets in May 1938, but unfortunately his early progress was brought to a dramatic halt by the outbreak of World War Two. When the Football League was suspended in September 1939, he had yet to make his senior bow for the club.

Mather's debut was not long delayed, and he lined up at left-back in the opening match of the North West Regional League in October 1939. Ironically, the opposition that day was Bolton Wanderers, but Mather did sufficiently well to anchor his place in the team for the remainder of that campaign. He only missed a couple of games during 1940–41, but wartime service restricted his availability for selection. He guested for Plymouth Argyle, Charlton Athletic and Heart of Midlothian while stationed in different parts of the country and returned to Turf Moor whenever he could. He returned to occupy the left-back spot at Burnley on a regular basis in 1945–46, the final season of wartime football. He featured in both FA Cup ties

against Stoke City that season, and the first of these, played at the Victoria Ground, is regarded as his senior debut for the club as other wartime games were not considered first-class matches. In 1946 he was also selected to represent the Navy against the RAF at Hampden Park.

Mather made his League debut on the opening day of 1946–47, when Coventry City visited Turf Moor. He was one of seven League debutants that day but struck up an immediate understanding with Arthur Woodruff, who operated at right-back. He quickly cemented his role in what was known as Cliff Britton's 'Iron Curtain' defence, and the first season of peacetime football resulted in the Clarets winning promotion to the First Division and a place in the FA Cup Final.

Mather remained the undisputed first choice at left-back throughout the remainder of the 40s and early 50s. There was little flamboyance about his play, just a steady consistency week in and week out as he became part of the bedrock of the Burnley defence. Ultimately, Father Time was the one opponent that began to get the better of him, and in the latter stages of 1953–54 he found himself overlooked in favour of Doug Winton.

Mather then embarked upon a coaching career that began at nearby Nelson in February 1955. He then moved to work with former Claret Bob Brocklebank, who was manager of Hull City, before trying his hand at management with Kettering Town. He then had spells with Portadown and Limerick in Ireland before he trained for his coaching badge at Lilleshall.

In 1960 Mather left for South Africa to coach at Pietermaritzburg and East Rand United. In between those coaching assignments he returned to Lancashire to complete a short stint with Padiham FC. In the summer of 1962 he became manager of Accrington Stanley, who had recently fallen from the Football League, and two years later he became manager at Nelson before retiring from the game.

Mather continued to retain his roots in Burnley until his tragic death in 1999. Sadly, he suffered a fall while recuperating from a knee injury and broke his hip. He passed away in hospital at the age of 78.

Trevor Meredith

Date of birth: 25 December 1936, Stottesdon

Burnley record:
Appearances: League 37, League Cup 1
Goals: League 8
Debut: League, 9 April 1960 v Nottingham Forest (a) won 1–0

Also played for: Kidderminster Harriers, Shrewsbury Town

During his five and a half years at the club, Trevor Meredith made fewer than 40 senior appearances. Furthermore, his seasonal total only reached double figures in terms of League appearances on two occasions. He didn't feature in any FA Cup campaigns and, in truth, was a peripheral figure in the Turf Moor first-team squad of the early 60s. However, when he scored the winning goal at Maine Road on the final day of the 1959–60 League campaign, he not only clinched the Championship for Burnley but also carved his own niche in the history of Burnley Football Club.

Meredith had made his debut for the club just a month before his all-important goal against Manchester City. He had gained his opportunity against Nottingham Forest at the City Ground in April 1960 because John Connelly was away on international duty with England. He had enjoyed a rather quiet debut in a somewhat drab affair that was played in difficult conditions, with a swirling wind and bumpy end-of-season pitch not really conducive to good football. Nonetheless, a single Ray Pointer goal was enough to give the Clarets an important victory. Meredith might well have added to this in the closing stages, but the ball bobbled on the uneven surface and his shot sailed over the bar.

Connelly returned six days later for the Good Friday encounter with Leicester City at Turf Moor. The England international winger scored the only goal of the game, but in the closing stages he received an injury that would keep him out of action for the rest of the season. It was an injury that provided Meredith with the opportunity to make his own mark on the Championship finale.

The day after Connelly's injury, Meredith took his place on the right wing for the visit of Luton Town to Turf Moor. He enjoyed a brilliant game and even won a penalty, which enabled Jimmy McIlroy to score the third goal in a comfortable 3–0 victory. Two days later he scored his first goal for the Clarets but couldn't prevent the team from slipping to a 2–1 defeat at Leicester City.

Five days after the defeat at Filbert Street, Meredith was on hand again to give the Clarets the lead in their meeting with Blackpool at Bloomfield Road. Although the game ended in a 1–1 draw, the point proved vital as it took Burnley to within two points of leaders Wolverhampton Wanderers, with the Clarets also having played two games fewer than their rivals from Molineux.

The next game at Birmingham City again brought a vital contribution from Meredith. The diminutive winger beat two defenders before his cross was converted by Brian Pilkington for the only goal of the game at St Andrews.

After a goalless draw at home to Fulham, the Clarets went into their final match of the season knowing that nothing short of victory would bring the Championship to Turf Moor. The defining moment of Meredith's football career occurred after 31 minutes when Ken Branagan, the City defender, sliced the ball into his own penalty area, and the ever alert Meredith pounced on the loose ball in a flash. Retaining his poise despite the intense pressure of the situation (the game stood at 1–1), he sent the ball smartly into the net just inside the post. It was a goal that clinched the Championship and guaranteed his place in Burnley's history.

Meredith was signed from Southern League Kidderminster Harriers, and under the tutelage of Billy Morris, the former Burnley Welsh international, he began to develop into a skilful young winger. He became a regular with the reserve side and won two Central League Championships and three Lancashire Senior Cup-winners' medals while at Turf Moor.

However, while medals were accumulated with some regularity, a first-team place continued to remain elusive even after his heroics in the closing stages of 1959–60. Meredith covered for Connelly whenever the England winger was injured or on international duty, but it was not until the 1963–64 campaign that he forced his way into the team in his own right. During a period of transition, Connelly was moved to the left flank, and Meredith was given an opportunity to establish himself at outside-right. Unfortunately, the emergence of the immensely talented Willie Morgan meant that he was again reduced to the role of understudy.

In April 1964 Meredith opted to join Shrewsbury Town and went on to enjoy a long and successful career at Gay Meadow. He made 235 League appearances for Shrewsbury, and during his latter period at the club he played on a part-time basis so he could attend teacher training college. Teaching became his new career when he finally hung up his boots and remained so until his retirement from the profession in 2001.

Brian Miller

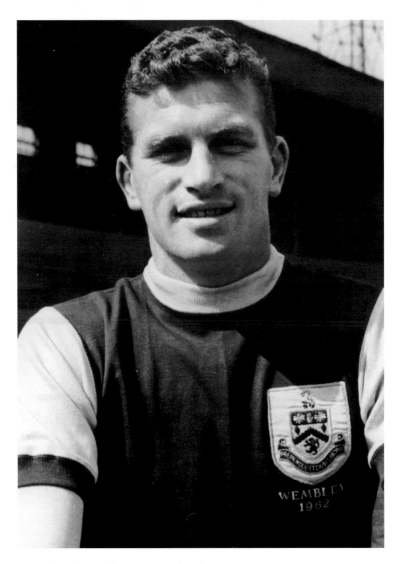

Date of birth: 19 January 1937, Burnley

Burnley record:
Appearances: League 379, FA Cup 50, League Cup 13, Charity Shield 1,
Europe 12
Goals: League 29, FA Cup 4, League Cup 1, Charity Shield 1, Europe 2
Debut: FA Cup, 1 February 1956 v Chelsea (a) drew 1–1
Manager: October 1979–January 1983 and July 1986–January 1989

Also played for: England (1 cap), England Under-23 (3 caps), Football League (2
appearances)

The majority of Brian Miller's working life has been spent in the service of Burnley Football Club. As a player, coach, manager and scout, he has witnessed the highs of a League Championship success and an FA Cup Final appearance at Wembley and the depths of fighting for League survival at the bottom of the Fourth Division. Throughout it all, he remained totally committed to the Clarets, and as a result he has achieved legendary status at Turf Moor.

Recruited from schoolboy football, Miller joined the office staff and progressed to sign as a professional in February 1954. His debut came during the colossal struggle with Chelsea in a fourth-round FA Cup tie in 1955–56. The tie went to four replays and Miller made his debut in the first replay, which was at Stamford Bridge. He also featured in the second replay and made two League appearances that season. He scored his first senior goal in a 1–1 draw with Sheffield United at Turf Moor in February 1956.

However, it wasn't until the start of 1959–60 that Miller started a season in the first team. That season he appeared in every game as the League Championship was won for the first time since 1920–21. He figured at both centre-half and left-half, although it was in the latter position that he would finally settle. As a sturdy and tough-tackling half-back, his style perfectly complemented the likes of Jimmy Adamson and Jimmy McIlroy.

Miller's consistency was rewarded with appearances for the Football League team and three England Under-23 caps. Surprisingly, he only played for the senior England team on one occasion. In May 1961 he and John Angus appeared in the 3–1 defeat by Austria in Vienna. He travelled as a reserve on a number of occasions, but Ron Flowers, of Wolverhampton Wanderers, was regarded as the first choice at left-half.

In 1961–62, Miller missed only four League games when the Clarets finished as runners-up to Ipswich Town, and he also featured in the FA Cup Final against Tottenham Hotspur. He remained a wonderfully consistent performer until he damaged his cruciate knee ligament at Villa Park in April 1967. It was an injury that brought his playing career to an end.

Miller then joined the backroom staff and served in various capacities before his appointment as manager in October 1979. The club was involved in a battle against relegation that ultimately ended with the Clarets falling to the Third Division for the first time in their history.

The directors kept faith with Miller, and in 1981–82 he delivered the Third Division Championship. Sadly, success proved to be fleeting, and the following season found the club embroiled in yet another relegation battle. In January 1983 he was axed on the morning of his 46th birthday: the day that Burnley enjoyed an unprecedented 4–1 win against Tottenham Hotspur at White Hart Lane in the Football League Cup.

A revolving door might well have been fitted to the manager's office after Miller's departure as Frank Casper, John Bond, John Benson, Martin Buchan and Tommy Cavanagh all came and went with alarming speed. In July 1986 the directors again turned to Miller and appointed him manager of a club that was now languishing in the Fourth Division.

The situation was not great when Miller took over. 'I inherited just 13 players, two of them 'keepers and a centre-back, Joe Gallagher, who had a dodgy knee. So I brought in Leighton James and Billy Rodaway on frees, and I remember having to go cap in hand to the bank manager to see if we could pay their wages. It was that desperate,' he recalled.

Ultimately, the future of the club came down to one match: the meeting with Orient on the final day of the season. Victory, of course, ensured the club's survival, and for Miller the emotions were overwhelming, as he explained 'When we got the result the relief was unbelievable. Tears, laughter, joy. Emotionally, everybody was drained, but we'd come through our darkest hour together.'

In May 1988 Miller took the club to Wembley for the Final of the Sherpa Vans Trophy but, sadly, couldn't return with the trophy as the Clarets went down 2–0 to Wolverhampton Wanderers in front of a crowd of 80,841.

In January 1989 Miller was again replaced by Frank Casper, but he remained at the club to take up the role of chief scout. During his first tenure as manager, he had the distinction of introducing his son, David, to first-team action at Turf Moor and also in the Clarets squad at the time was Derek Scott, his son-in-law. There can be no doubt that his involvement with Burnley Football Club has been a love affair that has lasted a lifetime. Quite simply, Brian Miller is a Burnley legend.

Willie Morgan

Date of birth: 2 October 1944, Sauchie, Alloa

Burnley record:
Appearances: League 195+1, FA Cup 13, League Cup 15, Europe 8
Goals: League 19, FA Cup 1, League Cup 2
Debut: League, 23 April 1963 v Sheffield Wednesday (a) won 1–0

Also played for: Fishcross FC, Manchester United, Bolton Wanderers, Chicago
Sting (US), Minnesota Kicks (US), Blackpool, Scotland (21 caps),
Scotland Under-23 (1 cap)

When Harry Potts switched John Connelly from his favoured right wing to the opposite flank for the visit to Hillsborough in April 1963, few could have realised the significance of the move. Gordon Harris, the regular number 11, was missing, and Potts moved Connelly to allow Willie Morgan to make his debut at outside-right. Although it wasn't realised at the time, it proved to be the changing of the old guard in more ways than one. Connelly, an England international, was a product of the 50s: a fleet-footed winger who was the very epitome of the professional footballer of his era. Morgan, on the other hand, was a product of the swinging 60s: a non-conformist with strong opinions and, ultimately, his own fan club.

Morgan had joined the Clarets as an amateur and signed as a professional in October 1961. He wasn't a regular in the team that won the Central League title in 1961–62, but the following season he picked up a medal as Burnley retained the Central League Championship. After spasmodic appearances with the first team, he became a regular in December 1963.

Morgan was a different type of winger to Connelly. His game had more reliance on his dazzling dribbling skills and instant ball control. He could fire in crosses with the unerring accuracy of the best of wingers, but he was also capable of dropping back into midfield and winning the ball. He was a bundle of tricks and flicks, and the crowd loved him.

When Connelly left to join Manchester United in April 1965, Morgan became the supplier in chief to Andy Lochhead and Willie Irvine. In 1965–66 the pair notched 60 League and Cup goals between them, and Morgan was the architect of a good number of them. The Clarets finished third in the First Division that season and captured a European place. The fans, who recognised Morgan's contribution to the club's success, worshipped him, and a fan club was set up in his honour – believed to be the first of its kind.

Morgan won a Scottish cap in October 1967 when he was selected to face Northern Ireland in Belfast and also became the target of bigger clubs. Matters were not helped when he expressed his views during negotiations over a new contract, and, as a result, relations with Bob Lord became somewhat strained. Indeed, the Burnley chairman banned Morgan from the training ground for a time. In August 1968 he left Turf Moor to join Manchester United for £117,000.

Morgan was in his element in the city of Manchester, but he found a rival for the adulation that he had enjoyed at Turf Moor in George Best. He didn't enjoy the best of fortunes during his early period at United, and for a time he found himself out of the team. However, he rediscovered his form and returned to the wing for a United team that was full of star names, albeit that several of them were beginning to enter the twilight of their careers. Morgan's influence on the United team began to grow, and he became an integral part of things at Old Trafford when Frank O'Farrell moved him from the wing and gave him a midfield role.

The adventurous attacking qualities of his game were suited to Morgan's new role, but the fact that he could tackle and had a huge capacity for work made the switch to a deeper role all the more successful. When he arrived at Old Trafford the club had just won the European Cup, but in 1973–74 United slipped into the Second Division. Nonetheless, during that relegation campaign, he remained one of the most consistent performers and succeeded George Graham as captain under the management of Tommy Docherty.

After just one season out of the top flight, United returned, with Morgan appearing in 34 League games as United carried off the Second Division Championship in 1974–75. However, he and Docherty clashed, with the result that Morgan was allowed to leave Old Trafford to return to Burnley.

There is a saying in football that 'you should never go back', and for Morgan this turned out to be true, for his second spell at Turf Moor was particularly disappointing. After just 13 League appearances – 12 starts and 1 substitute outing – he was sold to Bolton Wanderers.

The move rejuvenated his career, and Morgan enjoyed a glorious 'Indian Summer' at Burnden Park. He helped Bolton to the Second Division Championship in 1978, after a couple of near misses. In 1976–77, the Wanderers also reached the semi-final of the League Cup with Morgan in sparkling form.

After Bolton, Morgan moved to America to parade his skills in the North American Soccer League before ending his career with a couple of seasons at Blackpool. On hanging up his boots, he left the game to concentrate on a successful career in marketing and promotions.

Tony Morley

Date of birth: 26 August 1954, Ormskirk

Burnley record:
Appearances: League 83+13, FA Cup 3+2, League Cup 3+1, others 2
Goals: League 5, FA Cup 1, League Cup 1
Debut: League, 7 February 1976 v Ipswich Town (h) lost 0–1

Also played for: Preston North End, Aston Villa, West Bromwich Albion, Birmingham City, Seiko (Hong Kong), Den Haag (Holland), West Bromwich Albion, Tampa Bay Rowdies (US), Hamrun Sports (Malta), Sutton Coldfield Town, Bromsgrove Rovers, Stratford Town, England (6 caps), England B (2 caps), England Under-23 (1 cap)

In February 1976 the Clarets were fighting a desperate rearguard action to avoid relegation to the Second Division. Jimmy Adamson had been replaced by Joe Brown as manager, and the team had just enjoyed a 3–2 win at Goodison Park. It was into this environment that Tony Morley, Preston North End's skilful young winger, arrived at Turf Moor. As an England Youth international, he had become an important member of the North End team, and in January 1975 he had been capped at Under-23 level by his country. The North End directors were reluctant to part with such an exciting young prospect, and it took a fee of £100,000 to bring him to Turf Moor.

Unfortunately, Morley could do little to sway the season's outcome, and, having spent the majority of the campaign in the drop zone, it came as no surprise when the Clarets finally lost their relegation battle. Initially, Morley, who had appeared in 99 League and Cup games for Preston, struggled to find his feet at Turf Moor and drifted in and out of the team. Indeed, many of the Burnley supporters had begun to question the wisdom of investing a sizeable sum in a player who was untested at the highest level. By the end of the season he had only started eight League games and made one other appearance as a substitute, in a team that was destined for relegation.

However, it was a different Tony Morley who appeared before them at the start of the 1976–77 campaign – quite literally as he had shaved his head. Suddenly, the exceptional wing play that had earned him such plaudits at Deepdale returned. The fans rapidly took a liking to their new hero. Not only was he quick, but he was extremely comfortable on the ball. At times he appeared to be in cruise mode, as he rode challenge after challenge but still retained complete control over the ball. Having left defenders trailing in his wake, he also had the ability to send in pin-point crosses that invited his colleagues to soar to meet them. Furthermore, like all the best wingers, he could unleash shots that would trouble even the best of 'keepers. The Tony Morley who figured for the Clarets in 1976–77 looked a totally different proposition than the youngster who had stuttered his way through the previous campaign.

In truth, views on Morley's value to the team continued to be mixed. Those who admired his skilful trickery realised the potential he possessed and hoped it could be honed at Turf Moor. Others felt that, despite his undoubted ability, he had a tendency to remain on the periphery of the action and, as result, had little impact or influence on the outcome of a game. Indeed, with the Clarets marooned in mid-table mediocrity in the Second Division, it appeared as if his style of wing play was a luxury the club could ill afford. Despite his individual flashes of brilliance, there was little to suggest that he would become a future England international. A few good performances were invariably followed by a slump in form, with the result that he was in and out of the team.

Ultimately, it took a move to Aston Villa before Morley found the consistency that turned him into an international player. Even then, his first season at Villa Park following his £200,000 move from Burnley in June 1979 was an indifferent affair. However, in 1980–81 he finally found his feet and enjoyed an outstanding season, featuring in every game as Villa lifted the First Division Championship. The following season he was a member of the Villa team that won the European Cup, and he was also selected for England. In 1982–83 he helped Villa win the European Super Cup and also appeared in the World Club Championship in Tokyo, when Penarol beat Villa 2–0.

In December 1983 Morley left Villa Park to join West Bromwich Albion for £75,000. Unfortunately he made little impact at the Hawthorns, and so he embarked on a series of moves that took him around the world and brought him back to Turf Moor for a short loan spell in October 1988. He brought a sparkle to the Burnley attack during his brief return before jetting off to play in America, Malta and New Zealand. When he returned to England, he became involved with the game at non-League level.

Billy Morris

Date of birth:	30 July 1918, Llanddulas, near Colwyn Bay
Died:	2 January 2003, Bodelwyddan, near Rhyl

Burnley record:

Appearances:	League 211, FA Cup 19, Wartime 25
Goals:	League 47, FA Cup 6, Wartime 15
Debut:	League, 28 January 1939 v Norwich City (h) won 3–0
Also played for:	Old Colwyn Youth, Llanddulas FC, Llandudno Town, (wartime guest for Wrexham), Wales (5 caps)
Managed:	Wrexham

Billy Morris had just broken into the senior team at Turf Moor when the outbreak of World War Two put his career on hold for seven years. He served in the Far East, having enlisted in the Royal Welsh Fusiliers, and reached the rank of sergeant. It was while serving in Kohima, Burma, that he was wounded in the neck by a Japanese bullet. Fortunately, he made a full recovery and even managed to play football for a services team. However, his military service meant that he made only fleeting appearances on the wartime stage at Turf Moor. After featuring in three games during 1939–40, he didn't reappear in the team until late November 1945, although he did make 23 appearances for Wrexham during the first season of wartime football while undergoing his military training at a barracks in the Welsh town.

When the Football League re-opened in 1946–47, Morris began the campaign at inside-right, one of only five pre-war Burnley players to participate in first-team football during the season, the others being George Bray, Arthur Woodruff, Jack Marshall and Freddy Taylor. While Marshall and Taylor had only a peripheral role, making just one appearance each, Bray, Woodruff, and Morris featured prominently in the new team that Cliff Britton had constructed.

Morris quickly struck up an excellent understanding with Jackie Chew on the right wing. Both players registered nine goals apiece as the Clarets clinched promotion to the top flight. Morris, who also hit four goals in the FA Cup as the club reached the Final, won his first international cap for Wales in April 1947 when he featured against Northern Ireland in Belfast. It proved to be the first of five Welsh caps, with his final appearance for his country coming against the Rest of the UK at Cardiff in December 1951.

Morris, although not the tallest of men at 5ft 4in, was blessed with a deft touch that enabled him to bring the ball under immediate control. Workmanlike in his approach, he was constructive in possession and was capable of making darting runs beyond opposition defences. The unpredictability of his movement made him a difficult opponent to mark.

Although not a prolific marksman, he had the happy knack of being on hand to finish off the odd half chance, but he proved more proficient in front of the goal during the closing stages of his career at Turf Moor. In 1950–51 he notched 11 goals in 38 League games while the following campaign produced 18 goals in the League, making him the club's top goalscorer.

Morris's playing career was finally blighted due to the affects of malaria, which he had contracted during the war. As increasing arthritic problems began to take their toll, he made the transformation from player to coach when he took charge of the club's promising youngsters in the A team in 1952. He was hugely successful in this post, as Jimmy Robson explained at the time of Morris's death: 'He was a good coach and knew a lot about the game. He helped me a lot because he was one of the old style inside-forwards, which I went on to become. When I went to the club he was one of the first people I met, and he was a special, special man. He took us for training in the mornings and afternoons and he did a lot for the young lads who were coming through at the time. He was a pleasure to work with.'

In June 1960 Morris left Turf Moor to return to his native Wales to take over as manager of Wrexham. Sadly, his hip problems worsened, and after just one season at the Racecourse Ground he resigned and turned his back on football to run a boarding house in Llandudno.

In March 1965 Morris was invited back to Wrexham following the departure of Ken Barnes from the managership. He remained at the helm until October of the same year, when three wins from the opening 14 matches of the 1965–66 season brought about his downfall.

Once again Morris turned his back on the game and ran a grocers and off-licence in Lystaen. He then took a job with the Isle of Man Steamship Company and later worked for the local council before his retirement in 1976. He had both his hips replaced and continued to live in the Colwyn Bay area until his death in 2003. He had the distinction of being the last surviving member of Burnley's 1947 FA Cup Final team.

Eddie Mosscrop

Date of birth: 16 June 1892, Southport
Died: 14 March 1980, Southport

Burnley record:
Appearances: League 176, FA Cup 21, Wartime 35, others 1
Goals: League 19, FA Cup 1, Wartime 6
Debut: League, 7 August 1912 v Glossop (h) won 2–1

Also played for: Blowick Wesleyans, Shepherds Bush, Middlesex, Southport
                   YMCA, Southport Central, (wartime guest for Reading), England
                   (2 caps), Football League (2 appearances)

Eddie Mosscrop was an outstanding player in what may be regarded as Burnley's first golden era. Burnley won promotion from the Second Division in 1912–13, the FA Cup the following season and the League Championship in 1920–21, and he played his part in what was a halcyon period in the history of the club.

Curiously, Mosscrop, in his younger days, had played for Blowick Wesleyans, the same junior club in Southport that was also home to Billy Watson, who also played a leading role in this monumentally successful period in Burnley's history. Both players came to Turf Moor from Southport Central, although Mosscrop came by a more complex route.

Mosscrop was still a teenager when he left his native Southport to move to London. While in the capital he played junior football before returning north to join Southport Central. In the summer of 1912 he signed amateur forms for Burnley while continuing to work as a schoolteacher. Initially, he came to Turf Moor as an outside-right, and for a time he vied with Billy Nesbitt for the right-wing position. He made his debut on the opening day of 1912–13 in the home win over Glossop and went on to make 22 appearances that campaign, as the Clarets clinched promotion to the First Division as runners-up to Preston North End.

However, it was during the following season, when the Clarets embarked on a successful run in the FA Cup, that Mosscrop really made his mark at the club. He spent the first part of that season on the right flank but later crossed over to the left to allow Nesbitt to operate on the right. He found the outside-left role to his liking and contemporary scribes began to extol the virtues of the young winger from Southport. 'Lightly built and speedy, has good ball control and centres well,' was the judgement of one writer for the *Lancashire Daily Post Football Annual*.

Not only did Mosscrop pick up an FA Cup-winners' medal in 1913–14, but he also won international recognition when he was capped by England against Wales in March 1914. He received his second England cap the following month when he appeared against Scotland at Hampden Park. On both occasions he formed a left-wing partnership with Joe Smith of Bolton Wanderers. He might well have won more international honours but for the outbreak of World War One.

The match against Scotland on 4 April 1914 was the last England international until the meeting with Ireland in October 1919. Only 'keeper Sam Hardy retained his place, and Mosscrop, like so many others, found that the war had robbed him of what should have been the most productive years of his career.

During the war Mosscrop, who saw active service in Salonika, managed to make 35 appearances and score six goals for Burnley in the regionalised competitions that replaced the Football League. It was the 1915–16 season that brought the majority of his appearances, 25 in all, as the Clarets finished second in the principal tournament and won the subsidiary competition.

When the Football League was restored in 1919–20, Mosscrop was quickly back to his best, as one local wordsmith commented when he wrote that he 'is a polished player, and on his day there are few better left-wingers.' However, in March 1920 he lost his place to Walt Weaver, a recent recruit from South Liverpool.

As the Clarets embarked upon their 30-match unbeaten run in 1920–21, Mosscrop was kept on the sidelines. In January 1921 he was restored to first-team action and went on to play in 14 games, as the club clinched the First Division Championship and he won a Championship medal to go with his FA Cup-winners' medal.

Having fought his way back to regain his left-wing spot, Mosscrop retained his place during 1921–22 until a bout of illness kept him out of action. Ultimately, his failing health brought an end to his playing career. On his retirement from football, he became a schoolteacher and then a headteacher at schools in the Southport area, where he lived most of his life.

Mosscrop was the last surviving member of the 1914 FA Cup-winning team when he died at a Southport nursing home after a short illness at the age of 87 in March 1980. Throughout his life he had kept an active interest in Burnley, and the Turf Moor flag flew at half mast as a mark of respect to one of its all time great players. The Burnley secretary, Albert Maddox, said of him at the time of his death, 'He was a great character who retained strong links with Burnley Football Club throughout his life.' Like so many players, he found that Burnley got into his blood and became a life-long commitment.

Jimmy Mullen

Date of birth: 8 November 1952, Hedworth, Jarrow

Burnley record:

Manager: October 1991–February 1996

Played for: Hedworth Celtic, Sheffield Wednesday, Rotherham United,
                 Preston North End, Cardiff City, Newport County, Aberdeen

Also managed: Newport County, Blackpool, Sligo Rovers, Telford United,
                 Merthyr Tydfil, Little Drayton Rangers, Bridgnorth Town,
                 Colwyn Bay, Ludlow Town, Bromsgrove Rovers

Jimmy Mullen had spent the majority of his playing career with Sheffield Wednesday and Cardiff City, before taking his first steps in management with Newport County. He had gained promotion from the Third Division on three occasions during his career, with Sheffield Wednesday, Rotherham United and Cardiff City. Thus, when he arrived at Turf Moor in August 1990 as assistant to Frank Casper, he had plenty of experience of lower Division football. He also had some management experience behind him, as not only had he managed Newport County, but he had also been in control at Blackpool during 1989–90.

When Mullen accepted the position of assistant manager at Turf Moor, the club was about to embark upon its sixth season of Fourth Division football. However, the combination of Casper and Mullen almost brought that period in the wilderness to an end, with the Clarets narrowly missing out on promotion by losing a Play-off semi-final against Torquay United.

The 1991–92 campaign opened disappointingly and Casper tendered his resignation in October 1991. With the Clarets stranded in mid-table, Mullen was given the opportunity to become manager at Turf Moor, with promotion seemingly as far away as ever.

However, Mullen brought an immediate transformation, with the first nine League games under his charge all being won. Suddenly, the club rocketed to the top of the table, and it was a position that was rarely relinquished between that point and the end of the season.

Mullen appeared to be the right man to motivate the players, and he transformed them into a tight-knit group that refused to be beaten. Steve Davis and John Pender were the rocks upon which he built the defence, while Mike Conroy and Roger Eli were his cutting edge in attack. The club clinched the Fourth Division Championship as Jimmy restored pride and passion back into the club.

Mullen's attempts to build upon promotion were hit by early season injuries to Conroy, Eli and Davis in 1992–93. By mid-September 1992 the Clarets had won only one of their opening six games in the newly constructed Second Division. However, the return of Davis and Conroy brought an improvement in results as Mullen entered the transfer market to make a couple of crucial signings. The arrival of Marlon Beresford solved the goalkeeping problems, while the experienced

Adrian Heath arrived to lend support to Conroy. By Christmas, Mullen had steered the team to a comfortable mid-table position, and during the first couple of months of 1993 the Clarets flirted with a Play-off place before they finally fell away and finished in 13th position.

After a season of consolidation, Mullen spent somewhere in the region of £400,000 to strengthen his squad. Warren Joyce, Kevin Russell and David Eyres arrived as Mike Conroy, Ian Measham and Steve Harper departed, as he shuffled the pack at Turf Moor. However, no matter how he tinkered with his team, the results continued to be mixed. At Turf Moor the Clarets were virtually unbeatable with no fewer than 17 of the 23 League games ending in a Burnley victory. However, on foreign soil it was a different story, with only four wins being achieved away from home all season.

Despite these Jekyll and Hyde performances, the Clarets were able to clinch the final place in the Play-offs. It was then that there was a remarkable turn around in form. After a goalless draw with Plymouth Argyle at Turf Moor, Mullen's team enjoyed a remarkable 3–1 win at Home Park and then celebrated promotion with a 2–1 win over Stockport County at Wembley. Thus, he had achieved two promotions in three years and was the toast of Burnley fans everywhere.

Sadly, football can be a fickle mistress, and within 12 months of celebrating promotion the club were again faced with relegation. Suddenly, Mullen's heroic status changed to villain as the Clarets lost their First Division status after only one season. From that point on, matters went from bad to worse, as the 1995–96 season found the Clarets flirting with relegation at the bottom of the Second Division. Four straight defeats in January and early February 1996 found Mullen under intense pressure from the supporters.

The home defeat by Crewe Alexandra on 10 February 1996, proved to be the end of Mullen's reign at Turf Moor, and within a couple of days he had been sacked. After leaving Burnley he has continued to coach and manage at various levels within the game, including a spell in Ireland with Sligo Rovers. His last job in a managerial position was with Bromsgrove Rovers in the Southern League Division One West, which came to an end in January 2006.

Billy Nesbitt

Date of birth:	22 November 1891, Portsmouth, near Todmorden
Died:	January 1972, Halifax

Burnley record:

Appearances:	League 172, FA Cup 19, Wartime 73, others 1
Goals:	League 19, FA Cup 1, Wartime 23
Debut:	League, 12 February 1912 v Barnsley (h) won 3–0

Also played for: Cornholme, Portsmouth Rovers, Hebden Bridge FC, Bristol City, Clapton Orient

Billy Nesbitt failed to make much impact following his arrival at Burnley from Hebden Bridge in September 1911. He was very much an unknown quantity, a quiet man who shunned the limelight, no doubt due to the fact that it was said he was deaf from birth. He and Eddie Mosscrop spent the 1912–13 season vying for the outside-right spot that had been so admirably filled by Jonathan Morley. Indeed, many supporters were aghast when Morley was allowed to move to Preston in December 1912, as neither Nesbitt nor Mosscrop had looked totally convincing out on the wing. Certainly, during the promotion season of 1912–13, Mosscrop looked the better of the two, and Nesbitt was restricted to just nine League outings that campaign.

Nesbitt enjoyed a few outings on the left wing during the first half of 1913–14, before it was decided to switch Mosscrop to the left and give the outside-right berth to him. Suddenly, he became an indispensable member of the team and hit his best form as Burnley embarked upon a successful FA Cup run. In the third round he made all three goals as Bolton were demolished 3–0 at Turf Moor. In the semi-final, it was his cross that Tommy Boyle converted to give the Clarets a narrow 1–0 win over Sheffield United. Against Liverpool in the FA Cup Final, played at the Crystal Palace, it was due to another brilliant cross from him that Bert Freeman scored the only goal of the game and ensured the trophy was won for the first time in the club's history.

Like so many wingers of his generation, Nesbitt combined an arsenal of tricks and the ability to cross the ball with unerring accuracy. It made him a potent force in the Burnley attack. He was reaching the peak of his form when the outbreak of war put his career on hold, for what should have been his most fruitful years within the game. He featured prominently for the club during the wartime games, but the competition was fairly meaningless and not a real test of the devastating ability that he possessed.

When the Football League was restored in 1919–20, Nesbitt was still in his prime, and he helped the Clarets to finish in second place in Division One.

The following season, when the Championship was won, he missed only two matches and was a model of consistency on the right wing. Although he only scored five goals, he created numerous goals for Joe Anderson, Bob Kelly and Benny Cross during the club's 30-match unbeaten run. On the final day of the season, when Sunderland visited Turf Moor, the correspondent of the *Burnley Express* commented that 'Nesbitt had the Sunderland defence in a hopeless tangle and seemed able to do just as he liked.'

The 1921–22 season found Nesbitt again at his best as the Clarets fought hard to retain their title. However, injury kept him out of action from February 1922 and this, combined with other injuries to key personnel, resulted in the club drifting out of the Championship race and having to settle for third place. Injury restricted him to just eight games during 1922–23 and the arrival of Peter Bennie from Albion Rovers in June 1923 signalled the end of his reign on the right wing at Turf Moor.

Curiously, for a player who contributed so much in terms of club success, international honours eluded Nesbitt. He was drafted into a trial match just before World War One, when he represented England against the North, but after the war he appeared to have been forgotten by the selectors. Yet, it was his partnership with Bob Kelly, on the right flank, that was such a major factor in the Championship success of 1920–21.

Nesbitt left Burnley to join Bristol City but was again hampered by injuries, and after just 30 League and Cup appearances he was released. An abortive attempt to resurrect his career with Clapton Orient came to nothing and failed to produce a first-team appearance.

In a team that contained the likes of Jerry Dawson, Tommy Boyle, Billy Watson, Bert Freeman and Bob Kelly, it is perhaps understandable that Nesbitt was often overshadowed by more famous colleagues. However, in the annals of Burnley Football Club, the contribution of Billy Nesbitt to both Championship and Cup success is well remembered and respected and will be for all time.

Keith Newton

Date of birth: 23 June 1941, Manchester
Died: 16 June 1998, Blackburn

Burnley record:
Appearances: League 209, FA Cup 14, League Cup 14, others 16
Goals: League 5, FA Cup 1, League Cup 1
Debut: League, 12 August 1972 v Carlisle United (H) drew 2–2

Also played for: Spurley Hey Youth Club, Blackburn Rovers, Everton, Morecambe, Clitheroe, England (27 caps), England Under-23 (4 caps), Football League (5 appearances)
Managed: Clitheroe

Jimmy Adamson pulled off a major coup in June 1972 when he persuaded Keith Newton to drop into the Second Division and join Burnley. Newton, a tall, elegant, classical full-back, had been an integral part of Alf Ramsey's England team that had reached the quarter-finals of the 1970 World Cup in Mexico just two years earlier. He had collected a First Division Championship medal with Everton in 1969–70 and was the proud possessor of 27 England caps. He also possessed a wealth of experience, having appeared in 357 League and Cup games for Blackburn Rovers prior to making 59 senior appearances with Everton.

A rift between Newton and Harry Catterick, the Everton manager, had led to him being released at Goodison Park. Adamson moved swiftly to ensure that his experience was placed at the disposal of the young team that he was building at Turf Moor. Newton's widow, Barbara, revealed in an interview for the *Lancashire Evening Telegraph* with Burnley teammate Martin Dobson why the England international threw in his lot with Burnley. 'Keith was anxious to get away from Everton. He didn't see eye to eye with the manager Harry Catterick, and when Jimmy Adamson came to see him he really sold Burnley to him. Jim talked about the potential of the side, but also about how important it was to have a steadying influence at the back. I remember Keith being very impressed during those initial talks, and both agreed on how the game should be played.' The latter point was always important to Newton. At Blackburn he had been noted for his performances as a footballing full-back, one who would prefer to play his way out of trouble and use a constructive pass rather than just the long ball forward.

Newton's first season at Turf Moor was more successful than anyone could have expected, with the Clarets lifting the Second Division Championship. He featured in every game at left-back and instantly brought a calming influence to the Burnley defence. Never flustered, no matter how great the pressure, he was always looking for the constructive pass, and if his pace had been slightly tempered by age he more than compensated with his masterful reading of the game.

When Burnley returned to the top flight they relied on Newton's vast experience to help guide the younger players. Peter Noble remembered the influence that he had upon the squad: 'Brilliant fella. When I came into the Burnley team I played out of position at right-back, but Keith talked me through the game – where to go, which position to take up. I wasn't the only one to improve my game. Leighton James was another who developed his game through Keith's promptings, and he improved on all fronts. He was respected by all the players.'

Newton, throughout his time at Turf Moor, missed very few games, and in 1976–77 he was happy to switch to left-back to allow the emerging talent of Ian Brennan to take over on the right flank. He remained the perfect professional and the perfect clubman. He made his final appearance for the Clarets on 11 February 1978 against Brighton & Hove Albion at the Goldstone Ground. At the age of 36 he was released by the Clarets and called time on his League career, dropping into local non-League circles.

Perhaps the greatest compliment that can be paid to Newton is the fact that the supporters of both Burnley and Blackburn Rovers, two clubs that enjoy such an intense rivalry, can happily share him as one of the legends of both clubs. He carved his own niche in the history of the two clubs and made an immense contribution to football in East Lancashire, a fact that is happily recognised by the fans.

After his retirement from football, Newton continued to live in Blackburn and work locally until his untimely death at the age of 57.

Peter Noble

Date of birth: 19 August 1944, Sunderland

Burnley record:
Appearances: League 241+2, FA Cup 15, League Cup 19, others 24
Goals: League 63, FA Cup 1, League Cup 8, others 8
Debut: League, 25 August 1973 v Sheffield United (a) won 2–0
(substitute)

Also played for: Consett, Newcastle United, Swindon Town, Blackpool

Once again, like Keith Newton before him, Peter Noble (fondly known as 'Nobby' to those at Turf Moor) was sold to Burnley by the persuasive tongue of Jimmy Adamson. Noble recalled how he came to Turf Moor in an interview with Martin Dobson for the *Lancashire Evening Telegraph*: 'Swindon were struggling and letting a lot of good players go, so I thought it best to look elsewhere. I didn't ask for a move, but a few clubs came in for me, such as Aston Villa, Birmingham and QPR, but the reason I came to Burnley was Jimmy Adamson. He was from the North East like me, and, as Burnley had just gone up to the First Division, it was an exciting time.'

'Jimmy told me I wouldn't be in the team straight away, and I must be prepared to knuckle down and fight for a place, but in the first game at Sheffield United Mick Docherty got an injury and Jimmy turned to me on the bench and said "can you play right-back?" I said "no problem, gaffer," despite never having played there before, and I stayed there all season.'

There can have been few more popular players at Turf Moor than this likeable Wearsider. He quickly won the fans over with his dynamic performances, which reflected his wholehearted approach to the game. Although he began his Burnley career at right-back, he was also utilised very successfully in midfield and as a forward.

Noble had started his football career in his native North East with Consett in the Northern League, while working as a painter and decorator. Although Sunderland was the team that he supported, it was Newcastle United that gave him his opportunity to break into the Football League. He scored valuable goals that helped Newcastle steer clear of relegation in both 1965–66 and 1966–67, before the arrival of Albert Bennett and Wyn Davies, together with the emergence of Bryan Robson, spelt the end of his time at St James' Park. Matters were not helped when he suffered damage to his medial and lateral ligaments, which resulted in his knee being put in plaster for many months.

Despite the injury, Noble moved to Swindon Town in January 1968 for a bargain fee of £8,000. It was during his time with the Robins that he proved to be a thorn in the side of Burnley. Nonetheless, he enjoyed his time at the County Ground as the club clinched promotion to the Second Division and pulled off a giant-killing act to win the League Cup against Arsenal at Wembley in 1968–69. It was during this League Cup run that he inflicted a devastating blow to the Clarets over a two-leg semi-final.

'We won the game at Turf Moor 2–1 when I scored, then Burnley beat us at the County Ground by the same score. In the replay at WBA we won 3–2 after extra-time, and I scored the winner,' recollected Noble.

Following promotion to the First Division, Jimmy Adamson only signed one new player as the Clarets faced life in the top flight again. That man was Noble, and the £40,000 fee now seems an absolute snip. It was during the 1974–75 campaign that he was switched to midfield, in the wake of the departure of Martin Dobson, to which he responded by netting 12 goals. Ironically, he scored his first hat-trick for Burnley on 23 November 1974 when his former club, Newcastle United, visited Turf Moor and were thrashed 4–1.

In 1975–76 Noble was joint leading goalscorer with Ray Hankin, both men scoring 13 League goals, but couldn't prevent the Clarets from being relegated to the Second Division. In the summer of 1977 he succeeded Keith Newton as club captain, and in December 1978 he led the Clarets to success in the Anglo-Scottish Cup.

Sadly, during these later years at Turf Moor, Noble witnessed the departure of a number of the club's brightest stars with the result that fortunes on the field began to wane. The 1979–80 season was a disastrous campaign for the Clarets, with the club being relegated to the Third Division for the first time in their history. Noble, who had lost his place in November 1979, was no longer at the club when relegation came as he was sold to Blackpool in January 1980.

Noble made over 100 senior appearances for the Seasiders before finally hanging up his boots. On retirement from the game, he concentrated on his sports shop in Burnley's Market Hall but finally retired from the business in the wake of increased competition from the major sports retailers.

Geoff Nulty

Date of birth: 13 February 1949, Prescot

Burnley record:
Appearances: League 123+7, FA Cup 9, League Cup 4+1, others 8+1
Goals: League 20, League Cup 1, others 3
Debut: League, 16 August 1969 v Sunderland (h) won 3-0 (substitute)

Also played for: Stoke City, Newcastle United, Everton

The career of Geoff Nulty ought to be an inspiration to all those young players who are faced with the disappointment of being rejected early in their careers. He was one of those who found himself on the equivalent of football's scrapheap when Stoke City discarded him without offering him the chance to prove his worth at first-team level.

'I had an early set-back in my playing career,' Nulty later recalled. 'I got a free transfer from Stoke City. Burnley gave me a trial, and within days I was travelling with the youth squad to a tournament in Germany. Burnley then offered me a one-year contract. I was on edge all season wondering if I'd done enough to get another one because once you've had a "free" it never leaves you. In fact, it kept me on my toes throughout my career.'

It was Harry Potts who brought Nulty to Turf Moor, but he had to spend a season in the Central League before being given his first-team debut as a substitute against Sunderland. He only made a handful of appearances in 1969–70, but the following season, with the Clarets fighting against relegation, he finally won a place in the Burnley side and was utilised in defence as well as midfield.

With Adamson's young side relegated, Nulty spent 1971–72 acting as understudy for the left-back position. Harry Wilson, Eddie Cliff and Jim Thomson all had spells in that position ahead of him, and after Adamson signed Keith Newton in the summer of 1972 his future at Turf Moor looked rather bleak.

However, the sudden departure of Dave Thomas to Queen's Park Rangers in October 1972, gave Nulty another opportunity to prove his worth. It wasn't an opening that he would allow to close. As the Clarets swept to the Second Division Championship, he rose to the challenge and chipped in with half a dozen League goals.

With the Clarets restored to the top flight, Nulty continued to impress and notched nine goals from midfield in 1973–74, being the only player to figure in every game.

'I felt Burnley were developing into something special, and the prediction made by Jimmy Adamson that Burnley would be the team of the 70s was coming to fruition,' reflected Nulty.

Sadly, that prophecy never materialised as Nulty was one of a number of young stars who were sold when approaching their prime. In December 1974 he was sold to Newcastle United for £120,000 – a pretty good profit for a player who had cost nothing.

The move to St James' Park merely emphasised to Nulty how farsighted the set up at Turf Moor, under Jimmy Adamson, had been. 'Newcastle, for instance, at that time, were so far behind the Clarets in organisation and preparation it was unbelievable,' he recalled. 'Every player at Burnley knew exactly what was required. They knew their responsibilities and what was expected on the pitch. An object lesson in how to run a football club.'

Nulty was immediately installed into the midfield at Newcastle, and, following the arrival of manager Gordon Lee in the summer of 1975, he was appointed club captain. The bond with Lee was to be a strong one, and in July 1978 he followed Lee to Goodison Park where he was reunited with former Claret Martin Dobson.

Sadly, a tackle from Jimmy Case during a Merseyside derby left Nulty with a knee injury that was to end his playing career. Lee offered him the opportunity to join the coaching staff at Everton, and when Lee joined Preston North End Nulty joined him at Deepdale as assistant manager.

After a couple of years his spell at Deepdale ended unhappily, and Nulty, who had a degree in Social Sciences from the Open University, turned his back on the game. He bought a convenience store in St Helens and then developed wider business interests including property investment. His successful careers in football and business prove that with the required determination, early setbacks need not be an obstacle to success.

Brian O'Neil

Date of birth: 4 January 1944, Bedlington

Burnley record:
Appearances: League 231+4, FA Cup 18, League Cup 21+1, Europe 7
Goals: League 22, FA Cup 1, League Cup 1, Europe 1
Debut: League, 30 April 1963 v West Bromwich Albion (h) won 2–1

Also played for: Southampton, Huddersfield Town, Bideford Town, Taunton
Town, Salisbury City, Bishop's Waltham, England Under-23 (1
cap), Football League (1 appearance)
Managed: Bideford Town

Brian O'Neil was very much a product of his time. He came to the fore when football was undergoing a tactical transformation, and the role of the midfield destroyer was becoming increasingly important. Every team wanted a player who could man-mark an opposing playmaker, who could win the ball in the centre of the field; and, above all, who could run and harry the opposition and never give them a minute's rest. It was a role that O'Neil undertook with relish, and fully justified his nickname of 'The Bedlington Terrier'. No respecter of reputations, he was not only an aggressive defender, but he was also blessed with a football brain that allowed him to be just as constructive when in possession of the ball as he was destructive when the opposition had it. In short, he was the perfect midfield dynamo.

When O'Neil joined the groundstaff at Turf Moor, he came under the protective wing of George Bray, the old Burnley half-back who was on the coaching staff. '...he had great belief in me and encouraged me all the way,' reflected O'Neil. 'I remember one training session when he called me over. "Hey Fettler. I'll show you what tackling's all about," and he dropped a medicine ball between us! "Now let's see what you're made of. Try and get that off me."'

O'Neil responded well to his mentor's coaching, and in April 1963 he made his debut against West Bromwich Albion at Turf Moor. By October 1963 he had been installed as a regular in the Burnley midfield and soon won over the fans with his no-nonsense approach to the game. He never ducked a challenge, never gave less than total commitment, and the Turf Moor fans quickly warmed to him. He partnered Gordon Harris in midfield during the mid-60s, and their contrasting styles seemed to complement each other perfectly.

O'Neil won an England Under-23 cap in April 1965 when playing in a 2–0 win over Turkey at Ewood Park, Blackburn. In October 1965 he lined up alongside Harris in the Football League team that trounced the League of Ireland 5–0 at Boothferry Park, Hull.

O'Neil continued to be at the hub of the Burnley midfield for the remainder of the 60s, until the decision was taken to sell him to Southampton in May 1970. He was not totally surprised by the £70,000 move to the south coast, as he later reflected 'I think it was on the cards that I was about to leave. All the players knew sooner or later they'd be transferred because that was

the policy of the club, but you never think it's going to be you.'

O'Neil was having a few problems at the time, and with other youngsters coming through the system it seemed an ideal opportunity for Bob Lord to cash in on him.

O'Neil gave excellent service at The Dell and thoroughly enjoyed his time on the south coast: 'Southampton was a homely club, similar in many ways to Burnley. The capacity at The Dell was only 15,000, and the crowd were right on top of the action, which I always felt gave us a good start. Most seasons we struggled to hold onto our First Division status but always survived, which was a great achievement.'

O'Neil remained at The Dell until Southampton's relegation in 1973–74. Now past 30 and reaching the twilight of his career, he moved to Huddersfield Town in October 1974. Despite his best efforts, he could not prevent the Yorkshire club from falling into the Fourth Division at the end of his first season at Leeds Road. However, the following season he almost achieved promotion, with Town falling just a couple of points short of making an immediate return to Division Three.

O'Neil retired from League football, and in September 1976 he took up the post of player-manager at non-League Bideford Town. He continued to feature in the non-League game for a while, after making his home on the south coast.

Vince Overson

Date of birth: 15 May 1962, Kettering

Burnley record:
Appearances: League 213+6, FA Cup 19, League Cup 10, others 22+1
Goals: League 6, League Cup 1
Debut: League, 3 November 1979 v Orient (h) lost 1–2

Also played for: Long Buckby FC, Birmingham City, Stoke City, Shrewsbury Town, Halifax Town, Padiham
Managed: Padiham, Ramsbottom United

Vince Overson was another former favourite, for whom the lure of Turf Moor proved too strong to resist on more than one occasion during his career. He had two spells at the club as a player, and he was appointed the head of youth development and centre of excellence manager.

Overson served his own apprenticeship at Turf Moor before turning professional in November 1979. He made his debut in the same month against Orient at Turf Moor, and in the Burnley team that day was his older brother Richard, who came on as a substitute for Jim Thomson. It was only the second time that a pair of brothers had represented Burnley in League football – Jack and David Walders having appeared for the club between 1904 and 1906. Richard however, didn't go on to establish himself at Turf Moor and left the club in May 1980 to join Hereford United.

Overson, who made 22 League appearances during the ill-fated relegation season of 1979–80, became one of the regular centre-backs at the club. A tough and uncompromising defender, his lionhearted approach was well suited to the Third Division, and he quickly became a favourite with the supporters.

Overson's resolute defending was one of the cornerstones of the successful promotion campaign of 1981–82. He made 36 appearances during that Third Division Championship-winning season, and he won many admirers for his indefatigable spirit. A rugged opponent, he was particularly strong in the air and was never afraid to put his body in the way of danger when defending his goal. As a result of his unflinching approach, he picked up more than his fair share of injuries. Indeed, he was sidelined for much of the 1982–83 campaign when the Clarets were relegated after just one season back in the Second Division. Unquestionably, the loss of Overson was a major factor in the club's plight that season.

John Bond made him one of his key players when he arrived at Turf Moor. At this point he was partnering the blossoming talent of Mike Phelan in the centre of defence, and their performances were one of the high points in an otherwise difficult period for the club.

Bond left Burnley in August 1984, and Overson continued to excel in defence, under the management of John Benson in 1984–85. However, despite his many outstanding displays, he couldn't prevent the Clarets from being relegated to the Fourth Division at the end of the season.

During the following season Overson played under two different managers: Martin Buchan and Tommy Cavanagh. He also played on a weekly contract, as he refused to sign a new deal with the club in the summer of 1986. Clearly destined for football at a higher level, he left Turf Moor in June 1986 to join Birmingham City – then managed by John Bond.

Life at St Andrews was not always easy for Overson, but, nonetheless, he clocked up 181 League appearances for City and appeared at Wembley when he helped City win the Leyland DAF Trophy in 1991. He left St Andrews in June of that year and signed for Stoke City for £55,000.

Once again, Overson found himself playing for a former manager. Lou Macari had moved to Stoke from Birmingham. His time in the Potteries was very successful, with Stoke reaching the Third Division Play-offs at the end of his first season at the Victoria Ground. He again stepped out at Wembley and helped Stoke beat Stockport County. A year later he captained the Potters to the Second Division Championship. He made 216 League and Cup appearances for Stoke before returning to his beloved Burnley in August 1996.

Adrian Heath, the Burnley manager at the time, had no doubts as to the qualities that Overson possessed: 'Vince Overson is a leader of men, and we've been short of that quality recently. In fact, he is just the sort of motivating character we need in the side.'

Unfortunately, Overson was plagued by injury after arriving back at Burnley, and it restricted his impact upon the team. He spent a short spell on loan to Shrewsbury Town before being released in May 1998.

Overson joined Halifax Town, in August 1998, but only made one substitute appearance for the Shaymen. He then became involved in the non-League game, holding managerial posts at Padiham and Ramsbottom United while running the centre of excellence at Turf Moor. In May 2004 he stepped down at Ramsbottom because of his increasing workload at Burnley. In December of that year he was appointed head of youth development at Turf Moor.

Louis Page

Date of birth:	27 March 1899, Kirkdale, Liverpool
Died:	12 October 1959, Prenton, Birkenhead

Burnley record:

Appearances:	League 248, FA Cup 11
Goals:	League 111, FA Cup 4
Debut:	League, 29 August 1925 v Aston Villa (a) lost 0–10

Also played for:	South Liverpool, Stoke, Northampton Town, Manchester United, Port Vale, Yeovil & Petters United, England (7 caps)
Managed:	Yeovil & Petters United, Newport County, Liverpool (wartime manager), Swindon Town, Chester

Louis Page earned a special niche in the history of Burnley Football Club on 10 April 1926 when he notched a double hat-trick in the 7–1 thrashing of Birmingham. His first three goals came after 29, 44 and 58 minutes and were separated from his second three, which came after 60, 62 and 86 minutes, by a strike from Jack Bruton. However, what made the feat even more remarkable was that Page had been switched from his normal spot on the left wing to lead the attack on that day. As the correspondent of the *Burnley Express* recorded, '...one thing, above all else, which contributed to a sensational revival was the superb leadership of Louis Page, the gifted left-winger, who, as a last resort, was moved to centre-forward in the hope that there would be a punch in the attack to speed change of fortune.'

Page scored 26 goals that season, a major factor in the Clarets being able to scramble to 20th place in the First Division and avoid relegation. It was a notable achievement for a man who had only just stepped up from playing his football in the Third Division South of the Football League.

The somewhat exotically named Louis Antonio Page was a native of Kirkdale, Liverpool, and a member of a family of footballing brothers: Jack and Tom Page both played League football for Everton in the years immediately prior to World War One. He also had a trial with the Goodison Park club but wasn't taken on and was playing with South Liverpool when Stoke snapped him up in May 1919.

After three years in the Potteries, Page moved to Northampton Town where he featured in 122 League games before joining Burnley in May 1925 as part of the deal that took Jack Treasdern from Turf Moor to the County Ground as player-manager.

A speedy and talented outside-left, Page quickly settled into his new surroundings and a higher standard of football. The Clarets soon found that they had not only signed a winger, but they had also bought a player who was a fine opportunist whenever he got near the opposing goal. It was just unfortunate that he should arrive at the club at a time when Burnley were about to enter a dip in fortunes. Indeed, his debut coincided with the team suffering a traumatic 10–0 reversal at Aston Villa. It was a day when the Clarets fell foul of the new offside law, and their problems were exacerbated when Jack Hill, Burnley's centre-half, had to leave the field with an injury after only 30 minutes.

The impressive form that Page was producing on the left flank of the Burnley attack caught the eye of the England international selectors in 1927. Between February and November of that year he won all of his seven international caps and scored his only international goal in the 9–1 win over Belgium in Brussels in May 1927, on the day that Dixie Dean scored his first hat-trick for his country.

As the dark clouds of relegation hovered around Turf Moor, Page continued to sparkle with his dazzling displays of wing play. However, not even he could prevent the club from dropping into the Second Division at the end of 1929–30. He had again finished as top goalscorer, with 15 League goals, but defensive frailties undermined his efforts, and the Clarets dropped out of the top tier of English football.

Page continued to shine in the lower Division until he was snapped up by Manchester United in March 1932. The deal was done on the deadline for transfers, and he cost United £1,000. Sadly, the move signalled a decline in his personal fortunes. He was appointed captain at Old Trafford for the start of the 1932–33 campaign, but within two months he had been sold to Port Vale. His return to the Potteries was a bleak affair as he was unable to find the form that had taken him to the heights of English football. After just one season with Port Vale he embarked upon a coaching and managerial career, which took in several clubs and ended with a stint at Chester between June 1953 and June 1956. He then took up a scouting role with Leicester City but sadly passed away at the age of 60 after a prolonged illness.

Andy Payton

Date of birth: 23 October 1967, Whalley

Burnley record:
Appearances: League 115+41, FA Cup 6+2, League Cup 4+2, others 6
Goals: League 69, FA Cup 3, League Cup 6, others 3
Debut: League, 17 January 1998 v Bristol Rovers (a) lost 0–1

Also played for: Hull City, Middlesbrough, Glasgow Celtic, Barnsley,
                    Huddersfield Town, Blackpool, Stalybridge Celtic

Andy Payton was a player with whom the fans could readily identify. The 'Padiham Predator' has had a love affair with Burnley all his life, despite being released by the club while still a trainee. Undeterred, he carved out a very successful career in the game before finally getting his dream move, in January 1998, when Chris Waddle brought him to Turf Moor. For a 'Natural Born Claret', it was the only place he wanted to play his football.

Payton remains philosophical about his early rejection by the Clarets: 'It was John Bond who let me go, but, the way I saw it, I could do one of two things: I could deal with the rejection and bounce back or I could give up football and find a job. In many ways that early setback helped me because it gave me the burning desire to prove I could do it. It was difficult getting knocked back, leaving home for Hull when I was 16 and only getting home once every three months. But having to start all over again could have been the making of me.'

Payton served his apprenticeship at Hull and made his senior debut as a substitute at Stoke City in April 1987. He started 116 League games for Hull and made a further 27 appearances from the bench. Although not the biggest of forwards, he had the pace to take him away from defenders and scored 55 League goals for the Tigers.

In November 1991 Middlesbrough paid £750,000, their record fee at the time, to take Payton to Ayresome Park. Unfortunately, he enjoyed mixed fortunes on his debut. A goal in the fourth minute was followed by an injury that necessitated his departure from the game before half-time. His time at Middlesbrough was not a happy period of his career. As the club marched towards promotion to the newly established Premier League, he found himself confined to the bench. In August 1991 he left Middlesbrough and joined Celtic for £600,000. He became an instant hit with the Celtic fans when he scored the winning goal in a derby clash with Rangers, but, once again, he struggled to establish himself, and in November 1993 he returned to England to join Barnsley.

In Yorkshire Payton soon found his shooting boots and scored 41 goals in 108 League outings for the Tykes. However, scoring a winning goal against the Clarets at Turf Moor was undoubtedly his least favourite moment as a Barnsley player, as he recalled

'Even though I had scored I did not want to celebrate. I did not run around giving it the big one, it would not have felt right.'

Payton switched to Huddersfield Town in July 1996 and continued to score goals until a change of management and hernia problems led to his move to Burnley in January 1998. At the time the Clarets were at the bottom of the Second Division and fighting against relegation. Although it was a dream move for him, it was not without a certain amount of trepidation that he agreed to join Burnley, as he explained 'I was a local lad who loved the club... I knew that if I didn't score the goals the club would be relegated. But I came in, struck up a good partnership with Andy Cooke and scored 13 goals as we stayed up by beating Plymouth.'

Stan Ternent took over as manager in the summer of 1998 and during his first year at the helm it was Payton's goals that once again helped the club avoid relegation. However, in 1999–2000 his goals helped the Clarets to win promotion and his niche as a cult hero was assured.

During his time with the Clarets Payton scored 69 League goals, his highest tally at any of the clubs he represented. It remains a remarkable scoring record when one remembers that he only started 115 League games and was used as a substitute on no fewer than 41 occasions. In total he scored 81 goals in all competitions for the Clarets, although he readily admits that 'The goals I got basically came in about three seasons.' After that, he was restricted to cameo roles from the bench.

Ultimately, time caught up with Payton as a succession of injuries, combined with new arrivals, meant his first-team opportunities became increasingly spasmodic. Unfortunate personal problems, coupled with an unsuccessful loan spell at Blackpool, couldn't disguise the fact that he remained one of the greatest goalscorers in the club's history.

'Andy is one of the best strikers that Burnley Football Club has ever seen,' said Stan Ternent when Payton left the club at the end of 2002-03. 'His record speaks for itself, and he has been a top-class striker all of his career, wherever he has played. He is a top-class lad as well, and I think the world of him.' It was a fitting tribute for a true Legend of Burnley Football Club. Andy Payton – 'A Natural Born Claret'.

John Pender

Date of birth: 19 November 1963, Luton

Burnley record:

Appearances: League 171, FA Cup 17, League Cup 11, others 21
Goals: League 8, FA Cup 1, League Cup 1, others 1
Debut: League, 14 September 1990 v Stockport County (a) drew 2–2

Also played for: Lichfield Social, Wolverhampton Wanderers, Charlton Athletic,
Bristol City, Wigan Athletic, Rochdale, Republic of Ireland
Under-21 (1 cap)

As a defender of the old school, there was little of the spectacular in John Pender's game, but throughout his career he proved himself to be a solid, reliable defender who performed with great consistency. However, the highlight of his career was undoubtedly his spell at Turf Moor, during which time he led the club to two promotions in three years, including a Play-off victory at Wembley.

Ironically, it was as a goalscoring centre-forward in Sunday League football with Lichfield Social that Pender caught the eye of Wolverhampton Wanderers. He joined the Molineux club as an apprentice in 1979 and turned professional two years later. However, by this time he had been converted into a defender – a case of poacher turned gamekeeper! He became a fixture in the Wolves defence of the early 1980s and clocked up 117 League appearances before moving to Charlton Athletic in July 1985.

In his first season at Charlton, Pender helped the London club to achieve promotion to the First Division as runners-up to Norwich City. He made a total of 41 League appearances for the Addicks before moving to Bristol City in October 1987. Once again, he proved a lucky charm and helped the Ashton Gate club gain promotion to the Second Division.

Initially, Pender left Ashton Gate to join the Clarets on loan in September 1990, and a month later he made the move permanent in a £70,000 deal. During his first season at Turf Moor, he formed an impressive partnership with Steve Davis in a team that took Burnley to the Play-offs. Sadly, the Clarets lost out to Torquay United at the semi-final stage, but Pender had made a favourable impact on the Turf Moor faithful.

Pender became the Burnley skipper following the departure of Davis in the summer of 1991. However, as one Steve Davis departed another arrived in the form of Southampton's Steve Davis. Once again a Pender–Davis partnership performed heroically at the heart of the Burnley defence.

Indeed, the new defensive partnership was, if anything, even more impressive than the one it replaced. Pender's solid, no-nonsense approach blended perfectly with the more adventurous style that Davis employed. Together they were a major factor in the club capturing the Fourth Division Championship in 1991–92. Although not as cavalier as Davis, Pender was a threat from set pieces and grabbed three goals during that Championship-winning campaign.

Pender's consistency remained undiminished in a higher grade of football. He continued to provide a reliable defensive barrier week in and week out. On more than one occasion he picked up injuries but refused to be unbowed and insisted on being patched up and thrust back into the fray. It was an attitude that endeared him to the supporters.

In 1993–94 Pender was again at the heart of things as the Clarets challenged for yet another promotion. Ultimately, the club had to settle for a place in the Play-offs, but Pender led them to success over Stockport County at Wembley. It meant he had led the team to two promotions in the space of three years, a feat that ensured him a place in the history of Burnley Football Club.

However, victory at Wembley proved to be the peak of Pender's career at Turf Moor. He was now the wrong side of 30, and the club began to look for a younger option to partner Davis in defence. The introduction of Mark Winstanley meant that he became a peripheral figure during the 1994–95 campaign, a season which resulted in the Clarets losing the First Division status that he had worked so hard to achieve.

Pender made one appearance in 1995–96 before he left Turf Moor to join Wigan Athletic for £40,000. He was quickly appointed captain at his new club, and in 1996–97 he helped steer Wigan to the Third Division Championship, despite suffering a severe knee injury in January 1997.

Pender left Springfield Park to join Rochdale in July 1997, but, sadly, the knee problems he had suffered at Wigan reoccurred and forced him to quit League football.

Mike Phelan

Date of birth: 24 September 1962, Nelson

Burnley record:
Appearances: League 166+2, FA Cup 16, League Cup 16, others 11
Goals: League 9, League Cup 2, others 2
Debut: League, 31 January 1981 v Chesterfield (a) lost 0–3 (substitute)

Also played for: Barrowfield Celtic Boys Club, Norwich City, Manchester United, West Bromwich Albion, Blackpool, England (1 cap)

Born in Nelson and a Clarets' fan in his youth, Mike Phelan joined Burnley as a schoolboy and graduated through the apprentice ranks to sign professional forms in July 1980. His promotion at Turf Moor was quite rapid, and he made his senior debut in January 1981, when he appeared as a substitute against Chesterfield at Saltergate.

Phelan retained his place in the first team during the latter part of 1980–81, and the following season he picked up a Third Division Championship medal. However, injuries hampered his progress that season as he suffered a broken ankle and a depressed fracture of the cheekbone.

Fortunately, Phelan was restored to full fitness for the start of 1982–83 and featured in every game. Although the club suffered mixed fortunes – relegation to the Third Division being accompanied by two excellent Cup runs – he established himself as a rising star with a series of impressive performances. Indeed, he ended a disappointing campaign on a high note when he was not only voted Young Player of the Year but also picked up the Player of the Year award at Turf Moor.

During his time at Turf Moor, Phelan demonstrated his versatility by being used at full-back, centre-back, and in midfield. The fact that he could undertake each of these roles with equal aplomb merely emphasised the talent he possessed. As a youngster, he proved himself to be amazingly consistent. He was always cool and calm under pressure and rarely allowed himself to be harassed into making errors. His calm persona was a rare commodity in one so young and inexperienced.

Four managers, Brian Miller, Frank Casper, John Bond and John Benson, all appreciated the qualities that Phelan brought to the team. Unfortunately, this was one of the bleakest periods in the club's history, and at the end of 1984–85 the club slipped into the Fourth Division. Having suffered two relegations, while at the same time establishing a reputation as one of the outstanding young players in the game, it came as no surprise when he left Turf Moor in July 1985. A £70,000 move took him to Carrow Road, and in his first season at Norwich he helped the club to clinch the Second Division Championship. While at Carrow Road, he also succeeded Steve Bruce to the

captaincy of the club, such was the esteem in which he was held.

Phelan appeared in a total of 194 League and Cup games for Norwich and was on the brink of international honours when he moved to Manchester United in June 1989 for a fee reputed to be in the region of £750,000.

At Old Trafford, Phelan continued to adopt the same style of play that had served him so well at Burnley and Norwich City. His was the unspectacular role, the player who covered in both midfield and defence and gave total commitment. He was a popular and valued member of the United squad because of his versatility. Unfortunately, it was this versatility that eventually counted against him at Old Trafford as new players arrived and he found his opportunities become increasingly limited.

However, during his early period at the club Phelan collected his fair share of silverware. In 1989–90 he picked up an FA Cup-winners' medal, and the following season he was part of the team that won the European Cup-winners' Cup. In 1991–92 he completed his set of Cup medals when he was part of the United team that beat Nottingham Forest in the Football League Cup Final. Phelan, who had been capped on six occasions for the England Youth team, received a senior England cap when he replaced Bryan Robson, his Old Trafford teammate, in a goalless draw with Italy at Wembley in November 1989.

By 1992–93, when Manchester United won the inaugural Premier League Championship, Phelan had become a familiar sight on the substitutes' bench. He started five League games that campaign and made another six appearances as a substitute, although he remained unused on numerous occasions. The following season he had become an even more peripheral figure, and in July 1994 he moved to West Bromwich Albion.

In December 1994 Phelan returned to Carrow Road in a backroom role that was to be the start of a successful coaching career. After a brief interlude at Blackpool, he was appointed assistant manager with Stockport County in July 1997 before returning to Old Trafford in June 1999 as a youth coach. He then coached at various levels at Old Trafford before becoming coach to the senior team, a post that he still holds today.

Brian Pilkington

Date of birth: 12 February 1933, Leyland

Burnley record:
Appearances: League 300, FA Cup 33, League Cup 3, Europe 3, others 1
Goals: League 67, FA Cup 7, League Cup 1, Europe 2
Debut: League, 27 September 1952 v Tottenham Hotspur (a) lost 1–2

Also played for: Leyland Motors, Bolton Wanderers, Bury, Barrow, Leyland
Motors, England (1 cap), England B (2 caps), Football League (2
appearances)
Managed: Leyland Motors, Chorley

Short and stocky Brian Pilkington was perhaps not everyone's idea of the perfect athlete. However, Pilkington, or 'Pilky' as he was popularly known, was a winger who possessed a blistering turn of pace, and his direct style quickly found favour with the Turf Moor faithful. At Leyland Motors, where he was serving his apprenticeship as a coach painter, he had impressed scout Tommy Thornber sufficiently for him to recommend that Burnley signed him on, and in April 1951 he signed a contract at Turf Moor. He was just 19 when he was given the opportunity to make his first-team debut for the Clarets, due to Billy Elliott being away representing the Football League. Thus, he came face to face with Alf Ramsey, the England right-back, at White Hart Lane on his debut. Such was the level of his performance that Frank Hill, the Burnley manager, allowed Elliott, who was hugely popular with the Burnley crowd, to move to Sunderland the following summer.

During his first full season of senior action, Pilkington impressed everyone with his direct running and eye for goal. He opened his goalscoring account on the first day of the season, during the 4–1 demolition of Wolves at Turf Moor, and went on to score nine League and Cup goals during the campaign, strangely all of them on home soil. The 1954–55 season brought him 11 goals, second only to Bill Holden in the goalscoring charts.

In October 1954 Pilkington won an England cap when he featured in the 2–0 win over Northern Ireland in Belfast. He also won two England B caps and made a couple of appearances for the Football League team but, surprisingly, was never again selected for England. He was unfortunate that the legendary Tom Finney was operating on the left wing at that time, otherwise he would surely have added to his solitary England cap.

While deprived of the opportunity to parade his talent on the international stage, Pilkington continued to enrapture the public of Burnley with his electrifying brand of wing play. As the Clarets marched inexorably towards the Championship, it was the level of consistency that he achieved which impressed most observers. During the mid-50s he had formed an excellent understanding with Albert Cheesebrough on the left wing, before striking up an even more successful partnership with Jimmy Robson.

It was on 2 May 1960 that Pilkington's career with Burnley reached its peak, when Burnley clinched the First Division Championship at Maine Road. Indeed, it was Brian who set the team on its way when he beat Bert Trautmann in the Manchester City goal after only four minutes.

The following season Pilkington continued as automatic choice on the left wing and gave some impressive performances against foreign opposition in the European Cup. However, his brace of goals against SV Hamburg in a thrilling 3–1 win at Turf Moor proved to be the beginning of the end of his time at the club. Although a regular during the first part of the campaign, he found himself rested on a couple of occasions in favour of young Gordon Harris.

In January 1961, although he hadn't requested a transfer, Pilkington made no secret of his disenchantment with the situation at Turf Moor: 'I have been nearly 10 years at Burnley and with some eight years' first-team experience I consider that I could be more useful to a club than playing in the reserves. Burnley are a fine club. They have treated me well, and I have no complaints about that, but my career is at stake and I am not satisfied to be a reserve.'

With the likes of Blackpool, Preston North End, Everton and Bolton Wanderers all monitoring the situation, Pilkington was left out of the derby match with Blackburn Rovers at Turf Moor in late February 1961. A few days later he accepted the chance to join Bolton Wanderers in exchange for £25,000.

Pilkington's arrival at Burnden Park coincided with a downturn in the fortunes of the Wanderers, and in February 1964 he moved to Bury as Bolton headed towards relegation. His stay at Gigg Lane lasted just 12 months before he moved to Barrow, where he brought his career to an end in 1967.

Pilkington then became involved in the game at non-League level with Leyland Motors and then Chorley. Away from football, he ran his own estate agency business for over 30 years and spent a similar amount of time serving as a local magistrate.

Ray Pointer

Date of birth: 10 October 1936, Shankhouse

Burnley record:
Appearances: League 223, FA Cup 35, League Cup 7, Europe 4, others 1
Goals: League 118, FA Cup 13, League Cup 2
Debut: League, 5 October 1957 v Luton Town (a) lost 2–3

Also played for: Cramlington Welfare, Dudley Welfare, Bury, Coventry City, Portsmouth, Waterlooville, Blackpool Rangers, England (3 caps), England Under-23 (5 caps), Football League (1 appearance)

Ray Pointer was once described as 'Mr Perpetual Motion', which is probably a fair assessment of him as a player. During the course of their history, Burnley Football Club might well have had more skilful centre-forwards, but the club can rarely have had a more wholehearted competitor than Pointer. What he lacked in ball playing ability, he more than made up for by his speed, stamina and guts. He was blessed with that happy knack of scoring goals – and scoring them prolifically!

Another of that band of players from the North East who arrived at Burnley in the 50s, Pointer was playing for Dudley Welfare when he signed amateur forms for the Clarets in 1955 before turning professional in August 1957. He made his League debut at Luton, just five days after his 21st birthday, and shared the centre-forward duties during 1957–58 with Alan Shackleton. However, 27 goals in 37 League appearances the following season installed him as the undoubted first choice for the lead role in attack. It was the highest seasonal goal tally from a Burnley player since George Beel's 30 goals in 1928–29.

Pointer's familiar shock of blond hair made him an easily recognisable figure as he developed into the archetypical centre-forward. He willingly chased every ball, no cause was ever hopeless, defenders were harried into submission and the goal was attacked with venom. The harder he worked, the more the goals flowed, and ultimately they flowed more for him than any other post-war goalscorer at Turf Moor. Indeed, only George Beel has scored more goals for the Clarets than him.

Pointer's all-action game quickly caught the eye of the international selectors. In May 1959 he won the first of five England Under-23 caps when he was selected to face Italy in the San Siro Stadium in Milan. It proved to be a personal triumph for him, as he notched two goals in a 3–0 victory.

During the Championship-winning campaign of 1959–60, Pointer was an ever present and bagged 19 goals as the Clarets climbed to the summit of English football. So many of his goals proved vital, like the one he scored at Nottingham Forest in April 1960, which gave the Clarets a narrow 1–0 win.

Pointer continued to score goals with a consistent regularity, and in September 1961 he won his first full England cap when he was chosen to lead the attack against Luxembourg at Highbury in a World Cup qualifying match. He marked his England debut with a goal in a 4–1 win, and he was on target again a month later when he and John Connelly scored England's goals in a 2–0 win over Portugal at Wembley, in yet another World Cup qualifier. In between these World Cup matches, he also played for his country against Wales at Ninian Park but didn't get on the score sheet. Hopes that Pointer may make England's World Cup squad for Chile in the summer of 1962 were dashed when he was overlooked in favour of Gerry Hitchens and Alan Peacock. Nonetheless, his qualities remained clear for all to see, and it was in 1961 that the correspondent of the *Burnley Express* paid a glowing tribute to the boundless energy that he possessed: 'One continues to be amazed at the non-stop, full-speed chasing by Pointer, retriever of lost causes and the taker of unexpected half-chances!'

During 1962–63, the number-nine shirt at Turf Moor was passed to Andy Lochhead, and Pointer was switched to inside-right. However, in the meeting with Nottingham Forest at Turf Moor in April 1962, he received a serious injury when he chipped a bone in his ankle. When he returned to fitness the following campaign it appeared that the injury had taken something from his game. He struggled to find his form and consequently made just 10 League appearances that season.

The 1964–65 campaign proved even more disappointing for Pointer, with him making just three League appearances. Bury, who had been rumoured to be interested in him in March 1965, finally signed him in August of that year for £8,000. He quickly found his feet in the Second Division, and by December he had scored 17 goals in 19 League games. Jimmy Hill, the Coventry City manager, stepped in with a bid of £20,000 and took him to Highfield Road. He scored a further 11 goals for Coventry that season, taking his total for 1965–66 to 28, the highest seasonal tally of his career.

He moved to Portsmouth in January 1967, and it was there that he made the transition from player to coach by looking after the younger players while still scoring goals for Pompey. He joined Harry Potts, his former mentor at Turf Moor, as a coach at Blackpool in August 1973 and remained at Bloomfield Road until 1976. He then played and coached in local Leagues in the Fylde area for a time before he returned to Turf Moor as a youth coach in July 1978. Pointer's final coaching appointment came at Bury in the mid-1980s, and today he is happily retired and living in Blackpool.

Harry Potts

Date of birth: 22 October 1920, Hetton-le-Hole
Died: 16 January 1996, Burnley

Burnley record:
Appearances: League 165, FA Cup 16, Wartime 9
Goals: League 47, FA Cup 3, Wartime 5
Debut: League, 31 August 1946 v Coventry City (h) drew 1–1
Manager: January 1958–February 1970 and February 1977–October 1979

Also played for: Hetton Juniors, (wartime guest for Fulham, Bury, Sunderland), Everton
Also managed: Shrewsbury Town, Blackpool

As a player, Harry Potts was an influential factor in the club's post-war revival. As a manager, he took the club to the pinnacle of English football by winning the League Championship and reaching an FA Cup Final. However, McIlroy perhaps best captured the respect that this quiet player from the North East engendered when he said, shortly after his death, 'I'm proud to have been one of his players but even more proud to have had this gentle man for a friend.'

Potts first arrived at Turf Moor in 1937. He was just 16, and after a trial he was taken on as part of the club's developing youth policy. He played in junior football for the club but was sufficiently impressive to be offered professional terms in November 1937.

The outbreak of World War Two put Potts's career on hold, but he managed to make his first appearance at senior level during 1940–41 when he appeared in the 2–2 draw with Bolton Wanderers at Turf Moor on 12 April 1941. Service with the RAF in India meant that he made relatively few appearances during the wartime period. However, when the 1946–47 campaign began he was installed at inside-left by Cliff Britton.

Potts missed just two games during that first season after the war, as the Clarets won promotion to the First Division and reached the FA Cup Final. He and Billy Morris proved to be the perfect combination at inside-forward, with his more naturally defensive inclinations blending well with the attacking creativity of Morris.

Potts proved just as impressive in the top Division and continued to give excellent service until the opening months of 1950–51. With Frank Hill now in charge at Turf Moor, he became unsettled and asked to be placed on the transfer list. Cliff Britton, his former mentor at Burnley, wasted no time in taking him to Everton for a fee of £20,000. Unfortunately, Potts was unable to lift the fortunes of a struggling Goodison Park outfit, and at the end of the season Everton couldn't avoid relegation to the Second Division.

The years that followed resulted in increasingly spasmodic first-team appearances for Potts, and so he turned to coaching the club's junior players. When Everton released him in May 1956, he joined the backroom staff at Wolverhampton Wanderers. However, in July 1957 he took his first steps in club management when he was appointed manager at Shrewsbury Town. His stay at Meadow Lane was brief, as in January 1957 he arrived at Turf Moor to take over from Billy Dougal who had resigned through ill-health.

Potts inherited a blossoming young team at Burnley and was fortunate to have the services of Dougal and Bennion on the backroom staff. With the addition of Alex Elder, he moulded the players he inherited into a team that would reach the summit of English football. He always encouraged his players to play football, and, as Jimmy McIlroy explained, 'In his sincere, enthusiastic way he got the best out of every player. His love and loyalty for this famous old club rubbed off on all of us.' Indeed, Potts proved that football management didn't have to be a cut-throat business, for he was a sensitive and fair-minded man who treated his players with respect and fostered a family spirit at the club.

Potts's approach proved successful, as he led Burnley to the Championship in 1959–60 and to the runners'-up spot in both the League and FA Cup in 1961–62. His popularity suffered slightly in March 1963, when he was criticised for his role in the departure of Jimmy McIlroy. However, the fact remained that he kept Burnley afloat in the top flight at a time when other Lancashire town clubs had slipped into the second tier of English football.

In February 1970 Potts moved upstairs to become general manager, while Jimmy Adamson took control of playing affairs. He remained in this capacity until June 1972 when he finally cut his ties with Turf Moor. He spent a short spell out of the game before becoming manager of Blackpool in December 1972.

Potts's time at Bloomfield Road was not the happiest period of his career, and in May 1976 he left the club. He wasn't out of work for long, for in July he was invited to become chief scout at Turf Moor. In February 1977 he stepped back into the manager's office when Joe Brown was sacked. He led the club to victory in the Anglo-Scottish Cup in December 1978, but, sadly, his second period in charge proved a difficult time for all concerned. In October 1979, with the Clarets entrenched at the foot of the Second Division, he was replaced by Brian Miller.

Potts later worked as part of the management team at Colne Dynamoes, looking for new talent for the ambitious non-League club. However, with the sudden demise of the Dynamoes, he left the game for good. He continued to live in Burnley until he passed away in January 1996 at the age of 75.

Jimmy Robson

Date of birth: 23 January 1939, Pelton

Burnley record:
Appearances: League 202, FA Cup 29, League Cup 6, Europe 4, others 1
Goals: League 79, FA Cup 14, League Cup 4, Europe 3
Debut: League, 6 October 1956 v Blackpool (h) drew 2–2

Also played for: Blackpool, Barnsley, Bury

Goals seemed to come naturally to Jimmy Robson on the big occasions of his career. He crashed home a late equaliser for Burnley on his senior debut, bagged a goal against West Germany on his England Under-23 debut, and, of course, he became the first Burnley player to score for the club at Wembley when he scored in the 1962 FA Cup Final. That Wembley goal also ensured his place in the record books as it was the 100th goal in Finals at Wembley. Not that he took much satisfaction in that particular milestone: 'I know I scored the 100th goal in a Cup Final, but at the time I had no idea and it's a small consolation when you end up with a losers' medal.' He also became the holder of a rather more obscure record in August 1961 when he was selected for the FA XI, facing the double-winning Tottenham Hotspur in the FA Charity Shield match. In doing so, he became the only Burnley player to hold two Charity Shield medals, having also featured for the Clarets against Wolverhampton Wanderers the previous August.

Like so many who went on to give excellent service at Turf Moor, Robson was spotted by the club's talent scouts in the North East. He duly progressed through the junior ranks and signed professional forms on his 17th birthday in January 1956. He got his first opportunity to taste senior football when he was drafted into the team to cover the absence of Jimmy McIlroy, who was away on international duty. However, with McIlroy and Cheesebrough in possession of the inside-forward positions, he had to bide his time in the Central League.

It was during the 1958–59 season that Robson began to edge ahead of Cheesebrough in the battle for the inside-left position. He was seen to offer a slightly more potent threat in front of goal and Harry Potts was sufficiently impressed to allow Cheesebrough to move to Leicester City in the close season, and entrust Robson with the number-10 shirt. He fully justified the manager's faith in him and notched 18 goals in 38 appearances as the Clarets lifted the First Division Championship. His feat was all the more remarkable as he was working at Bank Hall Colliery as a part-time electrician. With conscription coming to an end, he and four other Burnley players, Adam Blacklaw, John Angus, John Connelly and Brian Miller, were given the option

of going into the local pit for a year instead of the normal two-year conscription.

'It's amazing to think we all won the First Division title while we were part-time, but that's how things were,' reflected Robson when looking back on the strangest of arrangements. 'In midweek we would go out to the pit at 7am, come out at three, go to bed for a couple of hours and then play for the first team at night. Training used to be Tuesdays and Thursdays full-time, but we still had to go down the pit before and after.'

In 1960–61 Robson topped the goalscorers with 25 League goals as well as 12 Cup goals, including three in the European Cup. He was again a regular scorer the following season as the Clarets chased a League and Cup double and, of course, ended that campaign with his historic goal in the FA Cup Final. Sadly, the Clarets had to settle for the runners'-up spot in both competitions and the subsequent years brought a gradual decline as the team began to break up.

A new wave of younger players began to challenge for places in the forward line, and Robson found his position under threat. In 1964–65 he made just five appearances in the League, and in March 1965, despite being only 26, he reluctantly departed to Blackpool for £10,000. 'I was settled in the town and any move from Burnley was a backward step then because you were leaving a team that were Champions a few years earlier.'

Robson spent three years at Blackpool, but his time at Bloomfield Road coincided with a downturn in fortunes for the Seasiders. Relegated to the Second Division in 1966–67, Robson found himself on the fringe of things the following season and moved to Barnsley in January 1968. In August 1970 he switched to Bury and ended his playing career at Gigg Lane, where he linked up with John Connelly, his former teammate from the Championship-winning team at Burnley.

When he retired from playing, Robson returned to Turf Moor to join the coaching staff and embarked on a long and successful career coaching young players at Burnley, Huddersfield Town and Rochdale. After a spell in non-League football, he returned to Burnley in the summer of 1998 to work with the club's centre of excellence.

Billy Rodaway

Date of birth: 26 September 1954, Liverpool

Burnley record:
Appearances: League 245+2, FA Cup 13, League Cup 18, others 25
Goals: League 3
Debut: League, 25 April 1972 v Preston North End (h) won 1–0

Also played for: Peterborough United, Blackpool, Tranmere Rovers, Runcorn, Altrincham, Colne Dynamoes, Runcorn
Managed: Accrington Stanley

When Billy Rodaway was beginning to establish himself in the Burnley defence in April 1974, he was playing in a team that finished the season in sixth place in the First Division. He was surrounded by such luminaries as Alan Stevenson, Keith Newton, Colin Waldron, Martin Dobson, Leighton James and Frank Casper. His final appearance for the club came on that day in May 1987, when victory over Orient enabled the Clarets to cling to their Football League lifeline by the narrowest of margins.

During his two spells at Turf Moor, Rodaway sampled life in all four Divisions of the Football League, and yet despite the club's fall from grace he remained a popular player with supporters. They recognised that while he might not have been the most skilful defender to don the Claret and Blue, his gritty determination and workrate more than compensated for other failings in his game.

A former England Schoolboy international, Rodaway joined the Clarets as an apprentice before turning professional in September 1971. He understudied Colin Waldron in the final two games of 1971–72 but didn't appear in the first team the following season when the Clarets won the Second Division Championship.

Rodaway was drafted in to appear in matches against Everton and Manchester United during the autumn of 1973 before replacing Jim Thomson, in the centre of defence, during the closing stages of the season. He formed a solid defensive partnership with Colin Waldron during the following campaign as the Clarets finished in 10th place in the top flight.

Rodaway spent much of 1975–76 on the sidelines, while Waldron and Thomson re-emerged as the first-choice defensive partnership. However, he was reintroduced during the latter stages of the campaign that ended with the Clarets being relegated from the First Division.

The departure of Waldron enabled Rodaway to form a new partnership with Thomson, and the two created a formidable defensive barrier in the seasons that followed. Although not the tallest of central-defenders at 5ft 9in, his unquenchable enthusiasm and boundless energy more than compensated for a lack of height. He was a member of the team that won the Anglo-Scottish Cup in December 1978 and remained at the heart of the Burnley defence until the 1980–81 campaign, although he only made 28 League appearances during the previous season when the Clarets were relegated to the Third Division.

Rodaway was continually overlooked in 1980–81, and in July 1981 he left Turf Moor to join Peterborough United. He became a key figure in the 'Posh' defence during the next two seasons and was made captain. He even had a spell as player-coach under the managership of Martin Wilkinson. In total he made 81 League appearances for the London Road club, but in August 1983 he rejected the offer of a new contract, and instead he returned to Lancashire to join Blackpool. He spent just one season at Bloomfield Road before he left to return to his native Merseyside to join Tranmere Rovers.

Having spent two seasons at Prenton Park Rodaway returned to Burnley in August 1986, when Brian Miller signed him for a Burnley team that was about to embark on its second season of Fourth Division football. It proved to be a disastrous campaign, which culminated in the fight for survival against Orient on the last day of the season. With Football League status retained, Rodaway was released in May 1987.

He returned to Merseyside and worked as a scaffolder in Liverpool while being part of the management team at Runcorn. He then embarked on a playing, coaching and management career in non-League football.

Derek Scott

Date of birth: 8 February 1958, Gateshead

Burnley record:
Appearances: League 277+8, FA Cup 23, League Cup 24, others 24
Goals: League 24, League Cup 3, others 2
Debut: League, 19 April 1975 v Manchester City (a) lost 0–2

Also played for: Bolton Wanderers, Colne Dynamoes, Burnley Bank Hall

Derek Scott spent a decade at Turf Moor during some of the most turbulent times in the club's history. He sampled life in three different Divisions with the Clarets and suffered four relegation campaigns. On the opposite side of the coin, he picked up a Third Division Championship medal in 1981–82, and only injury robbed him of featuring in the Anglo-Scottish Cup-winning team in December 1978.

An England Schoolboy international, Scott served his apprenticeship with the club before joining the professional ranks in February 1975. At that time he was a dashing right-back and was given an early opportunity to sample life in the First Division when he appeared in the final two games in 1974–75. However, at the time the Clarets were blessed with several outstanding full-backs, and he found himself behind Keith Newton, Mick Docherty and Ian Brennan in the pecking order for first-team football.

In January 1976 Scott edged ahead of Docherty for the right-back position and spent the remainder of the season partnering Newton at full-back. Sadly, it proved a dreadful campaign, with the Clarets slipping into the Second Division. Life in the second tier of English football started with Scott and Terry Pashley at full-back, but after an unimpressive start to the season manager Joe Brown brought in Newton and Brennan to replace them.

It wasn't until December 1977 that Scott was restored to the right-back position on a regular basis. Newton was approaching the end of his career, and he was installed as the new partner for Brennan. In 1978–79 he may have featured in the Anglo-Scottish Cup victory over Oldham Athletic but for an injury, which sidelined him for several games, in November and December 1978.

Scott was not the classical type of full-back that Newton had been. He was a rugged and tough-tackling full-back who liked to make attacking runs at the opposition. Indeed, it was these qualities that made more than one manager utilise his strengths in midfield rather than at right-back. Brian Miller drafted him into midfield during the closing stages of 1979–80 when the Clarets fought a desperate, and ultimately unsuccessful, battle against relegation.

When Burnley began life as a Third Division club, Scott was switched to midfield with Brian Laws coming in to fill the vacancy at right-back. his battling qualities made him an ideal choice for the hurly burly of Third Division midfield play.

In 1981–82 Scott featured in 30 League games as the Clarets won the Third Division Championship under Miller. However, hopes that the club had begun a permanent revival were quickly dispelled, as the Clarets became embroiled in yet another relegation battle. Curiously, while life in the Second Division proved difficult, the club enjoyed a successful run in the League Cup that took them all the way to the semi-final. The highlight of this run was a 4–1 victory over Tottenham Hotspur at White Hart Lane, with Scott in the thick of things in midfield. He featured in both legs of the semi-final clash with Liverpool but, sadly, missed two reasonable opportunities to get on the score sheet in the first-leg meeting at Anfield, and ultimately the Clarets were brushed aside 3–0. However, he did have the consolation of scoring the only goal of the game in the return meeting at Turf Moor.

Back in the Third Division, the Clarets endured a traumatic season under the managership of John Bond in 1983–84. Scott spent spells at both full-back and midfield, and did the same the following campaign under Bond's successor John Benson. In January 1985 he was appointed club captain but was unable to guide the club to safety, and at the end of the season the Clarets dropped into football's basement.

While Burnley prepared to ply their trade in the Fourth Division, Scott was subject to a £20,000 move to Bolton Wanderers in July 1985. Used predominately at full-back during his first season at Burnden Park, he helped Bolton reach the Freight Rover Trophy Final at Wembley. However, a 3–0 defeat by Bristol City, coupled with a final League placing of 17th in the Third Division, was followed by relegation to the Fourth Division at the end of 1986–87. Scott who had played in 36 League games that season, also featured in both legs of the Play-off semi-final defeat against Aldershot that sealed the club's fate.

Bolton made an immediate return to the Third Division with a third-place finish in 1987–88, with Scott appearing in 40 League games. However, when he was subsequently released by Bolton he opted to play non-League football and then pursued a new career in the Police Force.

Bobby Seith

Date of birth: 9 March 1932, Coatbridge

Burnley record:
Appearances: League 211, FA Cup 27
Goals: League 6
Debut: League, 3 October 1953 v Manchester United (a) won 2–1

Also played for: Monifieth Tayside, Dundee
Managed: Preston North End, Scotland Youth, Heart of Midlothian

For almost 40 years, Bobby Seith remained the forgotten man of the 1959–60 Championship-winning squad. He played in 27 of the first 34 League games of that season as well as in all eight FA Cup games. However, following a 6–1 defeat at Wolverhampton Wanderers and a 3–3 home draw with Sheffield Wednesday, he was axed from the team. Tommy Cummings was restored to the centre of defence, Brian Miller was moved to left-half, and Jimmy Adamson switched to take Seith's position at right-half. The game with Sheffield Wednesday proved to be his last appearance for the Clarets, as a disagreement with chairman Bob Lord resulted in him being placed on the transfer list and denied the Championship medal that he so richly deserved. Fortunately, matters were put right in October 1999 when Barry Kilby, the Burnley chairman, presented Bobby with his medal prior to a home game with Bristol City. The rousing reception he received from the Burnley faithful proved that his contribution to the history of Burnley Football Club was still treasured, even by a different generation of supporters.

Seith was just 15 when a Burnley official travelled to Scotland to watch him in action for Monifieth Tayside. His father, a former amateur with Queen's Park, encouraged him to take the plunge and accept the opportunity of a trial at Turf Moor. He signed amateur forms for the club, but admits in the early days he was badly affected by homesickness. 'I went to Burnley and found it very difficult to settle down. We only had one other youngster of my age, Tony Hapgood... living in digs, and not knowing anyone in the town can be pretty grim for a youngster,' he told *Football Monthly* magazine in the 50s.

Fortunately, Seith stuck it out, and after playing at wing-half in the A team he graduated to the reserves at the tender age of 16. He turned professional in March 1949 shortly before he began his National Service in the RAF, but as he was stationed in Gloucester he could only manage occasional outings for the A team. Even after his demobilisation, he struggled to establish himself at the club and suffered a great deal of frustration before being given his senior debut at Old Trafford in October 1953.

Seith made 23 League appearances as he gradually took over from the veteran Reg Attwell at left-half. The following season he struggled to make much of an impression, as manager Alan Brown switched Les Shannon to left-half from inside-left. It proved a frustrating campaign for him, with only 13 senior appearances to his name. It was during 1955–56 that he finally clinched a place in the team, while playing at right-half, and he was to remain a fixture in the side until his departure.

Seith was a superb defender, whose tough tackling made him a popular figure with the Burnley crowd. Yet, he was also capable of initiating attacking moves thanks to his accurate passing ability, and he enjoyed a distinguished career at Turf Moor before his controversial departure in the summer of 1960. In the modern game he would have been regarded as the ideal midfield dynamo.

In truth, as Seith readily admitted during an interview in the early 60s, the departure of Alan Brown from Burnley had had an effect on him. He had the highest regard for Brown as it was under his tutelage that he blossomed at Turf Moor.

On leaving Burnley, Seith returned to his native Scotland to join Dundee, and in 1961–62 he collected a Scottish League Championship medal. Thus, although denied the opportunity to play European Cup football with the Clarets, he was able to sample European football at Dundee.

When he hung up his boots, Seith stayed in the game and joined the coaching staff at Dundee, before taking up a coaching position with Glasgow Rangers. In November 1966 he returned to Lancashire to take over as manager of Preston North End from Jimmy Milne. Sadly, he was unable to improve the fortunes of the Preston club that had become becalmed in the lower reaches of the Second Division. At the end of 1969–70 Preston slipped into the Third Division for the first time in the club's history, and Seith was axed.

On his return to Scotland, he took charge of the Scottish Youth international team before one final stint in club management with Heart of Midlothian. Today he still lives in Dundee and has enjoyed a successful career as a chiropodist in the city.

Les Shannon

Date of birth: 12 March 1926, Liverpool

Burnley record:
Appearances: League 262, FA Cup 19
Goals: League 39, FA Cup 5
Debut: League, 27 December 1949 v Blackpool (a) lost 0–2

Also played for: Liverpool, England B (3 caps)
Managed: Bury, Blackpool

After an abortive trial with Everton where he was discarded for being too small, Les Shannon joined Liverpool as an amateur in 1943 before signing professional forms in November 1944. Ironically, he made his debut for Liverpool against Everton on 2 April 1945 and scored his side's goal in a 3–1 defeat. He made 15 appearances for Liverpool during the final stages of wartime football, but once the Football League was restored in 1946–47 he found himself unable to progress beyond Central League football. Yet, it was because of his performance for a Central League Select XI that he first came to the attention of Burnley manager Frank Hill. The Clarets, as reigning Central League Champions, faced a Central League Select XI at Turf Moor in October 1949. Shannon made a good impression on Hill, and the following month he joined the Clarets in a deal that was said to be worth £6,000.

At Liverpool, Shannon had played the majority of his games on the right wing, and it was in this position that he made his Burnley debut. He was drafted into the team to replace the injured Jackie Chew at Bloomfield Road in December 1949. He made eight senior appearances, all on the right-wing, during his first season at Turf Moor. However, the 1950–51 season found him completely confined to Central League football, with both Jackie Chew and Roy Stephenson ahead of him in the queue for the right-wing berth.

The following season Shannon began the campaign on the left wing until the arrival of Billy Elliott pushed him back into the reserves. However, an injury to Jimmy McIlroy gave him an unexpected opportunity to prove his worth as an inside-forward. It was a chance he grasped with both hands, and when McIlroy returned he was moved to inside-right so that Shannon could continue his role at inside-left. Indeed, so impressive was his form that he was selected for the England B team that faced a French team in Le Havre in May 1952. Sadly, the English were crushed 7–1, and there was to be no immediate recall to international duty for him.

In 1952–53 Shannon featured in every game and hit 15 League goals as the Clarets jumped to sixth spot in the First Division. As an inside-forward, he played somewhat deeper than the norm and proved the ideal foil for Jimmy McIlroy. He not only showed an eye for goal himself but was also hugely productive in creating goalscoring opportunities for his colleagues.

In March 1954 Shannon was awarded the second of three England B caps when he was selected to play against West Germany B in Gelsenkirchen. He celebrated his second call up with a goal in a comfortable 4–0 win and looked completely at home playing alongside promising youngsters like Duncan Edwards and Johnny Haynes.

When Alan Brown replaced Frank Hill at the helm at Turf Moor, there was to be a switch in position for Shannon. He was asked to fill the void at left-half that had been created with the departure of Reg Attwell. As the Clarets made a steady improvement during the 1950s, he was an automatic choice in his new role. It was as a left-half that he won his final cap for the England B team, lining up with Tommy Cummings against Scotland B at Dens Park, Dundee, in February 1956.

Shannon continued to hold down the first-team spot until age began to dim his influence. Harry Potts had become manager in January 1958 but kept faith in him until the end of the season. However, as Potts restructured his side during the early stages of 1958–59, Shannon found himself out of first-team contention. He made his final bow in League football in the home draw with Luton Town on 20 September 1958. At the age of 32, he was asked to help guide the younger players in the Central League team, and this he did until he joined the coaching staff of Everton in August 1959. It proved to be the start of a long and successful career in coaching and management. After a spell on the coaching staff at Arsenal, he became manager of Bury in 1966 and then took control of Blackpool in May 1969. The early 1970s found him in demand as a coach on the continent, with appointments at PAOK Salonika, Iraklis and Olympiakos Piraeus appearing on his CV.

Len Smelt

Date of birth: 10 December 1885, Rotherham
Died: 8 February 1933, Burnley

Burnley record:
Appearances: League 229, FA Cup 18, Wartime 14, others 1
Debut: League, 30 August 1919 v Notts County (a) lost 2–0

Also played for: Gainsborough Trinity, Sutton Junction, Rotherham Town, Chesterfield Town, Gainsborough Trinity, (wartime guest for Rotherham County, Leeds City), Barrow, Frickley Colliery, Hurst

'One of the most dependable of players, Leonard Smelt served Burnley Football Club as a right-back in a most praiseworthy manner. His judgement was generally sound and his strong kicking a feature of his virile displays, which were marked by a commendable keenness to keep all opposition out.' This contemporary pen-picture of Len reveals the importance of his contribution to the club in the 1920s.

Smelt first appeared for the Clarets on 17 March 1917 in a wartime game at Bolton Wanderers. He made two other appearances that season and featured again on one occasion in 1917–18. During the wartime period he also helped out Rotherham County and Leeds City as well as the Clarets, as clubs often experienced difficulties in raising a team. However, as the final season of wartime football was coming to a close the Clarets opted to sign him for a fee of £10 on the recommendation of Jimmy Wilde, one of the Burnley players.

Smelt's 'official' debut came on the opening day of 1919–20, and he went on to appear in every game of that season. There was little of the intricate about his style: he was a tough tackling full-back who performed with great consistency on a weekly basis. Smelt's was a high energy game: non-stop running and robust challenges were the main weapons in his defensive armoury. The master of the sliding tackle, he was a popular member of the team that lifted the First Division Championship in 1920–21. His loyalty to the Burnley cause was beyond reproach, and on one occasion he went to extraordinary lengths to ensure he didn't miss a game. When the train on which he was travelling from Rotherham to a match was held up, he simply got off and walked five miles to catch another train further along the line.

Although Smelt arrived from Chesterfield Town, playing in the Midland League, Burnley did not give him his first experience of life in the Football League. Way back in 1908, he had made his League debut for Gainsborough Trinity when he featured in their Second Division clash with Birmingham. He played a total of seven League games for Trinity before dropping out of the League to play with Sutton Junction. He moved to Midland League club Rotherham Town and from there he found his way to Chesterfield Town in the summer of 1913.

Smelt was part of a footballing dynasty at Chesterfield as he had three other brothers, Alf, Tom and John, who all played for the club at one time or another. Indeed, during the 1914–15 season Alf partnered Len at full-back while brother Tom, a goalscoring centre-forward, played for Accrington Stanley at the same time as Len was plying his trade at Turf Moor. Indeed, Tom also had a spell on the books at Burnley but never made it into the first team.

After the Championship-winning campaign, the Clarets began to lose their way during the 1920s. However, Smelt continued to deliver his high level of consistency for another four seasons. He played his final League game for the club on 18 April 1925, when Burnley crashed to a 5–0 defeat at Arsenal. By this time Smelt was well into the veteran stage of his career, and he spent a season coaching the A team before being released by the club in 1926.

Smelt opted to revive his playing career at that juncture and joined Barrow in the Third Division North. He made 37 League appearances for the club during 1926–27, before dropping out of League football to play in non-League games.

In addition to his football duties, for a time he was also an assistant cricket coach at Rossall college. In the summer of 1932 he rejoined the coaching staff at Turf Moor, but, tragically, within six months he was taken ill and died in January 1933 at the age of 47. He was buried in his native Rotherham but the funeral cortege from Burnley paused for a few minutes outside Turf Moor, his spiritual home and the scene of so many of his triumphs on a football field.

Trevor Steven

Date of birth: 21 September 1963, Berwick-upon-Tweed

Burnley record:
Appearances: League 74+2, FA Cup 13+4, League Cup 10
Goals: League 11, FA Cup 4, League Cup 1
Debut: League, 14 April 1981 v Huddersfield Town (h) won 4–2
    (substitute)

Also played for: Everton, Glasgow Rangers, Marseille (France), Glasgow
    Rangers, England (36 caps), England Under-21 (2 caps)

Trevor Steven was yet another in the long line of North East youngsters who were groomed in the Burnley youth system. However, like so many of the players the club produced post-1960, it was others who benefitted from the schooling he had received at Turf Moor. In Steven's case he enjoyed a spectacularly successful career that brought two League Championships, an FA Cup-winners' medal, a League Cup Finalist medal, a Full Members' Cup-winner's medal and four Charity Shield appearances with Everton. In Scotland, his two spells with Rangers brought six Premier Division Championships, three League Cup wins and one League Cup Finalist medal. In between his two spells with Rangers, he found time for a Championship medal with Marseille in France. Added to this are 36 appearances for England. Without a doubt, he remains the most successful former Claret of them all in terms of winning silverware.

There can be no denying that, in his prime, Steven was one of the finest midfield players of his generation. In many ways he was the complete footballer. He could run at defenders and produce moments of mesmerising skill that would completely open up an opposing defence. Although not the most prolific of goalscorers, he still managed a respectable total and was always liable to unleash a ferocious drive given half a chance. Yet, when he wasn't in possession he was prepared to do his bit defensively, and he would willingly toil away in midfield, chasing and harrying for possession.

Burnley fans knew the skills that Steven possessed – his blistering pace and deft footwork – as he had demonstrated them from the very moment that he made his senior debut for the club. He had joined the Clarets as an apprentice in the summer of 1980. He had hardly played for the Central League team before being given his debut from the bench in the home match with Huddersfield Town in April 1981. He signed professional forms in September of that year, and in the same month he made his first full League appearance at Bristol Rovers. During that campaign he went on to appear in 36 League matches as the Clarets lifted the Third Division Championship.

While the Clarets struggled for survival in the Second Division the following season, Steven looked quite at home in higher company. Certainly, his performances in the two Cup runs that season suggested a player of immense potential, despite his youth. An England Schoolboy and Youth international, he was clearly destined for a bright future.

Unfortunately, that future was not to be at Turf Moor. The period following relegation to the Third Division was one of change at the club, and the arrival of John Bond signalled the end of Steven's stay with Burnley. In truth, the decision to part with him had been made before Bond arrived, but the departure of the club's brightest star set the tone for the upheavals that were to follow. However, the offer of £325,000 from Everton was unlikely to have been refused no matter who was manager. While Burnley fans expressed their dismay, Steven went on to enjoy a glittering career and the fortunes of Burnley entered a downward spiral.

At Everton Steven was a prominent member of a team that dominated English football in the mid-1980s. Goodison Park provided him with a suitable stage on which to display his skills to the maximum, and he fully justified the hefty fee that Howard Kendall paid for him.

Steven's sparkling midfield displays brought him international honours, although, in truth, many believed that he ought to have won many more England caps than he actually did. Nonetheless, he was selected for the England squad for the 1986 World Cup Finals in Mexico and the 1990 World Cup Finals in Italy. In Mexico he appeared in the infamous 'Hand of God' match in the Azetec Stadium, when Maradona scored a goal of true genius as well as gaining notoriety with his deliberately 'handled' goal. However, although part of the squad in Italy, he didn't see any of the action, and his final England appearance came against France in June 1992.

Steven enjoyed a career of virtual non-stop success, and he remains one of the finest players that Burnley Football Club has ever produced.

Alan Stevenson

Date of birth: 6 November 1950, Staveley, Chesterfield

Burnley record:
Appearances: League 438, FA Cup 33, League Cup 36, others 33
Debut: League, 22 January 1972 v Orient (a) lost 0–1

Also played for: Chesterfield, Manchester City, Rotherham United, Hartlepool
United, England Under-23 (11 caps)

Alan Stevenson was one of those individuals blessed with a natural athleticism. As a youngster, his cricketing ability was sufficiently impressive for him to be invited for trials by Derbyshire. Indeed, he made the county's Second XI, and at Staveley Works, his local club, he performed heroics as a wicketkeeper and batsman, so much so that he hit a record score of 147 not out in one match in the Bassetlaw Cricket League. Stevenson also represented his local clubs at both tennis and table tennis, such was his all-round ability. However, it was football that remained his first love, and it was in football that he ultimately made his career both on and off the pitch.

Stevenson played as a goalkeeper in schoolboy football in Chesterfield, no doubt aspiring to follow in the footsteps of the legendary Gordon Banks who was a fellow native of the town. He signed amateur forms for Chesterfield while working as an apprentice fitter at Staveley Works, before moving up to the professional ranks in October 1969. Ironically, prior to joining the Saltergate club he had gone to Burnley for a trial but had failed to catch the eye.

The circumstances surrounding Stevenson's debut in League football were somewhat unusual. Chesterfield were due to play at Scunthorpe United on 4 October 1969 when first-team 'keeper Alan Humphreys failed a fitness test on the morning of the match. As a result, the coach taking the Chesterfield team to Scunthorpe had to call in at Stevenson's home to pick up the aspiring young 'keeper. With little time for nerves to set in, he helped his side to a 2–1 win and retained the goalkeeping position until he left for Burnley in January 1972. He ended his first campaign at Saltergate with a Third Division Championship medal in his pocket and appeared in 116 League and Cup games for his club prior to joining the Clarets.

When Stevenson arrived at Turf Moor, the goalkeeping situation at the club had become one of major concern. The Clarets had slipped into the Second Division, with veteran Tony Waiters having to come out of retirement to cover for the injured Peter Mellor. When Mellor returned, his form fluctuated to the point where Jimmy Adamson began to cast his net for a new 'keeper. Ultimately, Stevenson was the man chosen and his potential meant that Burnley had to pay a fee of £50,000 to bring him to Turf Moor.

Once Stevenson had found his feet at the club, he helped to stabilise the defence. The final six matches of the season were all won with just two goals being conceded. This paved the way for the successful Second Division Championship-winning campaign of 1972–73, when the Clarets conceded a meagre total of 35 goals with Stevenson appearing in every game.

His heroics between the posts quickly brought him international honours. In November 1972 he succeeded Peter Shilton as the England Under-23 goalkeeper when he played against Wales at the Vetch Field, Swansea. It proved to be the first of 11 England Under-23 caps that he was awarded. Unfortunately, he failed to make an appearance for the full England team, the nearest he got being a place on the bench when England faced Portugal in Lisbon in April 1974. It was also the game that Martin Dobson made his international debut and Alf Ramsey's final game as national coach.

The only blip in Stevenson's career at Turf Moor came during the 1975–76 season when he lost his place to Gerry Peyton. However, he regained the goalkeeping position at the end of October 1976 and continued as the number-one custodian until leaving the club in the summer of 1983.

Stevenson played for the Clarets in three different Divisions and won both Second and Third Division Championships. He also won an Anglo-Scottish Cup-winners' medal in 1978. He was a brave and athletic 'keeper, who maintained a consistently high level of performance on a weekly basis. It was, therefore, a major shock when he was released just one game short of Burnley's post-war record of 439 League appearances, held jointly by Jimmy McIlroy and John Angus.

Stevenson had a trial with Manchester City but signed for Rotherham United in August 1983. The following season he moved to Hartlepool United, initially on loan, and then became that club's commercial manager. Stevenson then held a similar position at Middlesbrough, West Bromwich Albion and Huddersfield Town before becoming a sales manager at Wembley Stadium in May 1999. Later that year, it was reported that he had decided to auction all of his football memorabilia with the agreement of his family.

Jimmy Strong

Date of birth: 7 June 1916, Morpeth
Died: 11 October 1989, Burnley

Burnley record:
Appearances: League 264, FA Cup 21, Wartime 103
Debut: League, 31 August 1946 v Coventry City (h) drew 1–1

Also played for: Pegswood Villa Juniors, Choppington Welfare, Pegswood United, Hartlepools United, Chesterfield, Portsmouth, Gillingham, Walsall, (wartime guest for Blackpool, Rochdale)

Burnley is fortunate to have been blessed with many fine goalkeepers throughout its history, and Jimmy Strong stands favourable comparison with any of them. Indeed, he was the first in a long line of excellent goalkeepers that played for the club after World War Two. What makes him so remarkable is that due to the hostilities he had already celebrated his 30th birthday before he made his League debut for Burnley. Yet, he went to feature in 220 successive League and Cup games for the club between 31 August 1946 and 24 March 1951. In truth, he was already a veteran of over 100 games for the Clarets before he made his League debut. However, as those games were played during wartime, they are not regarded at first-class appearances.

In his younger days Strong had been a fine athlete, who combined sprinting with playing full-back in junior football. Once he had switched to goalkeeping he was snapped up by Hartlepools United and made his League debut in a 3–3 draw with neighbouring Gateshead in February 1934. The following summer he moved to Chesterfield on a free transfer and enjoyed a run of 21 consecutive League and Cup games in mid-season when he replaced the injured Jack Moody. His form was sufficiently impressive for First Division Portsmouth to snap him up in March 1935. He went on to appear in 62 League and Cup games for Pompey before sampling life in the Southern League with Gillingham during 1938–39. In the summer of 1939 he switched to Walsall, but the outbreak of war brought a swift end to his career with the Saddlers.

Strong joined the RAF, and while stationed at Blackpool he appeared as a guest for both Blackpool and Rochdale. On 11 October 1941, he made his first appearance for the Clarets when he appeared as a guest player in the 4–2 win over Southport at Turf Moor. He made a further appearance in March 1942 when the Clarets enjoyed a 2–0 win over neighbouring Blackburn and became the regular first-choice custodian at the start of 1943–44.

The switch to Turf Moor was made permanent in January 1946 when the Clarets paid a fee of £450 to sign him. When the Football League was restored in 1946–47, Cliff Britton made Strong his automatic choice as 'keeper for his 'Iron Curtain' defence. A somewhat burly figure between the posts, he enjoyed an excellent first season of League football for the Clarets. The defence was particularly frugal, with only 32 League and Cup goals conceded in 51 matches. Promotion to the First Division was achieved, and he made a Wembley appearance in the FA Cup Final.

As the club re-established itself in the top flight, Strong proved to be the very epitome of reliability. On a weekly basis, he displayed the finer arts of goalkeeping at its best, and despite the robust nature of the game at that time he was able to withstand the torrid buffeting that he received from opposition forwards without succumbing to injury. Indeed, it was not until a clash with Chelsea's Bobby Smith on Good Friday 1951 that he received an injury which kept him sidelined. It ended his remarkable sequence of games, but the following weekend he was back between the posts, and despite his advancing years he remained as the first-choice custodian until December 1952.

Strong's final game for the Clarets was in the 1–1 draw with Arsenal at Turf Moor on 13 December 1952. The previous month the club had spent £7,350 to sign Des Thompson from York City, and Strong, who had seen off all other pretenders to his throne at Turf Moor, remained at the club until May 1954 but was unable to oust Thompson from the first team.

On his retirement from the game, Strong who never lost his north-eastern accent, ran his own poultry farm near his home on the outskirts of Burnley for some 20 years. He later worked at Grenfell and retired in 1979, but continued to live locally until his death in October 1989.

Stan Ternent

Date of birth: 16 June 1946, Gateshead

Burnley record:
Appearances: League 5
Debut: League, 6 May 1967 v Sheffield Wednesday (a) lost 0–7
Manager: June 1998–May 2004

Also played for: Carlisle United, Sunderland
Also managed: Blackpool, Hull City, Bury, Gillingham

Stan Ternent belongs to that select group of men who have served Burnley Football Club as both player and manager. In his case, he made far greater impact on the club as a manager than as a player. Indeed, his management style proved a breath of fresh air at Turf Moor, as he led the club out of the doldrums and into a position where Burnley were challenging for a place in the Premiership.

Ternent joined the Clarets as an apprentice in the summer of 1962, and 12 months later he turned professional. He was a hard-working half-back who endured a torrid introduction to League football with the Clarets slumping to a 7–0 defeat at Sheffield Wednesday on his debut in May 1967. The following season brought four League appearances, but, unable to carve out a regular niche in the team, he left for Carlisle United in May 1968.

Ternent enjoyed great success at Brunton Park and made 219 League and Cup appearances for the club before moving to Sunderland in May 1974. It was at Roker Park that he moved into coaching under Bob Stokoe, his former Carlisle United manager. When Stokoe moved to Blackpool as manager Ternent followed him, and in September 1979 he took the helm when Stokoe was sacked. Ternent himself was axed in February 1980, and after that experience he spent some time out of the game. However, in January 1987 he joined the coaching staff at Bradford City, marking the beginning of a managerial and coaching career that took in clubs as diverse as Crystal Palace, Hull City, Chelsea and Bury before he returned to Turf Moor as manager in June 1998.

When Ternent arrived he found a club that had only just escaped relegation. In the six seasons he was in charge he transformed the club from top to bottom. A promotion and two Play-off near misses meant that he took the club to within a whisker of Premiership football. At the same time he put Burnley in the national spotlight with audacious moves to bring Ian Wright and Paul Gascoigne to Turf Moor. He generated an excitement about the club that had, for far too long, languished in the doldrums. Incredibly, he achieved all this with relatively little in the way of expenditure.

Ternent shook the club up from the moment he walked through the door. Established names disappeared as he brought in his own men, and he ended his first campaign as manager with the club in a respectable 15th place in the Second Division, due largely to an 11-match unbeaten run at the back end of the season.

In 1999–2000 Ternent led the club out of the wilderness and achieved promotion to the First Division. On St Valentines Day 2000 he rocked the football world with the capture of Ian Wright, a move that generated an atmosphere around Turf Moor that had not been seen for many years.

First Division football brought new challenges for Ternent, as he was faced with operating on a different playing field from many of the wealthier clubs in the Division. Both neighbouring Blackburn Rovers and Bolton Wanderers were able to spend huge sums of money to ensure they won promotion to the Premiership. Ternent, meanwhile, had to operate on a more restricted budget, but he kept the club in the Play-off hunt until the closing stages of the campaign. Indeed, the club's seventh-place finish was a remarkable achievement for the manager.

The 2001–02 campaign again found the Clarets in the hunt for promotion. Ternent was able to spend £1 million to bring Robbie Blake to the club, while David Johnson and Paul Gascoigne both arrived on loan. Sadly, hopes of a Play-off place ended on the final day of the season, and once again the Clarets had to settle for seventh place.

Those two seasons challenging for promotion to the Premiership had seen a rise in expectations among the Turf Moor faithful. However, the financial situation meant that the club was unable to give the manager the funds required to continue to compete at this level. Players came and went as Ternent tried to mix and match a team that could achieve the dreams of the supporters, while keeping the demands of the bank manager happy. The Clarets reached the quarter-final of the FA Cup in 2002–03, but the League position worsened as the financial restraints impacted upon strengthening the squad.

As the 2003–04 season drew to a close, and with Burnley struggling at the wrong end of the table, it was announced that Ternent's contract would not be renewed. The final home game of the season brought out 18,852 fans as the Clarets faced Sunderland. He received a rousing send off from the Burnley fans, and in August 2004 he received a well-deserved testimonial when Alex Ferguson brought his Manchester United team to face the Clarets.

Ternent managed Gillingham for a season during 2004–05 but declined the invitation to continue at the helm at the Prestfield Stadium following the club's relegation from the Championship.

Dave Thomas

Date of birth: 5 October 1950, Kirkby-in-Ashfield

Burnley record:
Appearances: League 153+4, FA Cup 4, League Cup 16, others 2
Goals: League 19, League Cup 4
Debut: League, 13 May 1967 v Everton (h) drew 1–1

Also played for: Queen's Park Rangers, Everton, Wolverhampton Wanderers, Vancouver Whitecaps (US), Middlesbrough, Portsmouth, Bishops Stortford, Bognor Regis Town, England (8 caps), England Under-23 (11 caps)

Dave Thomas followed the well-trodden path from the North East to Burnley when he joined the club as a schoolboy in March 1966. He was actually born near Nottingham but had spent his childhood in West Auckland. On 13 May 1967, he became the youngest player to make his senior debut for Burnley when he was selected against Everton. He was 16 years and 220 days old and still registered as an apprentice. He turned professional in October 1967 and spent six years at the club before being sold to Queen's Park Rangers for £165,000 on his 21st birthday.

Thomas, nicknamed 'Ticer' after his grandfather who won an Amateur Cup-winners' medal with Bishop Auckland, got a taste of Turf Moor when he appeared for England in a schoolboy international. He had been invited for trials by both Blackpool and Preston North End, while Manchester United and Leeds United had kept tabs on him before he signed for Burnley.

A talented winger, Thomas always looked comfortable on the ball and relished taking on opposing defenders. In many ways he was a classic winger, sprinting past defenders, dummying them when necessary, and whipping in crosses from all angles but particularly from the dead-ball line. These attributes, coupled with a powerful left-foot shot, quickly made him one of the hottest properties in English football. He soon made his mark at Turf Moor, and aside from his early first-team debut he also helped the club's youth team win the FA Youth Cup in 1968.

Thomas became a regular in the first team in the wake of the departure of Willie Morgan in August 1968. Initially, he played on the left-wing, with Ralph Coates moving to fill the void left by Morgan on the opposite flank. However, at the beginning of October 1968 he was switched to outside-right, the position he would retain for the remainder of his time with the club. He gave many virtuoso performances in the Claret and Blue of Burnley and had a number of the leading clubs drooling with envy at the special talent that the Clarets possessed within their ranks.

In March 1970 Thomas made his England Under-23 debut when he appeared against Scotland at Roker Park in a match that was abandoned after 62 minutes because of snow. The 1970–71 season found him playing regularly for the England Under-23 team alongside the likes of Kevin Keegan, Trevor Brooking, Mick Channon, and Malcolm MacDonald. However, when the Clarets slipped into the Second Division at the end of that season it became clear that the club would struggle to keep him at Turf Moor.

Having spent a season playing Second Division football, Thomas made his final appearance for the club at Luton Town on 30 September 1972. Although his departure was not totally unexpected, it still came as a surprise when he moved to another Second Division club for £165,000. Indeed, it was particularly surprising that the Clarets should sell him to Queen's Park Rangers, one of Burnley's rivals for promotion.

Ironically, while Burnley won the Second Division Championship, Thomas's new club clinched the runners'-up spot. At Loftus Road, he found himself in the company of some well-known names including Frank McLintock, Terry Venables, Gerry Francis and Stan Bowles. He quickly adapted to life in the top flight, and in 1975–76 he missed only one League game as Queen's Park Rangers finished second in the First Division, just one point behind Champions Liverpool. Sadly, this was the season that the Clarets left the top flight of English football.

In August 1977 Thomas returned to the north-west when he joined Everton in a transfer said to be worth £200,000. It was to be the start of a nomadic period in his career, which brought another big money move to Wolverhampton Wanderers in October 1979 for £325,000. While the move to Goodison Park had been a success, with Everton finishing third in the First Division in 1977–78, his switch to Wolves was less successful. He was released in December 1980, after making just 16 senior appearances for the Molineux club. He sampled life in the North American Soccer League with Vancouver Whitecaps before returning to England to join Middlesbrough in March 1982 and then Portsmouth in July 1982.

It was while at Fratton Park that Thomas moved from player to coach, like Ray Pointer before him, when he took charge of Portsmouth's youth players. He had a spell as a coach in non-League football with Bishops Stortford and Bognor Regis Town before joining the coaching staff of Brentford. When he left football for good he became a PE teacher in a secondary school in Chichester and also dabbled with after-dinner speaking and radio commentary.

Harry Thomson

Date of birth: 25 August 1940, Loanhead, Edinburgh

Burnley record:
Appearances: League 117, FA Cup 5, League Cup 15, Europe 4
Debut: League, 20 March 1965 v Leicester City (a) won 2–0

Also played for: Shotts FC, Bo'ness United, Blackpool, Barrow

Harry Thomson proved his qualities as an outstanding goalkeeper during his time at Turf Moor. However, unlike his immediate predecessors at the club, Thomson had a temperamental streak and many believed that his stormy relationship with the hierarchy at the club prevented him from fulfilling his true potential.

A former pit worker, who had played his football in the Edinburgh and District League, Thomson had joined the Clarets in August 1959. However, with Adam Blacklaw and Jim Furnell ahead of him, he had to bide his time playing youth and reserve-team football. In 1962 Furnell moved to Liverpool, and Thomson stepped up to play Central League football on a regular basis. It was while he was reserve-team goalkeeper that the Clarets captured the Central League Championship and the Lancashire Senior Cup in 1962 and retained the Central League title in 1963.

The consistency of Blacklaw meant that Thomson had to wait until March 1965 before he made his debut in League football. He made his senior bow in the 2–0 win over Leicester City at Filbert Street. Goals from Willie Irvine and Ralph Coates and a penalty save from Thomson ensured the points for the Clarets. He featured in the final eight games of 1964–65, and the following season he began the campaign as the first-choice goalkeeper.

During the next two seasons Thomson and Blacklaw vied for possession of the goalkeeper's jersey at Turf Moor. Although smaller in build than Blacklaw, Thomson was just as brave and agile as his Scottish compatriot, and by the middle of the 1966–67 campaign he was finally acknowledged as the number-one custodian at Turf Moor. It was during this season that he performed heroically in the final stages of the Clarets' Inter-Cities Fairs Cup adventure. Blacklaw had featured in the opening four games in this competition, and Thomson took over for the games with Napoli. Having kept a clean sheet at Turf Moor, when the Clarets had won 3–0, Thomson gave one of the greatest performances of his career in the return fixture in Italy. He kept the Italian team at bay and saved everything that was thrown at him during a stormy affair. Once again, he proved his ability at saving from the penalty spot, and the correspondent of the *Burnley Express* was full of praise for his heroics: 'He was a god in a green jersey. Burnley's little Scot had one of those goalkeeping hours when the impossible seemed to have happened, not once, but frequently. Burnley survived the most one-sided game I have ever seen. And throughout it Thomson was brave, brilliant, lucky and, as 60,000 Neopolitan fans will confirm, sometimes fantastico!'

It was, undoubtedly, Thomson's finest hour with the Clarets, but the match was also remembered for the conflict that ensued after the final whistle. Thomson was spat at during the mêlée that followed it, and it was Blacklaw who dived to help his fellow Scot to the safety of the dressing room. Ironically, it was probably the performance that persuaded Harry Potts that Thomson had now superseded Blacklaw as the number-one goalkeeper at Turf Moor.

The summer of 1967 brought international recognition for Thomson, with selection for a Scottish FA touring party to Israel. Thus, in May 1967 he made his first appearance for a Scottish XI when he featured in the match against Israel in Tel Aviv. He was joined that day in the Scottish team by Willie Morgan, who was also making his international debut. Shortly afterwards, Blacklaw left Turf Moor to join Blackburn Rovers, which meant that Thomson was now the undisputed first-choice 'keeper at the club.

However, Thomson could be a tempestuous character, and on more than one occasion he became involved in controversy that led to him being censured by the club and axed from the team. In May 1969 the patience of officials was finally tested once too often, and he was dismissed.

Obviously, a player of Thomson's ability was quickly snapped up, and he spent the following season helping Blackpool gain promotion to the First Division. Unfortunately, success at Bloomfield Road couldn't be maintained, and Thomson lost his place in the team as the Seasiders slipped to relegation after just one season in the top flight.

Blackpool released Thomson in the summer of 1971 and he moved to Barrow. He spent a season at Holker Street as the first-choice goalkeeper, making 40 League appearances, before leaving the club in the summer of 1972.

Jim Thomson

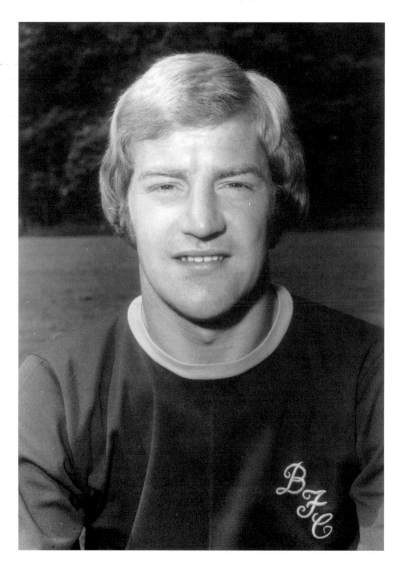

Date of birth: 1 October 1946, Glasgow

Burnley record:
Appearances: League 293+3, FA Cup 23, League Cup 21, others 23
Goals: League 3, FA Cup 1, League Cup 1, others 1
Debut: League, 5 October 1968 v Liverpool (h) lost 0–4

Also played for: Provenside Hibernian, Chelsea, Morecambe

The arrival of Jim Thomson from Chelsea for £40,000 in September 1968 merely underlined the shift in emphasis with regard to teambuilding at Turf Moor. Twelve months earlier Frank Casper had been bought from Rotherham United and Colin Waldron from Chelsea, while Doug Collins arrived from Grimsby Town at the same time as Thomson. Suddenly Burnley, the club famed for its youth policy, had resorted to buying young players rather than producing their own. While there were still some talented youngsters in the pipeline, to many Clarets supporters this period was a watershed in the club's history.

Thomson didn't enjoy the best of starts to his Burnley career, with the team being thumped 4-0 at home by Liverpool on his debut. Thomson, who had played at right-back, was replaced by Freddie Smith for the next game, and the Clarets embarked on an eight-match winning streak. For Thomson, it meant a season on the sidelines and just a handful of appearances. It had a depressingly familiar feel to it, as he had struggled to maintain a place in a Chelsea team that was littered with up and coming young players. He had appeared in 47 senior games for Chelsea after joining them as a 17-year-old in January 1965. He previously worked in the shipbuilding industry in his native Glasgow before embarking upon a career in professional football.

For the next three seasons Thomson enjoyed periods of prolonged first-team activity followed by spells out of the team. Indeed, it wasn't until the start of 1972–73 that Jimmy Adamson promoted him to partner Waldron at the heart of the Burnley defence. By this time the Clarets were a Second Division outfit, but he finally found his own niche in the team. He and Waldron enjoyed an impeccable season, with neither man missing a game as the Clarets clinched the Second Division Championship.

However, throughout his time at the club, Thomson had to face several challenges for his place in the team. Undeterred, he always responded and regained his place with a brand of gritty defensive play that made him a popular figure with those on the terraces. When Waldron left the club in June 1976, Thomson formed another impressive defensive partnership with Billy Rodaway, a youngster who had challenged for his place at one point. In December 1978 he was a member of the team that won the Anglo-Scottish Cup, but, sadly, that was the end of the good times at Turf Moor.

In 1979–80 the Clarets slipped into the Third Division for the first time, and Thomson found himself replaced at the heart of the defence by Vince Overson. He played just three games in the Third Division before being released in May 1981. Rumours of a testimonial failed to materialise, and he left to try his hand at management with non-League Morecambe.

Unfortunately, his career in management was one of the shortest on record. It ended after just two days! 'We played Mossley on the Saturday and lost 1-0, and when we got back to Morecambe I handed in my resignation. I had been notified the previous day that I had got a sales job I'd applied for,' explained Thomson, who had initially been doubtful of accepting the Morecambe job but did so when the Christie Park club were desperate for an answer.

Thomson returned to Turf Moor in June 1986 as commercial manager, when the club was in dire straits. At a time of financial stringency and with the club's fortunes at their lowest ebb, he had the thankless task of trying to generate interest in the club. The nadir was reached with the Orient game, and it was left to him to get the kick-off delayed, as thousands of fans queued to witness the most important game in the club's history.

With Football League status retained, Thomson left the club in September 1987 to return to the drinks industry. He continued to reside within the Burnley area and became the sales manager for a local brewery.

Colin Waldron

Date of birth: 22 June 1948, Bristol

Burnley record:
Appearances: League 308, FA Cup 14, League Cup 23, others 11
Goals: League 16, others 2
Debut: League, 28 October 1967 v Southampton (a) drew 2–2

Also played for: Bury, Chelsea, Manchester United, Sunderland, Tulsa
Roughnecks (US), Atlanta Chiefs (US), Rochdale, Philadelphia
Fury (US), Atlanta Chiefs (US)

At a time when a combination of funding by Roman Abramovich and shrewd management by Jose Mourinho have taken Chelsea to the summit of English football, it is, perhaps, difficult for younger supporters to believe that Colin Waldron's move to Turf Moor from Stamford Bridge proved to be the making of his career. Yet he turned his back on the bright lights of London, becoming a fixture in the Clarets defence and a true Burnley Legend.

Waldron had broken into League football in the more humble surroundings of Gigg Lane with Bury, but following his move to London he found it difficult to adapt to his new environment.

'I was a fish out of water, completely lost in London. It was a big city club. To be fair, Tommy Docherty threw me in at the deep end, and I sank. There's no other way of putting it,' revealed Waldron in a typically forthright manner. A £30,000 move to Burnley proved to be a lifeline for him. 'I was pleased to come back north. I didn't know about Burnley, but I quickly found myself liking the club, the town and the people. It was a homely club and the opposite of what Chelsea was,' he explained.

The blond hair of Waldron became a familiar sight in the centre of the defence, and the supporters quickly came to realise that he was a player of enormous potential. Following the departure of Andy Lochhead to Leicester City, Harry Potts handed him the club captaincy despite his youth and lack of experience. However, there were initial problems with him being a little too rash for his own good at times, and this led to Potts axing him from the team and the captaincy.

Fortunately, Waldron's career at Turf Moor was saved when Jimmy Adamson took charge of playing affairs in February 1970. One of his first acts was to restore Waldron to the centre of defence, but sadly, despite some inspired displays by him in 1970–71, he couldn't prevent the Clarets from falling into the Second Division.

Nonetheless, Adamson believed that Waldron was a player around whom he could build his defence. In 1972–73 he formed a new central-defensive partnership with Jim Thomson as the Clarets won the Second Division Championship and regained their place in the top flight.

Waldron believed that Burnley might well have fulfilled Adamson's prophecy of becoming the 'team of the 70s' with just a little more investment.

'I think we had a fairly good side, which I think may have warranted, at any other club, maybe signing a couple of quality players which might have given us a bit more depth. We came up with QPR. We sold two players, and they bought two. They finished second and we finished sixth,' Waldron recalled.

Unfortunately, Burnley had become a selling club by this time, and Waldron's hopes of a brighter future for the club rapidly faded. The departure of some of the club's brightest talent, coupled with the development of the stadium, led to a downward spiral that resulted in relegation at the end of the 1975–76 campaign.

Waldron, who had been a virtual ever present during the club's three-year stay in the First Division, ended his association with the club following relegation. He joined Manchester United but was never more than a squad player, and after four senior appearances he moved to Sunderland, firstly on loan and then permanently, in July 1977.

However, Waldron never really settled at Roker Park, and in April 1978 he joined the exodus to the North American Soccer League. He sampled football with Tulsa and Atlanta at a time when he ought to have been at the peak of his career in England.

'Looking back I probably prostituted myself. I left the greatest League in the world for the glamour and glitz of America,' Waldron confessed. Nonetheless, it gave him the opportunity to play with and against some of the greatest footballers in the world, albeit that many of them were in the autumn of their careers.

Waldron returned to English football in October 1979 when he joined Rochdale. Doug Collins, his former Turf Moor colleague, was the manager at Spotland Road and persuaded him to join Rochdale in the Fourth Division. However, shortly after his arrival his friend was sacked, and Waldron brought his association with the club to an end after just one season. He returned to America to play for Philadelphia and Atlanta before ending his playing career.

At 31 Waldron turned his back on football to pursue his career as a bookmaker in Nelson. It was a career that he was to enjoy for many years to come, while still retaining his close interests in Burnley Football Club.

George Waterfield

Date of birth:	2 June 1901, Swinton
Died:	October 1988, Bamber Bridge, near Preston

Burnley record:

Appearances:	League 371, FA Cup 23
Goals:	League 5
Debut:	League, 27 October 1923 v Sheffield United (h) 2–0
Also played for:	Picadilly FC, Swinton FC, Mexborough Town, Crystal Palace, England (1 cap)

When George Waterfield joined the Clarets in October 1923, the club's star was already on the wane. The halcyon days of FA Cup and League Championship glories were fading into memory as John Haworth's team began to break up. Indeed, Haworth himself would be dead within 14 months of Waterfield's arrival at Turf Moor. Thus, it was in a climate of change and uncertainty that he tried to establish himself at the club. Change was something that Waterfield had to quickly become accustomed to, with regard to his own role in the team. When he arrived from Mexborough it was as a dashing outside-left that he had caught the eye. In his youth, he had worked down the mines by day and played on a part-time basis for Mexborough in the Midland League.

Waterfield entered League football somewhat later than most, having already turned 22 before joining the Clarets. Haworth used him on 17 occasions on the wing, one of which was on the right flank, in 1923–24, and he fulfilled the same role the following season prior to Haworth's death. However, on Boxing Day 1924, shortly after Haworth's demise, He was asked to play left-back against Huddersfield Town at Leeds Road. Although the Clarets slipped to a 2–0 defeat, Waterfield had found the position that would make him a Turf Moor legend.

In May 1925 Andrew McCluggage arrived from Bradford to replace Len Smelt at right-back and thus form a partnership with Waterfield that would last for the next six years. He was a steady performer in defence, and it was his reliability that made him popular with the Turf Moor crowd. While the club struggled to maintain First Division status, Waterfield proved to be a beacon of light in troubled times. Indeed, his performances caught the eye of the England international selectors, and in February 1927 Waterfield made his England debut against Wales at the Racecourse Ground, Wrexham. He was unfortunate not to win more international caps as the regular England left-back, Sam Wadsworth, was coming to the end of his international career. However, the country was littered with excellent full-backs, and 'Taffy' Jones at Blackburn and Ernie Blenkinsop at Sheffield Wednesday edged ahead of him, with the latter inheriting Wadsworth's mantle.

Waterfield's quest for international football was not helped by the fact that he was playing in a team struggling to maintain their presence in the top flight. Two 19th-place finishes in 1927–28 and 1928–29, were followed by relegation to the Second Division.

Nonetheless, Waterfield continued to give excellent service to the club in the lower Division. His partnership with McCluggage came to an end in 1931, and he spent a season and a half partnering Billy Wood and Tom Willingham, before Gilbert Richmond made the right-back spot his own in the second half of the 1932–33 campaign. By this time, Waterfield's own career at Turf Moor was drawing to a close. In 1934–35, in his 12th season with the club, he became only the third Burnley player to feature in 350 League games for the Clarets. Indeed, today only nine men have featured in more Football League games for Burnley Football Club than George Waterfield.

Waterfield made his final appearance for the Clarets at St James' Park on 4 May 1935, and the following month he left to join Crystal Palace. He spent just one season with the London club before calling time on his football career as he approached the age of 35.

Billy Watson

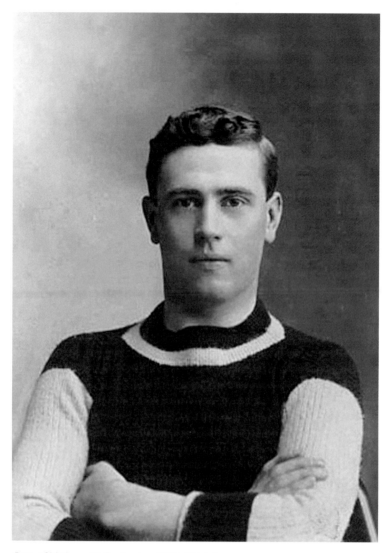

Date of birth: 11 September 1890, Kirkdale
Died: 1 September 1955, Southport

Burnley record:
Appearances: League 346, FA Cup 33, Wartime 44, others 1
Goals: League 18, FA Cup 2, Wartime 4
Debut: League, 3 April 1909 v Leeds City (h) drew 0–0

Also played for: Blowick Wesleyans, Southport Central, Accrington Stanley, Blackburn Rovers, England (3 caps+1 wartime cap), Football League (5 appearances)

When Burnley won the League Championship in 1920–21, Billy Watson, or Willie as he was sometimes known, featured in every game the Clarets played, and was the only player to do so. In addition, he also featured in the three FA Cup ties that were played that season. In December 1922, the *Lancashire Daily Post* remarked on the wonderful consistency of Watson: 'It is a rare thing indeed for Billy Watson to play even an indifferent game, or even rarer for him to be absent from his place in the side.' The article went on to extol the virtues of Watson '...he is a more complete artist than any other left-half of his time, equally good in defence and recovery, as in attack... his virtue of quiet workmanship veils some of his real strength.'

Watson had joined his home-town club of Southport Central in 1907, prior to linking up with the Clarets in March 1909. At that time the left-half position was in the possession of Hugh Moffat, and Watson had to bide his time with odd appearances as an understudy. However, on 1 October 1910 he was given the left-half role for a home game against Hull City. Although the match ended in a goalless draw, he remained as the automatic choice for the position from that point on.

During the latter part of 1912–13 Watson became one third of the famed half-back line with George Halley and Tommy Boyle, as the Clarets won promotion from the Second Division and reached the FA Cup semi-final. Watson's outstanding performances were rewarded with selection for the England team that faced Scotland at Stamford Bridge in April 1913. He certainly had plenty of company from his fellow Lancashire professionals that day, as Blackburn's Bob Crompton, Jock Simpson and Joe Hodkinson, together with Preston North End's Joe McCall, all featured in the 1–0 win.

The 1913–14 season brought a mid-table place for Burnley as the club established itself in the top flight. However, the main focus of the campaign had been in the FA Cup, with Watson featuring in all eight Cup ties and collecting his winners' medal after the 1–0 triumph over Liverpool at the Crystal Palace. Earlier in the season, in February 1914, he had been awarded his second England cap when he was in the team that was defeated 3–0 by Ireland at Middlesbrough. It was in October 1913 that he made the first of five appearances for the Football League team, when he played in the 2–0 victory over the Irish League at Cliftonville, Belfast.

Like so many professional footballers of his generation, the outbreak of war led to a barren period in Watson's career. He made numerous wartime appearances for the club, but the competition was a fairly soulless affair, and, of course, his international career was put on hold. He was called up for the Victory international against Wales at the Victoria Ground, Stoke, in October 1919, and the following week he made his final appearance for England when he played against Ireland in Belfast.

In 1919–20, as the Clarets finished second in the First Division, Watson notched five League goals, the highest seasonal tally of his career. However, it was in 1920–21 that he really proved his worth as the Clarets lifted the Championship, with Watson at the peak of his powers.

In 1921 Watson received his final representative honour when he was selected for the Football League team that travelled to Belfast to face the Irish League. However, he continued to maintain his high level of consistency for Burnley until he moved to Accrington Stanley in May 1925. He joined Accrington as player-coach to the reserve team but was called upon to make half a dozen appearances in the Third Division North for Stanley. In November 1926 he accepted a player-coach role with Blackburn Rovers but was not called upon by the first team at Ewood Park. Instead, he guided the club's younger players in the A team.

In later life Watson tried his hand as an ironmonger and a painter and decorator. He was also active in local politics in his native Southport and was elected as a local councillor.

Paul Weller

Date of birth: 6 March 1975, Brighton

Burnley record:

Appearances: League 199+53, FA Cup 8+6, League Cup 12+2, others 7
Goals: League 11, FA Cup 2
Debut: Football League Cup second round second leg, 4 October 1995
                   v Leicester City (h) lost 0–2

Also played for: Worthing, Rochdale, Leek Town, Stalybridge Celtic, York City,
                   Carlisle United, Workington

Paul Weller became something of an enigma with regard to his relationship with the Burnley faithful. A product of the youth scheme, he joined Burnley as a trainee and signed professional forms in 1993. He remained at the club until the summer of 2004 and made some 250 League appearances for the Clarets. Yet, in truth, he never really found favour with sections of the crowd. Despite overcoming serious stomach problems, which kept him sidelined for almost two seasons, Weller enjoyed a somewhat strained relationship with the fans before winning several Player of the Year awards in 2000–01.

Weller made the breakthrough into the Burnley first team during the autumn of 1995. Having made his debut in a League Cup tie against Leicester City, he retained his place on the right-hand side of midfield for much of the season. He proved himself to be a skilful player who could create opportunities in and around the opposing penalty area. However, at that time he was still regarded somewhat as a lightweight in terms of his physical presence.

During the two seasons that followed, Weller continued to give workmanlike performances on the right-hand side of Burnley's midfield. Although not always the most popular of players with supporters, he worked tirelessly on behalf of the team, and what he lacked in skill he more than made up for by the sheer effort he put into his game. In a team that often struggled in the lower Divisions, he proved to be one of the team's more consistent performers.

As the 1998–99 season approached, Weller was in protracted contract negotiations with the club. A trial with West Ham United came to nothing, and he reached an agreement to stay at Turf Moor. However, it proved to be a desperate time for the young midfielder, as a stomach problem laid him low and required surgery on more than one occasion.

Weller returned to first-team action in 1999–2000, but, initially, he found it difficult to regain his place, and continuing health problems meant that he didn't return on a regular basis until the following campaign.

Weller enjoyed a hugely successful season with the Clarets in the First Division in 2000–01. He again adopted his familiar role on the right of Burnley's midfield, either as a wing-back or in a more attacking role. Supporters gradually warmed to his tigerish approach, and he ended the season with several awards from different groups of supporters.

Weller continued to give excellent service to the club over the next three seasons, despite the fact that he was not always a regular, often due to injuries. His unspectacular approach didn't often catch the eye, but, nonetheless, his fetching and carrying in midfield proved invaluable to the team. During the 2002–03 campaign his battling qualities were put to use in the centre of midfield, and to good effect.

During the 2003–04 season, which proved to be Weller's last at Turf Moor, he was used almost exclusively as a 'holding' player in midfield. He was well suited to this role, and his appetite for work remained undiminished.

In May 2004 Weller was one of four established first-team players who were told that they would not be offered a new contract until a successor to Stan Ternent had been appointed. It was a major blow to a player who had served the club well for over a decade.

After leaving Turf Moor, Weller's career took a downward turn. He joined Rochdale in September 2004 but by November had dropped into non-League football with Leek Town. A spell with Stalybridge Celtic followed before he tried to revive his League career with trials at York City and Carlisle United during the summer of 2005. While with Carlisle, he was loaned to Workington to try to improve his fitness, but a permanent move to Brunton Park failed to materialise.

In November 2005 Weller returned to Turf Moor to take up a post with the Leisure and Community Department. As well as teaching students studying for their National Diploma of Football Studies with Myerscough College, he also became involved in coaching in the local area. In September 2006 he was appointed the club's new community manager.

Jock Winton

Date of birth: 6 October 1929, Perth

Burnley record:
Appearances: League 183, FA Cup 15
Goals: League 1
Debut: League, 29 November 1952 v Wolverhampton Wanderers (h)
           drew 0–0

Also played for: Jeanfield Swifts, Aston Villa, Rochdale, Scotland B (1 cap)

George Douglas Winton, known to all at Turf Moor as Jock, found himself in one of football's more bizarre situations shortly after transferring to Aston Villa in January 1959. As Winton had just purchased a house in Burnley, he opted to continue to train with the Clarets for part of the week. However, that situation became even more complicated when fate threw Burnley and Villa together in the sixth round of the FA Cup in February 1959. After a goalless draw at Villa Park, he enjoyed his return to Turf Moor as Villa left with a 2–0 win. Sadly for Winton, hopes of a Wembley appearance disappeared when Villa lost 1–0 to Nottingham Forest, the eventual Cup winners, in the semi-final.

Winton had originally been spotted as a 17-year-old with Scottish junior club Jeanfield Swifts. A Burnley scout offered him a trial at Turf Moor, and he signed amateur forms for the club in July 1945 before turning professional in September 1947. He was signed by Cliff Britton, who arranged for him to work as a joiner during his early days at the club.

At that time in his career Winton was regarded as an orthodox outside-left, and it was in this position that he was used in the youth team. However, on one occasion he was asked to play at full-back in a youth game against Barnsley. His opponent on the day was none other than Tommy Taylor, later of Manchester United and England fame, who tragically died in the Munich air crash in 1958.

Winton toiled for a number of years in youth and Central League football before being given his first-team debut against Wolverhampton Wanderers in November 1952. During his time with the reserves he had been tried at outside-right for a spell before being converted into a left-back, although, ironically, it was on the opposite flank that he made his debut at senior level.

Winton soon found that full-back was a position he enjoyed. 'I realised the advantages of being able to see more of the game, of going in to meet the ball instead of waiting for it, and of finding more room in which to work. I soon got into the habit of making a study of the wingers I was likely to come up against...their styles and technique, and then do the best I could to make them play the way I wanted them to,' he reflected in the later stages of his career.

As Burnley established themselves in the First Division in the 50s, so Winton established himself as the automatic choice at left-back in succession to Harold Mather. Indeed, he was sufficiently impressive to be capped by Scotland in the B international against England at St Andrews, Birmingham, in February 1957. Unfortunately, Scotland were beaten 4–1 and one of the England goalscorers that day was Brian Pilkington, Winton's colleague at Turf Moor.

Throughout his time as a regular in the first team, Winton had been faced with competition for his place from Dave Smith, a player who could operate on either flank. He appeared to have overcome that challenge when he suddenly found himself out of favour after the early stages of 1958–59. John Angus was preferred by Harry Potts at right-back with the result that Smith was switched to left-back in place of Winton.

In January 1959 Winton accepted a switch to Villa Park but never really settled in the Midlands, after an impressive start to his time at Villa. In 1959–60 he made just two League appearances as John Neal became the regular incumbent of the number-three shirt. Things improved during 1960–61 when he made 22 League appearances, before Gordon Lee edged ahead of him in the pecking order for the left-back spot.

In June 1961 Winton left Villa and returned to the North West to join Rochdale, a move that brought him nearer to his adopted home of Burnley. Although the Spotland club was in the Fourth Division, he enjoyed a successful run in the League Cup during his first season at the club. Rochdale reached the Final of the competition before being beaten by Norwich City in a two-leg Final. He brought the curtain down on his career in 1964 and has continued to make his home in Burnley.

Arthur Woodruff

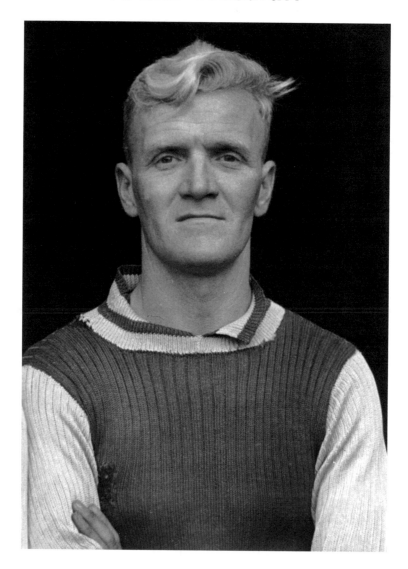

Date of birth: 12 April 1913, Barnsley
Died: 5 January 1983, Burnley

Burnley record:
Appearances: League 271, FA Cup 21, Wartime 245
Debut: League, 14 September 1936 v Plymouth Argyle (h) won 2–0

Also played for: Huddersfield Town, Halifax Town, Selby Town, Bradford City,
     Workington, Northwich Victoria
Managed: Northwich Victoria

The glamorous part of football is, of course, scoring goals. It is why goalscorers are worshipped as heroes, as it is through their deeds that games are won. Arthur Woodruff was not a goalscorer. He failed to find the back of the net in 292 senior appearances for the Clarets. Nonetheless, he was certainly a match winner as far as Burnley fans were concerned, for he brought to the table a range of defensive skills that were second to none. Quick and strong in the tackle, he was a formidable opponent for any forward to encounter. Before World War Two he was an outstanding young centre-half, and afterwards he developed into one of the country's best full-backs. When it came to the art of defending, he had few equals.

A Yorkshireman by birth, Woodruff's early career was spent in his native county as an amateur among the ranks of Huddersfield Town, Halifax Town, Selby Town – a Yorkshire League club – and Bradford City. He failed to make the first team at any of the League clubs, but in June 1936 he joined Burnley, then a mid-table Second Division side, and his career was transformed almost overnight. Manager Alf Boland installed him at centre-half, in place of Bob Johnson, for the game with Plymouth Argyle on 14 September 1936. He immediately became first choice for the position. Blessed with pace and impeccable timing, he proved to be an outstanding defender and appeared set for a bright future.

Alas, the outbreak of World War Two sent Woodruff's career into limbo as the League was suspended for the duration of the hostilities. The ebb and flow of players during the war years brought little continuity to the regionalised Leagues that had been formed. However, he was able to continue playing during the war years and clocked up a further 245 appearances, including the opening two League games of the abandoned 1939–40 programme. Needless to say, his name didn't register on the score sheet during the war years.

When Cliff Britton took charge of the club he founded his famous 'Iron Curtain' defence, in which Woodruff was to play a key role. During the final season of wartime football, Britton had moved him from the centre of defence to the right-back position. It was in this role that he featured prominently for the Clarets after the war. In Harold Mather, he found a full-back partner who had a similar approach to the game as himself. These were not attacking full-backs, and

Mather, like Woodruff, was not the type to get his name on the score sheet. Nonetheless, they provided a formidable barrier for any aspiring winger to pass.

Like his partner, Woodruff was a model of consistency at full-back. His pace enabled him to match the quickest of wingers stride for stride, while his timing of the tackle remained immaculate. He missed just two games as the Clarets won promotion to the First Division in 1946–47, and he played in all the FA Cup games that took the club to the Wembley Final that season.

Woodruff received representative honours when he was named at right-back for the Football League team that faced the League of Ireland in Dublin in April 1947. He retained his place the following October when the League enjoyed a 4–3 win over the Irish League in Belfast. He later came close to consideration for the England team, but a serious leg injury, sustained in 1950, deprived him of the opportunity to win further representative honours.

Woodruff had come under pressure from Joe Loughran during 1948–49 and, at 36 years of age, many may have been prepared to see the mantle pass to a younger man. However, he showed the same dogged determination as he had throughout his career, and before the season was over he was restored to the right-back position. Unfortunately, not even Woodruff could defy the march of time forever, and on 19 April 1952, just seven days after his 39th birthday, he made his final League appearance for the Clarets at Chelsea.

Woodruff was released in May 1952 and joined Workington as player-assistant manager. He played just 11 games in the Third Division North before leaving the Cumbrian club at the end of the season. He then took control at Northwich Victoria as player-manager before taking up coaching appointments with Cliftonville and Tranmere Rovers.

After leaving the game Woodruff returned to live in Burnley and for a spell had a greengrocery business. He later worked as a porter at Burnley General Hospital and was a frequent visitor to Turf Moor. He died suddenly at home on 5 January 1986 at the age of 69. Harry Potts, his former playing colleague, described him as 'one of the best two-footed players' he had ever seen. Former secretary Albert Maddox said that 'Arthur was a model professional. You could always rely on him to give a highly-competent performance, and I rarely remember him having a bad game.'

Ian Wright

Date of birth: 3 November 1963, Woolwich

Burnley record:
Appearances: League 4+11
Goals: League 4
Debut: League, 19 February 2000 v Wigan Athletic (h) drew 0–0

Also played for: Greenwich Borough, Crystal Palace, Arsenal, West Ham United, Nottingham Forest, Glasgow Celtic, England (33 caps), England B (3 caps)

When Stan Ternent signed Ian Wright in February 2000, it was a move that not only captured the national headlines but guaranteed that the crowds would flock to Turf Moor to support the club's push for promotion. At the time, the club was sitting comfortably in fourth place in the Second Division and in the thick of the promotion race. Ternent hoped that signing Wright would provide the impetus to take Burnley into one of the automatic promotion places. That it did, and coupled with his relationship with the fans it ensured that he became a cult hero at Turf Moor.

Wright, of course, needed no introduction to the Burnley fans. A larger than life character, he had come late to professional football after playing on a part-time basis with Greenwich Borough. He made his name initially with Crystal Palace, and it was at Selhurst Park that he and Stan Ternent first worked together. Wright went on to achieve enormous success with Arsenal, which resulted in him overtaking Cliff Bastin's record of 178 goals for the club in September 1997. While at Arsenal, he had won Championship, FA Cup and European medals, and, of course, during his career he was capped on 33 occasions by England.

Wright ended his stint at Highbury in the summer of 1998 with an impressive record of 185 goals from 288 senior appearances. On leaving Arsenal, he played for West Ham United, spent a short spell on loan with Nottingham Forest and then moved north of the border to join Celtic. However, his move to Scotland wasn't particularly successful, and he was seriously considering hanging up his boots when his friend Mitchell Thomas, the Burnley defender, suggested he try his luck with Burnley. Fortunately, he and Stan Ternent were also good friends from their days together at Selhurst Park and so the move was agreed.

The most immediate contribution he made was to attract thousands of missing fans to the club. The home game prior to Wright's arrival had been watched by a crowd of 13,526 while some 20,435 fans watched him make his debut against Wigan Athletic. His arrival created a genuine sense of optimism, and, of course, it enabled the club to raise extra funds through the marketing of such a 'big' star.

Initially, Wright struggled to score his first goal for the Clarets, with the result that he was placed on the bench after four games. It proved to be the role that he would occupy for the remainder of his time at the club.

Nonetheless, he made an immense contribution to the promotion push both on and off the field.

Wright scored his first goal for the club at Gillingham in March 2000, when his 86th-minute strike proved sufficient to rescue a point for the Clarets in a 2–2 draw. Four days later he scored his first goal at Turf Moor with the final goal in a 3–0 win over Reading. However, apart from his deeds on the pitch, Wright was also hugely popular with the other players, and he proved superb at keeping up morale in the dressing room.

The Clarets only lost one of their final 13 League games, with nine wins from those matches taking the club to second place in the Second Division and automatic promotion. Wright enjoyed a tremendous rapport with the Burnley faithful, who simply adored him.

With a place in the First Division assured, Ternent tried to persuade Wright to remain at Turf Moor for another season. However, he had become increasingly involved in media work and had reached the point in his career where the move to a full time role in the media was a natural one. Therefore, in the summer of 2000, he announced his retirement from football.

Although he only made a handful of appearances for the club, the impact that he had upon both the club and its supporters cannot be overestimated. His arrival sparked a rival of fortunes that captured the headlines. To the Burnley faithful, Ian Wright will remain a cult hero and a true Turf Moor Legend.